PILL HEAD

35465768960/200039837U
236476. OFFICIAL STATE PRESCIPTION .1

PILL HEAD

PRACTITIONERS DEA NUMBER

The Secret Life of a Painkiller Addict

Patient Name_____

Address_____

City_____ State_____ Age_____ Sex M F

Joshua Lyon

Prescribers Signature X_____

THIS PRESCRIPTION WILL BE FILLED GENERICALLY UNLESS PRESCRIBER WRITES DAW IN BOX BELOW

REFILLS ☐ None
Refills_____

HYPERION
NEW YORK

Some of the names and identifying characteristics of persons discussed in the book have been changed to protect their identities.

Library of Congress Cataloging-in-Publication Data

Lyon, Joshua.
  Pill head : the secret life of a painkiller addict / Joshua Lyon.
    p. cm.
  ISBN 978-1-4013-2298-4
  1. Lyon, Joshua. 2. Drug addicts—United States—Biography.
3. Analgesics—United States. 4. Narcotics—United States. 5. Young adults—Drug use—United States—Case studies. 6. Drug addiction—United States—Case studies. 7. Drug abuse—United States—Case studies. I. Title.
  HV5805.L96A3 2009
  616.86'320092—dc22

2008050297

Hyperion books are available for special promotions and premiums. For details contact the HarperCollins Special Markets Department in the New York office at 212-207-7528, fax 212-207-7222, or email spsales@harpercollins.com.

Design by Renato Stanisic

FIRST EDITION

10 9 8 7 6 5 4 3 2 1

THIS LABEL APPLIES TO TEXT STOCK

We try to produce the most beautiful books possible, and we are also extremely concerned about the impact of our manufacturing process on the forests of the world and the environment as a whole. Accordingly, we've made sure that all of the paper we use has been certified as coming from forests that are managed to ensure the protection of the people and wildlife dependent upon them.

For Stephanie Trong, Who Understood
Unconditional from the Very First Day.

And for Erin Hosier, Who Poured a Glass of Ice Water
Over Her Head at a Restaurant to Prove She Did Too.

0654

Acknowledgments

PLEASE FORGIVE ME IF I forget anyone here, since extended opiate use causes memory loss. And yes, I know that ·excuse has already gotten old.

Thank you to Brenda Copeland, my editor at Hyperion, for guiding me through this weird journey with a wicked sense of humor, an enormous heart, and no judgments. I knew we were destined to work together the second we met. To my friend and agent, Erin Hosier, from Dunow, Carlson & Lerner, thank you for believing in me for so long. You possess a mind and wit I would kill for. Stephanie Trong, I don't care if you're married at the time, I'm still living with you in a Florida condo when I'm an old man. Thank you for showing me that this world is inhabitable.

A massive thank you to everyone at Hyperion for your belief in this book, especially Ellen Archer, Will Balliett, Jessica Weiner, Betsy Plowman, Allison McGeehon, Pamela Peterson, Navorn Johnson, Kevin MacDonald, and Kate Griffin for dealing with all my anxiety-ridden emails.

This book wouldn't have been possible without enormous help from the following people: Melissa Kinsey, Loren Lankford, Chris

Steffen, and Tammy Tibbetts. I am forever indebted to all of you for your hard work and dedication.

Thank you to the following friends who have always had my back, no matter how bad things got: Melissa Plaut, Johnny Rauberts, Philippe Kane, and Erin Flaherty.

Thank you Timmy, Drew, and Jonah for your feedback on early versions of this manuscript. I will always love each of you.

Leslie Russo and Louise Yelin, thank you for being friends and mentors early in my career and making me believe I could accomplish anything I wanted to professionally.

Thank you Dr. Brian Meehan and Dr. Anthony Termine, for keeping me healthy and sane.

There are too many people to name individually who helped me get interviews with people who are normally hard to reach, but I want to extend a giant thank you to all of the hard-working assistants and media relations employees I worked with. And of course a huge thank you to all the brilliant experts from so many diverse fields who agreed to partake in this book, especially Dr. Carol Boyd, Dr. Alexander Bodkin, Alexander DeLuca, Mark Caverly, and all of the doctors, therapists, and volunteers at the Lower East Side Harm Reduction Center. Thank you also to Marion Ettlinger.

To my entire family, I hope I haven't made future reunions too awkward. I guess we have a lot to talk about now. I love you all. Special thanks to Mom and Peter for what I see as a whole new relationship. Dad, let's talk when you finish this. To my sisters, Erica and Nyssa—let's please all work harder to get together more often. Christopher, Francesca, Josie, Katie, and Ricky, I love you all and hope I haven't disappointed any of you. Bobby, thank you for the gifts of strength and language.

And to Emily, all I can say is onward.

Contents

This is why people OD on pills,
and jump from the Golden Gate Bridge.
Anything to feel weightless again.

—THE HANDSOME FAMILY

The medicine cabinet is your best friend.
I don't call that medicine,
I call it too much of too little, too late.

—HERMAN JOLLY/SUNSET VALLEY

We cannot learn without pain.

—ARISTOTLE

Prologue

I WAS FEELING NO PAIN.

I cared about nothing but this.

It wasn't just an absence of pain. It was warm waves pulsating through my muscle and skin. Breathing was hard, my chest felt weighted down by my own rib cage but I didn't panic because it's impossible to feel anxiety about anything when every inch of your body is having a constant low-grade orgasm.

I don't know how long I lay there on my bed, watching the blades of my ceiling fan slowly turn, lazily spinning tufts of dust before they floated down through the air around me like so much gray snow. Through half-lidded eyes I watched Ollie, my cat, go ape-shit chasing the dust balls, and it took every ounce of strength to turn my head toward the other side of the bed. I lifted an arm, ran my fingertips along the wall until they hit the mattress. I studied the blank wall. Its surface was pebbled under the paint. I'd always thought it was smooth. I got a sudden craving for an Orangina and, with a herculean burst of energy, sat up. Ollie freaked at my sudden movement, his eyes bulged out of his tiny skull and he went tearing out of my room in a manic frenzy. I heard him skid down the hallway, claws slipping on wood.

My skin itched. Everywhere. I stuffed my hands down the back of my shirt, pulled up my jean cuffs to get at my ankles, dug around the insides of my thighs. My fingernails sent jolts of red electricity down to the bone, but any discomfort washed away before it had a chance to really set in.

I kicked a pair of flip-flops out from under the bed and left my apartment. The usually harsh, trash-filled street looked soft as a meadow, and the light of the setting sun felt like a warm glow coming from inside *me* instead of the sky. In the bodega I found the Orangina and wandered up and down each aisle three times, picking up a bag of pretzels, putting it down. Opening the freezer, then shutting the door. Mr. Clean and I shared an intimate, prolonged stare. The cashier gave me a knowing smile and handed me my change.

Back upstairs I collapsed on the couch. Ollie dove into my lap, stayed there, warm against my stomach, writhing, trying to get closer. I reached for the TV remote, but it was a good six inches out of my grasp so I gave up. I felt my head roll back and hit the back of the sofa as another wave hit me, then I said out loud to Ollie, to myself: "This is what I've been waiting for my whole life."

Three Vicodin. That was all it took.

I was in love.

In the summer of 2003 my coworkers at *Jane* magazine and I began receiving massive amounts of email spam offering up Valium, Xanax, and Vicodin with "No prescription needed!" I kept hitting delete until the words actually sunk into my brain. It couldn't be that easy. My own physician wouldn't even prescribe a sleeping pill for a flight I had to take in the weeks immediately after 9/11. (In his typically reserved way, he told me to practice deep breathing and maybe have a cocktail, but no more than one.) So, strictly in the name of journalistic curiosity, I convinced my editor to let me try to buy these pills online. I wanted to see if it was just a scam or if it really was that simple to get controlled substances without a doctor's prescription. Everyone in the office—particularly the fashion and art departments—loved the idea and seemed unusually eager to hear the results. The story got approved as a small front-of-book piece in our pop culture section. Even better, I was given a $600 drug budget, courtesy of Fairchild Publications.

The Xanax and Valium were easy—I just had to fill out an online form. In the section where I had to explain why I needed the drugs, I wrote that I traveled a lot for work and I had a fear of flying. Within forty-eight hours I had two FedEx packages waiting for me on my desk: one with thirty brand-name Valium (the beautifully designed kind with the negative-space V in the center of each pill) and the other containing thirty alprazolam, the generic equivalent of Xanax. The two lots ran me $312 together.

The Vicodin order included an extra step: one of the online pharmacy staff doctors was going to call me for a consultation. I was also supposed to provide a phone number for my primary physician. I gave them a fake doctor's name and an unused telephone line at my office.

Their "doctor" called me first thing the next morning. The conversation went like this:

"You called to order Vicodin?"

"Hey, yeah, I, um, just had my appendix removed. I don't have insurance and your Vicodin prices seem pretty cheap."

"Yes, we do have good prices. We'll send it right out. Do you want thirty, sixty, or ninety?"

Ninety, of course. And it *was* a good price, only $223.

The third package arrived the next day. I wrote up a quick 250-word blurb about how frighteningly easy it was to order meds online, making a joke about slurring my words a lot ever since, and took the bottles home. It was a Friday, and they might have remained in the bottom of my underwear drawer forever if I hadn't received a frantic phone call from my editor around 8:00 P.M. I panicked when I saw her number on my cell phone screen, thinking that something disastrous had happened at work, especially since I knew that she was supposed to be at her place on the Jersey shore that weekend.

"What are you going to do with those pills?" she demanded as soon as I picked up the phone.

"I don't know," I said. "Give them away? I hadn't thought about it."

"I spent the entire train ride out here imagining you facedown on the floor somewhere," she said. "I can just see the headlines now: 'Magazine kills editor.' It's the last thing we need."

It was nice to know where I stood in the scheme of things.

"Don't worry, I'll get rid of them," I said.

"Promise?" she asked. "Flush them down the toilet."

"Yes, I promise," I sighed, but it was already a lie.

I have a problem. When someone tells me not to do something, I immediately go out and do it. It's an anti-authority streak that has been in me pretty much since birth. It first reared its head in my Montessori school when we grew a large crystal made from Epsom salt on a string. We were told not to touch it, but it ended up in my pocket. When it was discovered missing we all had to sit in a circle on the floor and received a stern, yet oddly sympathetic speech (a trademark Montessori method) about stealing. Our teacher told us all to reach into our pockets, see if it was there, and come clean if it was. I slipped my hand inside my red Garanimals shorts and felt the smooth sides of the crystal, with its comforting, sharp points. I kept my hand tightly clutched around it. It was mine now.

When I hung up with my boss, I pulled the bottles out of my bag and stared at them. The labels were pathetically generic and looked like they'd been created on a typewriter. The originating pharmacies were located in Florida, Arizona, and Colorado, and the addresses felt strangely cold: for some reason "Florida Drive" just screamed unmarked storefront with the blinds closed shut, located in a partially deserted strip mall, an empty soda can rattling around the parking lot, pushed by the wind.

The Vicodin bottle was fat, almost two inches in diameter. I'd never seen a pill bottle that large. I opened it up and removed the cotton. The pills were pressed together so tightly that when I stuck my finger inside I couldn't even get past the first layer. They were thick, the size of horse pills, and looked like they'd lodge directly in my windpipe if I tried to swallow one.

I took three.

That night I drifted in and out of sleep, but not in an unpleasant, restless way. It was more like a constant waking dream, and when the alarm went off the next morning I still felt a little high, but not at all hungover. That was all it took to seal the deal—I'd discovered my perfect drug.

CHAPTER 1

The How, the Why, and Let's Get High

I WAS NO STRANGER to drug use. I was twenty-seven, and pot, coke, whippets, Ecstasy, acid, and mushrooms had been an integral part of my life from age thirteen on. I was an expert at escapism. But as I'd hit my midtwenties, three beers were enough to leave me feeling like hell the next day. Even though I'd been a huge stoner in high school, pot now made me paranoid, silent, and terrified that I couldn't get enough air into my lungs. A lot of my friends have become unable to smoke pot after they left high school. I think there's something about being in your twenties and still trying to figure out your place in the world that makes pot just freak you out. When you're in high school you're usually too disinterested to care about your future, but suddenly you're in college and you're, like, "Oh shit, this is *real*. I've got to pay bills!"

I had gone through a big LSD phase during my senior year of high school and my first year of college. My high school grades were dismal and I couldn't get accepted anywhere except the local community college, where I suddenly started getting straight As, despite tripping my face off for most of that year. For half of it, I lived with a guy who dealt acid out of our freezer, but, like pot, acid lost its appeal once I realized I had to create some kind of real future for myself.

Plus, there was that night when I went with my friend Laura to a club where she was supposed to go-go dance on top of a lifeguard chair. While she was waving her arms around, she and the chair turned into a giant octopus as soon as "Cars" by Gary Numan came on. I was convinced that I had peed my pants in fear because it felt all hot and wet down there. Every time I looked at my pant leg I saw a dark, wet patch, but then I'd look up and see dark, wet patches *everywhere*, on every surface. For the rest of the night I would periodically stick my hand down my pants and then check my fingers to make sure they weren't wet. The very last time I did acid was, stereotypically enough, at a Phish show some friends dragged me to at the Saratoga Performing Arts Center. At a rest stop along the way my friends bought some acid from some hippies in the parking lot. When they showed me their purchase, I laughed, because the tabs looked like torn-up bits of toilet paper. "You guys just totally got ripped off," I said smugly. "There's no acid on these." To prove it I popped several in my mouth.

Six hours later, as my friends and I sat in the by-then empty parking lot, far too blasted to drive, I became convinced that the harsh concrete beneath us was actually billions of tiny needles injecting our asses with more acid. I swore off the stuff for good.

I'd only tried heroin once, when I was nineteen, and I only did it to impress a boy I thought did a lot of heroin himself. After we both snorted it, he told me that he had only done it because he thought *I* was a huge dope fiend and he was trying to impress me. I liked the warm, melting feeling it gave me, but we promised each other we'd never do heroin again. By that point I had transferred to SUNY Purchase, and in the late 1990s, it seemed like every cute person on campus was using. Heroin lost its appeal after two different girls overdosed in my bathroom, my roommate got kicked out of school for dealing, and a close friend of mine started bringing a vomit bag to class, which she would silently barf into in the back of Sociology 102.

Crystal meth was another drug I tried only once. I will never, ever touch that poison again. I thought it was like cocaine, so I snorted rail after rail at a fake Irish pub on the Lower East Side where a random friend of a friend had offered it to me. I didn't come down for three straight days. First I stayed locked in my room, trying in vain to masturbate even though there was absolutely nothing going on down there. On the second day I finally jumped in a cab to see an ex-boyfriend who lived in Brooklyn. He walked me around, got me soup, let me pace around his room, and basically took care of me until I came down. I went back to work the following Tuesday. I was coughing a lot, so I bought some cough syrup. I chugged some just as Jane Pratt, our editor in chief, stopped by my cube to ask me a question. I didn't know that one of the ingredients in the cough syrup was used to make meth, and the high kicked right back in as she was trying to explain something to me. I just stared and smiled and nodded as she went on, but I could feel that same sick high feeling rushing through my veins and my head felt like it was going to explode. As soon as she left I bolted from the office and ran down to Herald Square. I got through the turnstile and down to the subway platform before I realized that I would seriously lose it if I stayed underground for one more second. So I ran back out into the street, jumped in a cab, went home, and shivered in a corner of my bed until the next day.

I couldn't understand how anyone could become addicted to meth. It made me feel like someone had taken my brain and obsessively rolled it like a Play-Doh ball with their hands for seventy-two straight hours.

I loved cocaine, but, as with alcohol, my hangovers were always cloaked in a deep depression. Not to mention its physical side effects: my nose would spontaneously leak clear snot for up to three days anytime I went on a binge, which, around the time I discovered opiates, had been pretty much every weekend. On a typical Friday night I'd buy a six-pack of Corona, curl up by myself on my bed with the lights out, turn on my DVD of Rob Zombie's *House of 1,000 Corpses,* and do line after line of blow while chugging my beer. The film is an homage to 1970s gore and slasher flicks; it's filled with rapid-fire edits that, when I was on coke, made me feel like I was about to have a seizure—but in a good way. It wasn't the movie's violence that pulled me in. With most horror films, I become emotionally invested in the victims. I'm not watching the movie to get off on gore. I'm watching them to see what extreme survival instincts, albeit scripted and utterly implausible ones, do to a person.

By the time the film was done I'd be in a near manic state. I'd practice a "calm face" in the mirror by relaxing my facial muscles, head out to a bar, meet up with friends, do more drugs, have mindless conversations, stay out till dawn, and stumble home, either with a stranger or alone. I'd pay for the night for the rest of the weekend.

But that was behind me now. On Vicodin I felt fantastic, even when the high was over.

Over the next few weeks, as I began depleting my bottle in earnest, I discovered the other added bonus of Vicodin for me—zero social anxiety. I'd always suffered from a mild form of it, in that slightly paranoid way where you think everyone is looking at what you're wearing and laughing, but now when I went out in public I didn't care what anyone thought. Instead of worrying that whatever words were coming out of my mouth were quite possibly the dumbest sentences uttered aloud by anyone, ever, I found myself slipping into conversations with attractive strangers at parties and holding my own. I'd always been shy, which is, weirdly, one of the reasons I had been attracted to journalism and writing: it forced me to talk to people. And since I had a legitimate reason to talk to them, I never had to worry about whether the person I was talking to secretly wanted to get away from me, because even if they did, they'd still have to finish the interview.

I wasn't alone in my Vicodin abuse during this time. According to the National Survey on Drug Use and Health, in three short years, between 2002 and 2005, the number of Americans using painkillers nonmedically grew by over 3 million people; at last count that total number was 32.7 million. I started noticing certain statistics. For example, in 2004 there were more people in the United States using prescription painkillers recreationally for the first time than there were using either marijuana or cocaine combined. This wasn't surprising to me at all. Americans take pills for everything. According to the FDA, pharmacists filled 3.1 billion prescriptions in 2003, up 60 percent from ten years prior. Add to that the fact that every year, approximately 15 percent of the top two hundred largest selling pharmaceuticals are expensive new drugs, with no generic equivalents. Even our own beauty department at *Jane* magazine was starting to tout different pills as an effective way to treat skin problems, rather than creams or lotions. So why not use them to get fucked up too? At different times in my life I'd been put on antidepressants like Prozac, Parnate, and Zyprexa. They did little for my depression, but here was a pill that really worked, one that by curing the physical pain of simply being alive, cured my mental pain as well. Even better, it got me high.

Here's how. Humans have opiate receptors distributed throughout the brain, with higher concentrations of receptors in areas such as the basal ganglia and thalamus. These receptors are proteins located on the surfaces of nerve cells, or neurons. Neurons communicate with each other by sending out chemical signals called *neurotransmitters*. In the peripheral nervous system, nerve endings that deliver pain signals to the central nervous system are called *nociceptors*. For example, nociceptors in your fingertips might tell your brain that you've just touched a hot stove, or that the joint you're smoking has just burned down to your thumb and forefinger.

This pain signal is regulated by the rapid entry of calcium into the cells through calcium channels, cellular gatekeepers that control the release of neurotransmitters. Calcium channels concentrated in neural (nerve) tissue are called *N-type channels*. Scientists are trying to find new ways to treat pain by targeting these channels. The challenge is to control pathological pain (that is, pain that is not useful in helping a person avoid injury) without the undesirable, yet common, central nervous system side effects of respiratory depression and dependence.

Normally, opiate receptors are activated when your body produces endorphins, which are involved in a ton of normal body functions, such as respiration, nausea, regulation of hormones, and pain modulation. Morphine, heroin, and opioids (synthetic opiates) like Vicodin, OxyContin, and Percocet metabolize into replications of endorphin molecules that fit into pain receptors and flood into your body, making you feel euphoric. These endorphin replications differ, depending on the drug. Vicodin metabolizes into something called hydromorphone, and OxyContin, a controlled-release formulation of oxycodone, metabolizes into noroxycodone and other metabolites, but for all of these painkillers the end result on your body is similar. Your pupils constrict, your pulse slows down, your breathing becomes slower, and your blood pressure falls. Anxiety melts away and you feel utterly relaxed. Of course, pain goes away too. The reason why opiates can be so addictive is because after the brain starts getting them consistently, it stops producing endorphins on its own.

All of this, of course, depends on a lot of factors. Not everyone's body responds the same way to opioids. Variables can include age and weight, and in a lot of cases, totally unknown influences or something as simple as a sensitive stomach. I have a lot of friends who can't stand Vicodin because it makes them nauseated. Other people can overdose and die if they drink alcohol on even one or two painkillers, while a lot of people (myself included) have taken pills as strong as morphine and Dilaudid, gotten wasted on cheap beer and champagne, and woken up fine the next day. That's not to say it couldn't still happen to me. It's a total crap shoot, which makes these pills even more dangerous when used incorrectly.

Regardless of how or where someone gets their first taste of prescription painkillers (through a friend, a surgical procedure, a parent's medicine cabinet, or, say, a journalism assignment), the one common factor that can contribute to continued, abusive intake is that there's a presumed element of safety to prescription painkillers that doesn't exist with any other kind of drug out there, except maybe benzodiazepines like Valium or Xanax.

Even for the bravest thirteen-year-old, smoking your first joint is going to be a little bit terrifying, but that's part of the initiation, part of the excitement. It's the gateway to your cool older sibling's life or your foray into the bad kids' world that you've always looked at wistfully from afar. But with pills, you know that somewhere down the line, it came from a doctor. A safe, kindly doctor who knew just what you needed and would never distribute something that could potentially hurt you.

During my years of pill abuse after that initial first bottle, I knew

I wasn't alone in my use, so I didn't feel much shame. All I had to do was turn on the TV or go to the movies to see that everyone else was doing it too. The media hadn't dubbed us "Generation Rx" for nothing. In the American remake of the Japanese film *The Ring*, the doomed private-school girls in the opening scene aren't looking to raid the liquor cabinet when their parents aren't home—they just want to know where the mother hides her Vicodin. On the television series *House*, the brilliant doctor saves life after life while popping loads of Vicodin. The awesomely trashy ladies from *Sordid Lives* are downing Valium in practically every scene.

Pill use is a ubiquitous element in celebrity tabloids too. Witness Winona Ryder's inexplicable shoplifting spree in 2001: she was busted with several illegal bottles of prescription painkillers. According to *USA Today*, she had used six different aliases while seeking prescription drugs. She had thirty-seven prescriptions filled by twenty doctors over a three-year span, a method known as "doctor shopping."

Mischa Barton's younger sister has checked herself into rehab for painkiller abuse, as have Robbie Williams, Matthew Perry, Melanie Griffith, Jamie Lee Curtis, Charlie Sheen, and Kelly Osborne, just to name a few. Conservative kingpin Rush Limbaugh was booked on charges of doctor shopping for his Vicodin addiction. When Nicole Richie was arrested for driving the wrong way on the highway in Burbank she admitted to police that she had taken Vicodin that night (citing menstrual cramps). For a while, Lindsay Lohan's own father wouldn't stop talking to the press about his famous daughter's addiction to painkillers. And because the autopsy report showed Heath Ledger's death to be an accidental combination of oxycodone, hydrocodone, diazepam, temazepam, alprazolam, and doxylamine, the specter of pills will unfortunately always hang around his name.

John F. Kennedy Jr.'s use of methamphetamines and pills has been well documented. His supplier was a German refugee doctor named Max Jacobson. Max was one of the original famous "Dr. Feelgoods," a doctor who just doles out whatever pills you want without really taking into consideration any sort of actual diagnosis. (His other nickname was "Miracle Max.") Other celebrity clients of his included Tennessee Williams and Truman Capote, and it's rumored that he was Andy Warhol's Factory Kids' supplier as well.

So while I knew they were all around me, I never really questioned why there were suddenly so many pills everywhere. Even my short little *Jane* article was just out to prove that it was possible to get these pills, not why. But there are a number of social and economic factors that caused prescription painkillers to suddenly become America's latest obsession.

Carol Boyd is a professor of nursing and women's studies at the University of Michigan, director of the Institute for Research on Women and Gender, and a research scientist for the Substance Abuse Research Center. She has been studying the rise of prescription painkiller abuse since 2000.

"Listen," she tells me, over the phone from her Michigan office. "I'm a kid of the 1960s. Quaaludes and Valiums were swapped all the time, so it's not that prescription pill abuse is so unusual. Back in the 1950s and early 1960s, everyone was using Miltown, a tranquilizer that later became mostly replaced by benzos."

But in 2000, when she was focusing her drug research on Ecstasy and other "club drugs" like Special K and GHB, she witnessed something at a sports event that she went to with her son. "I saw two different kids use someone else's prescription asthma inhaler, and with impunity," she says. "They just tossed it over to the next person. I decided to start including more questions about prescription drug use in our questionnaires, and we were getting hits—hits that were throwing us way off," she said.

"Keep in mind, the National Institute on Drug Abuse had been asking about prescription pill use in their own monitoring surveys, but the wording was such that they weren't able to home in on what the specific pills were. Oxy and Vicodin were mixed into the same category as heroin and morphine. So our own federal questionnaires were completely off the dime and didn't catch the epidemic in time."

It makes sense that there would be some flawed data out there because of the methods used to obtain these numbers. We suddenly had 32.7 million people using painkillers nonmedically, but almost all studies are based on questionnaires or interviews. This method of data collection, called self-report, often lacks validity and reliability for several reasons. First, people tend to underreport their drug use, especially for legal but socially stigmatized drugs such as tobacco. They may also underreport drug use if they perceive a lack of privacy, as may happen when a survey is administered at school. Second, it's often difficult to get these surveys into the hands of the people most at risk, since drug users tend to fly under the radar. And finally, the fewer users there are of a given drug, the harder it is to count them. Take heroin, for example. According to the 2006 National Survey on Drug Use and Health (the most recent survey available when this book was published), 14.8 million people age twelve and older had used marijuana during the past month, and 2.4 million had used cocaine. By contrast, only 338,000 had used heroin. Reaching this sliver of the pie is complicated by the reality that many hard-core drug users lack a permanent address or are in prison.

Dr. Boyd also became convinced that Ecstasy and club-drug use was starting to decline. "They're just too dysphoric, they don't mellow you out enough. I think Ecstasy will be one of those drugs, like peyote, that comes and goes. It burns itself out, then comes back around, then burns itself back out again."

But prescription painkillers were different. She believes there were three things culturally that were going on that contributed to this sudden rise of painkiller abuse. The first was the rise of the Internet. We suddenly had more access to information. Say someone has a mole that looks funny; he can go online and get gobs of really important information on how to take care of it. The bad part of access to that kind of information is that you can easily find out about dosing and how to use prescription drugs to get high.

The second thing was September 11. It was harder to get other kinds of drugs into the country because of the overall security crackdown. The third was an upswing in prescribing by physicians. People with cancer were living longer, but they were also requiring more analgesics and benzos like Valium and Xanax for the pain and anxiety that comes along with debilitating diseases.

As a result, there are now more pharmaceutical drugs out there to be illegally diverted. "All of these things converge to make drugs more available and make the knowledge about how to use them more available," Dr. Boyd says.

Dr. Boyd believes there are four main kinds of pill users. The first group are *medical misusers*. "These are the people who have a prescription for Vicodin because, say, they had their wisdom teeth taken out. The doctor tells them to take one Vicodin every six hours, and they do it, but at night the pain is so great that they decide to take two pills every three hours or every two hours. On our initial surveys, these people showed up as nonprescription drug users, but they had a prescription and were self-treating. I would argue that that person is at risk, but probably stops taking the Vicodin when the pain goes away," she says.

She calls the second group *medicine abusers*. This is the group that has a legitimate prescription for Vicodin for the hypothetical wisdom teeth removal, but they save the leftover pills and take them recreationally when they want to go to a party and drink. That is abuse. It's not self-treatment. It's using specifically to get high or create an altered state, and mixing it with another drug. But both medicine abusers and medical misusers are *not* taking the medication illegally. They have their own prescriptions.

The third group she calls *prescription drug misusers*. This is, say, the girl who has really bad menstrual cramps but wants to go to the homecoming dance. Her mother feels bad for her and gives her daughter the Vicodin left over from her own wisdom teeth removal so she can take care of the cramps and go to the dance. It's a form of nonmedical use of prescription opiates. It's diverting a medication illegally to someone who doesn't have her own prescription and isn't using it for its intended purpose.

Dr. Boyd also argues that this group probably has fewer consequences. Albeit they are still at risk, but not as affected as the biggest group, the fourth one, *prescription drug abusers*. This is the group that takes or steals diverted pills from friends or family and uses them specifically to get high.

Dr. Boyd's concern is that when it comes to most drug research, these four different groups get lumped together, but it's not the same story for all four. They may all end up in the last category because they are all at risk for addiction, but their motivations are different and their access to the drugs is different. In order to really understand someone's drug use, you need to know his or her initial motivation.

My only disagreement with Dr. Boyd is her belief that prescription drug misusers (the girl who is getting pills from her mom) probably have fewer negative consequences. I think it's the opposite. Think back to that oh so quotable anti-marijuana ad from 1987, the one where the kid is banging away on invisible drums while wearing huge headphones, and his mustached dad bursts into his bedroom with the kid's drug stash and yells, "Who taught you how to do this stuff??" and the kid goes "YOU, all right? I learned it by watching YOU." It was genius as a pop culture idiom, but also totally true. I felt completely justified smoking pot in high school after I discovered my mom's old copy of *The Marijuana Cookbook* tucked away behind the equally stoner-esque recipe tome, *The Enchanted Broccoli Forest*. But she had only kept the former around as a cultural artifact from the 1960s. It wasn't until college that I discovered that recipes from the first book went transcendentally well with recipes from the second.

In Dr. Boyd's studies, she is finding that with prescription pill misuse, younger women are using more opioid analgesics than men, and more often they use these pills to self-treat. "It's surprising," she says, "because it's the first time that we've seen a popular drug that girls are using more than boys. The question is, why? We know that young women are more likely to experience depression, so it's possible that young women are trying to self-treat a mood disorder. Young women also are more likely to be sexually victimized [by incest and sexual assault] and sexual assault is thought, at least by some scholars, to be etiologic to a substance abuse disorder. So a desire to cope with the aftermath of assault might be another factor. Another is that during their lifetime, women see more physicians and, thus, get prescribed medications more often. It appears that mothers may be more sympathetic to their daughters' pain and give them diverted pain medication more liberally, maybe because it's easier for girls to admit that they have pain. So far the data doesn't show that girls and women become addicted to pain pills more than men, but under the age of twenty-five years, they more frequently become nonmedical users. But again, our original studies were exploratory and cannot answer all our suppositions; in the future our work will examine gender differences and the self-treatment hypothesis more thoroughly."

These initial findings came from two studies, the first conducted in 2003 among 1,017 ten- to eighteen-year-olds, and the second in 2005, where Dr. Boyd and her team surveyed 1,086 children in grades 7 to 12. There haven't been any large-scale longitudinal studies of addicts to see what sorts of patterns really evolve over the course of a lifetime. But the data that we do have makes it clear that the nonmedical use of prescription pain relievers has risen to scarily high levels, and the numbers have not yet begun to recede from this peak.

I obviously fall into the prescription drug abusers category. I could never be a prescription drug misuser, because that would mean giving away my stash for free. I don't care how bad someone's menstrual cramps are.

CHAPTER 2

"I Want Total Sensory Deprivation and Backup Drugs"

MY BEST FRIEND, EMILY, discovered pills when her father had a heart attack in 2001. Up until that point she smoked pot and drank socially. She had taken Ecstasy a few times in college and shared the occasional bag of cocaine with me. At twenty-six, she was a rising star at a large advertising firm in the city, and she got high the way you were supposed to. We'd met at a birthday party through a mutual friend at *Jane*. She told me she liked my articles; I told her I loved her hair. The bond was immediate and permanent, I think because despite our shallow cocktail talk we sensed a shared affiliation with contradiction and morbidity. I learned she'd grown up the cool high school cheerleader who secretly shuttled pregnant girls two counties over to get abortions. In college, she edited a zine that dealt with HIV-positive people maintaining a healthy sense of continued sexuality. She was obsessed with the Mütter Museum of medical oddities in Philadelphia. And then there was her hair. It was a shocking platinum blond, the kind only achieved with a bottle that would probably kill a small town if it ever leaked into the water supply. Think Marilyn Monroe under fluorescent lights. It was pure chemical shine.

When she got the call about her father's sudden heart attack a few weeks after 9/11, her boyfriend drove her back to the small town in Pennsylvania where she'd grown up. During the drive she got a message that her father wasn't going to pull through. He was brain-dead and in a coma. The paramedics had brought him back to life just so the family could gather around him and say good-bye. When they arrived, as Emily sat in the hospital waiting room, a nurse came in and slipped something small and round into her hand.

"Here, honey, you'll need this tonight," she said, patting her shoulder.

Looking back, Emily thinks it was probably a mild, generic benzo. Until that day in the hospital Emily had relied on Theraflu PM if she needed help sleeping. But that night, back at her father's house, the over-the-counter medicine was doing nothing to stop the noise in her head. She took the mystery pill and slept, deeply.

The next day, as the family made preparations for the funeral, Emily's boyfriend's well-meaning sister, the town's local pot dealer, pulled into the driveway. Emily walked out to greet her and was handed a clear sandwich baggie filled with several different kinds of pills of all shapes, sizes, and colors. "On the house, Em," she'd said. "I'm so sorry."

"What are these?" Emily asked.

The dealer repeated almost the same words as the nurse: "You're going to need them."

She took the pills inside, reached into the baggie, and swallowed the first one that touched her fingers. Her brothers and her mother were back at the hospital. She sat down on the couch. Her dad's ash-tray was on the coffee table, one and a half cigarettes ground inside a pool of ashes. As her mind settled and a warm comfortable haze enveloped her, she had a burst of practical insight and checked her father's computer. As Emily had suspected, there was enough porn on the hard drive to keep an entire fraternity occupied for a whole semester. She erased the files and canceled his accounts. She sat down in front of the answering machine and retrieved condolences from people who weren't even sure who they were leaving their messages for, knowing that the recorded voice they'd just heard was no longer there.

Emily doesn't remember what she did with the rest of the pills.

The dealer who gave them to her later became addicted to whatever it was she had been distributing and soon turned to heroin. What Emily does remember is the connection between mind-shattering emotional pain and the temporary solace the pills provided. And that's why, a few years later, in the midst of a brutal breakup with her musician boyfriend, Emily showed up at my apartment with tears streaming down her face and quoted our favorite line from *Ab Fab*: "I want total sensory deprivation and backup drugs."

Luckily, I had just the thing for her. I gave her two Vicodins and a cup of tea. We sat on opposite ends of the sofa. She hugged a pillow to her chest and didn't have to say anything. Instead of consoling her for her broken heart, I turned on a marathon of *America's Next Top Model* and let the pills do their work. We spent the next four hours in silence, in the dark, with only the light from the television to wash over our glazed eyes. We didn't need anyone, not even each other. I woke up the next morning, still on the couch. There was no hangover, no cocaine depression creeping around the corners of my brain like the Nothing from *The NeverEnding Story*. There was just a bottle of pills on the coffee table and Emily, stirring awake across from me.

"Hey, Em," I said, yawning and stretching. "Let's take pills and go look at art."

At first, the refills were easy. I'd already established a relationship with my original online pharmacy, so I never needed to re-fax my fake papers or talk to another doctor-for-hire. In fact, they called me to schedule refills (to this day, I *still* get calls from online pharmacies). I was making an associate editor's salary at the time, which meant I could barely afford food after I paid my rent and bills. Luckily the pharmacy took credit cards. It also helped that the pills kept me indoors on most nights, so I didn't spend money at bars.

The pharmacies that still call me these days are mostly offering mild sedatives or muscle relaxers. It's much harder to get anything stronger now, because of the Drug Enforcement Agency's crackdown. In 2003, as I was becoming more and more addicted to my FedEx'd

Vicodin, the DEA established a special pharmaceutical Internet coordination section. They had formally recognized online pharmacies as an epidemic as early as 2000, but prior to 2003, different DEA divisions handled the cases independently.

The DEA's Office of Diversion Control ("diversion" meaning controlled substances being illegally distributed, i.e., pharmaceuticals) was initially established as a regulatory arm of the agency. Its classification system for illegal drugs and legal controlled substances regulated by the federal government came about in 1970, when Congress passed the Controlled Substances Act. (The DEA wasn't actually created until 1973; prior to its formation, drug scheduling was overseen by the Bureau of Narcotics and Dangerous Drugs.)

This system assigns federally regulated substances to one of five categories, depending on how relatively safe or dangerous they are, how great a potential for abuse or likelihood of addiction they pose, and whether they have any medical value. Schedule I drugs are those that have high abuse potential and no currently accepted medical use; for example, heroin, Ecstasy, and psilocybin, a component of psychotropic mushrooms. Cocaine isn't on this list, because it still has a limited medical use as a local anesthetic for some eye, ear, and throat surgeries, so it falls under Schedule II drugs, which are legally available only by prescription. These drugs have a high level of abuse potential and users run the risk of physical dependency. Drugs in the Schedule II category also include narcotic painkillers like morphine, oxycodone, and codeine, and drugs used for attention deficit disorder (ADD), like the amphetamines found in Adderall. Vicodin and hydrocodone are classified as Schedule III controlled substances, meaning that they have been determined to have less potential for abuse relative to Schedule II drugs, but still may have the potential to be abused and to cause addiction or dependence.

The Office of Diversion Control initially started out inspecting large-scale drug manufacturers and distributors. But around the mid-1980s, the DEA began to see evidence of new kinds of pharmaceutical diversions, and the ODC began to change accordingly. It started to get more involved in criminal investigations and investigations of pharmacies and doctors who were illegally selling drugs they had access to. About ten years later, in the mid-1990s, the ODC started to see an even larger scale of diversion going on. Once Internet shopping became the norm, the volume of drugs being pumped out to consumers online exploded.

There are two main types of Internet pharmacies. The first is a legitimate, registered pharmacy that decides to make extra money by selling its wares nationwide. The pills originate from the usual supply medical chain: drugs manufactured in the United States that have been made available to the pharmacy through a distributor and have been accounted for. The pharmacy will align itself with a doctor or doctors who are willing to write bogus prescriptions for anyone with a credit card. Following a typical pattern, in 2004, a pharmacy in Fort Worth, Texas, that had been illegally employing doctors in the Caribbean to authorize its Internet orders was taken down by the DEA.

The other type relies on drugs that are manufactured in other countries and then smuggled into the United States. The DEA took down a major operation in 2003 whose supply source was in India. The leaders of the drug ring set up a receiving warehouse in Philadelphia, then moved the operation to New York to set up an order fulfillment center. They hired dozens of people to count pills, place them in packages, and send them to buyers via UPS.

My pharmacy fit the former model. The pharmacy address was featured prominently on my pill bottle, and the fact that I had to talk to a "doctor" meant the pharmacy was at least trying to put up a legitimate front. But suddenly my online pharmacy disappeared and its number was disconnected. The afternoon it happened I had noticed that my current bottle was getting low; I only had about ten pills left. My pharmacy was usually pretty good about sending products overnight, but sometimes there would be a delay of a few days, so I liked to reorder before I completely ran out. At this point I was up to about four or five pills a day. I'd take my first two Vicodin toward the end of the day at work, then keep popping extras as the night went on. There was no way I was going to let my last ten pills disappear before I had a supply lined up. So I simply made another Internet search for "buy Vicodin" and found another source. From then on, whenever I started to run low on my pills, I'd just call the pharmacy and reorder. If the pharmacy had been shut down, I'd do another Google search and start the whole cycle over again, with ever-increasing frequency.

Caleb likes to claim that his OxyContin addiction started with MTV.

When I first got to know him, he was twenty-five and living above his parents' garage in the suburbs of Los Angeles. He's your typical LA native—tall, blond, a splash of beach bum freckles across the center of his face. As a teenager he did tons of drugs—acid, pot, speed, coke. He doesn't even remember the first time he took Vicodin, but he knows that was the first pill he ever tried. It was just after he graduated high school, and he was bored with pot and how tired it made him feel. Someone gave him two Vicodins that he washed down with a beer. "I just got that sort of tired-wired buzz that I really like," he remembers.

After that night, he started asking around, bugging people who he had heard through the grapevine had their own prescriptions from dental work, broken limbs, minor surgeries. "The great thing about it was that I could do anything on Vicodin," he remembers. "Work on music or drive or whatever. But the problem was that I could never get it steadily. The pills would come and they'd go. At one point I got a bottle of a hundred that was prescribed to my sister, and when that bottle ran out it was the first time I felt withdrawal. I didn't even realize that's what it was, I just thought I had gotten the flu."

After about two years of taking all the Vicodin he could get his hands on, Caleb saw a show called *MTV True Life—OxyContin*. "I saw all these testimonials of people saying that Oxy was better than Vicodin," he remembers. "They called it hillbilly heroin. They explained that it was all the opiates of Vicodin without all the acetaminophen added."

Acetaminophen, the active ingredient in over-the-counter painkillers like Tylenol, is also found in prescription narcotics like Vicodin (hydrocodone and acetaminophen) and Percocet (oxycodone and acetaminophen). Yet acetaminophen is a much less powerful painkiller than the narcotic drugs with which it's combined. Eliminating it as an ingredient in these stronger painkillers lessens the damaging effects the pills can have on your liver and gives you a pure rush of the really powerful goods.

"I was like, 'Oooh, I want to try that,'" Caleb says. "Which is embarrassing because the show was about all these people who were having problems with it. They weren't making it appealing, but I already knew what it felt like to do pills, and I knew that if I could get a hold of this one, it would feel really good. The problem was, I couldn't find them anywhere."

Caleb went on a mission. He asked everyone he knew, specifically targeting people he'd gotten Vicodin from in the past and his regular pot dealers. Finally, a friend of a friend got a steady OxyContin supply because he knew a crew of people who were robbing trucks that delivered the pills to pharmacies. Hillbilly heroin was officially all over the California suburbs.

I take offense to the phrase "hillbilly heroin." Not just because I'm originally from Tennessee and have a strong sense of state pride, but because it's a contradiction. In most major cities, the current street value for pills usually follows the $1 per milligram rule, so an 80 mg pill of OxyContin usually goes for $80 if you're a first-time buyer (regular customers can usually work out discounts). The street value of a bag of heroin is around $10 to $20. If you go by the rules of the hillbilly stereotype, you'd assume that their version of heroin would be less expensive than the original. Like buying generic toothpaste instead of Crest. I understand that the media needed a cute, buzz-worthy phrase to document the rise of OxyContin abuse in rural areas, but in terms of street value for a similar high, OxyContin is more like sucker's smack.

I tried for weeks to land an interview with Dr. J. David Haddox, who is Purdue Pharma's (the makers of OxyContin) senior medical director and official spokesman. But Purdue's media relations department wouldn't let me near him. I imagine it was because I made the dumb mistake of telling them the title of this book. I was told curtly that there were enough third-party medical experts out there for me to talk to, but I think the main reason Purdue didn't want me to talk to Haddox is because the company got in a ton of trouble for the way it initially marketed OxyContin to doctors. Not to mention all the lawsuits that came a few years later.

In order to market the drug, Purdue targeted thousands of private-practice doctors and invited them to all-expenses-paid seminar weekends in warm locations like Florida and California to talk about pain management. The seminars stressed treating pain with their product, unfortunately a standard practice among some drug companies.

When the FDA approved OxyContin, Purdue's biggest painkiller was MS Contin, a controlled-release form of morphine. But there was resistance to treating chronic pain with morphine. It's a very strong narcotic derived from opium with a lot of stigma attached to it, and it wasn't too popular with doctors because of its potential for abuse. But OxyContin was a *synthetic* (man-made) form of morphine called oxycodone, and that somehow made it all right.

Like MS Contin, OxyContin is a controlled-released formula, so it lasts for twelve hours. Another advantage was that doctors could increase the patient's dosage over time because the drug didn't contain acetaminophen, which in larger doses can damage the liver and cause gastrointestinal bleeding. The FDA approved OxyContin for people with moderate to severe pain that went on for more than a few days. It's most often prescribed to people with severe pain brought on by cancer, a prolonged surgical recovery, or chronic pain syndromes, such as back pain.

What was quickly discovered was that if you chewed the tablets or crushed them and either snorted the powder or injected the dissolved product, the time-release aspect of the pill was destroyed and what you got was the full effect, all at once. Meaning you could get a giant rush similar to the effect of heroin, rather than the longer-lasting, gentle rolling waves of pain relief. No one is exactly sure how people got the idea to crush the tablets. But it's standard practice that if there *is* a way to abuse a drug, drug addicts will find it.

The U.S. Department of Health and Human Services has admitted as much:

At the time of OxyContin's approval the FDA was aware that crushing the controlled-release tablet followed by intravenous injection of the tablet's contents could result in a lethal overdose. A warning against such practice was included in the approved labeling. The FDA did not anticipate, however, nor did anyone suggest, that crushing the controlled-release capsule followed by intravenous injection or snorting would become widespread and lead to a high level of abuse.

It's debatable whether painkiller junkies got the idea to shoot the drug just by reading the label.

Caleb's first steady OxyContin supply—those friends of friends who were robbing the trucks that delivered the drugs from the manufacturer to a supply center—came from another fairly common form of diversion. The DEA recently handled a case where a group of thieves stalked the driver of an eighteen-wheeler as he left a drug manufacturer. They followed the truck, and then waited until the driver pulled into a truck stop. There is no official requirement for pharmaceutical companies to use GPS systems in their trucks, but many do so anyway because of the high value of their product. Sometimes they will place it with the truck, sometimes they will place it with the drug load. In this particular case, the thieves were smart enough to know about the truck's GPS device and disabled it. But they weren't sure if there was another one in the load, so they separated the trailer from the cab and parked it a few miles away in a vacant lot and left it there. The plan was to wait a few days to see if the cab was collected, and if not, make off with the haul. But before this happened, another trucker noticed the cab just sitting in the lot and called the police. Too bad for the thieves—the load was 16.6 *million* hydrocodone pills. The DEA believes the robbers had no idea just how large their haul would have been.

Caleb's friend who knew the guys who were robbing OxyContin delivery trucks kept up a successful diversion business for about eight months before it all came crashing down, though not through a typical bust. The man who was in charge of distributing the pills to buyers overdosed on methadone in Caleb's friend's house. Someone called an ambulance, but in his panic stupidly warned 911, "don't bring any cops." So of course the police showed up, searched the house, and found guns, $14,000 worth of marijuana, a hundred methadone pills, and tons of drug residue.

"He got locked up in the harshest of prisons," Caleb says. "He was the only white kid there, he went through withdrawal there, and I know he got fucked with. I don't know what eventually happened to him. But all I could think at the time, was, 'Damn, that was our hookup!'"

After the bust, Caleb got sick from Oxy withdrawal too. Since opiates stimulate the endorphin receptors in your brain and curb the release of the neurotransmitter norepinephrine, withdrawal symptoms are brought on by a surge of norepinephrine in the brain. (Most attention deficit disorder drugs, like Ritalin, are designed to *boost* norepinephrine and dopamine in a person's system.) But in an opiate user going through withdrawal, this norepinephrine surge can cause agitation, nausea or vomiting, abdominal pain, diarrhea, insomnia, increased blood pressure, and sweating. The first time I went through withdrawal it just felt like a bad cold. I was able to drink it away with hot toddies. By the time I was several years into my use, withdrawal became a full-on muscle spasm on the floor situation. But most people report feeling like they have the flu mixed with a crippling depression, muscle spasms, and, at least for me, the sensation that a razor blade is scraping away at your bones.

"But the withdrawal only lasted for a few days," Caleb says. He didn't consider himself to be addicted. Neither did I, in the beginning.

These days, pain specialists continue to feud over the distinction between dependence and addiction. Some experts believe the word *addiction* has negative connotations and should not be used. Others point out that a person who is physically dependent on a medication may not necessarily exhibit addictive behaviors. Having two terms allows clinicians to differentiate one kind of patient from the other.

The current edition of the *Diagnostic and Statistical Manual of Mental Disorders*, DSM-IV, does not recognize this distinction, however. Unfortunately, this blurring of the line has actually ended up stigmatizing patients with legitimate pain by encouraging physicians to view drug-dependent patients and addicts through the same lens. The definitions are being reconsidered and may be revised for the next addition of the DSM, which will come out in 2012.

I personally believe that, for the most part, there is a difference between the terms. I define *dependence* as the body's normal adaptation to repeated dosing of a central nervous system medication. It's an expected pharmacologic response characterized by increasing tolerance over time and by withdrawal symptoms if the drug is withheld. I define *addiction* as the compulsion to continue taking a drug despite the negative consequences of doing so. Addiction, which seems to have a genetic component, is characterized by an escalating loss of control as physical tolerance develops.

My own body is a perfect storm of these two situations. Addiction, as it's described above, runs deep in my family on both sides. But I never became dependent on any of the substances I'd abused in the past until I discovered painkillers. That's when addiction and dependency met inside me, becoming the chemical equivalent of Sid and Nancy.

But there will always be room for exception, and Caleb's case is a prime example of why this feud between pain specialists exists in the first place. After he went through withdrawal, he could go weeks without physically needing pills, but he was *always* on the hunt for them.

"Once the withdrawals were over I started asking around at parties to see if anyone was holding," he says. "But when that didn't pan out, a friend and I decided to take a trip down to Tijuana to see if we could score there. I was on a mission. I at least had to find some Vicodin, if nothing else. I didn't know anyone who had bought pills in Mexico before, but I heard that it was possible."

Officially, narcotic drugs are also classified as controlled substances in Mexico and require a doctor's prescription. But that didn't stop Caleb.

"We drove down, parked in San Diego, and walked across the border. We got a beer and I noticed that there were three pharmacies on every block. So I walked into every pharmacy, one by one, and said,

'Yo necesito OxyContin, Vicodin.' And they all said, 'No, no, no.' Then like, after the twenty-fifth pharmacy, they were like, 'Yep.' They sold me eighty-milligram OxyContins for $40 a pill. We bought thirty, and after that, started making regular trips down to TJ."

Caleb started a tradition with his Tijuana trips. "My friend and I would always go to the pharmacy first," he says. "It was so easy to buy. I even asked them once if they were scared of the cops, and they'd flat-out say no. After we'd scored, we'd go have a taco and a Corona and snort one pill to make sure we had a nice buzz going for crossing back over the border. Going in was never a problem—they don't give a shit what goes on there. All the security is coming back out. We kind of felt a little like James Bond, keeping the drugs hidden in our socks, going through the checkpoints, answering questions. But it was scary, too. Mexican prison is about the scariest thing I can imagine. *Any* prison is the scariest thing I can imagine, but a Mexican one would be worse. My life would be over."

Since walking back over the border to the United States always took longer than coming in (about an hour and a half on foot), Caleb and his friend found a quicker way to get across. One day, when the line stretched on forever, it was going to take them about five hours at least to walk it. "We were shitting ourselves," Caleb says. "Then we noticed these people riding little children's bicycles alongside the line. The cars were on the left, the sidewalk with the huge line was on the right, and in between we'd occasionally see someone ride by on a tiny pink bike. So we traced the path backward and found this little bike stand where you could rent a little girl's bike for $5 and skip the whole line. There was a person on the other side of the border who would collect the bikes once you crossed." Caleb's friend, who was six-foot-four, got the smallest bike of all, one that still had training wheels and ratty old streamers spilling out of the handlebars. The two of them whizzed past the line, high out of their minds under the Mexican sunset, cracking up the whole way.

CHAPTER 3

"I Meant for You to Take One or Two, Not the Whole Thing!"

AFTER ABOUT SEVEN MONTHS of taking Vicodin steadily, I quit my job at *Jane* and moved upstate to work on a documentary series for the Sundance Channel about transgender college students, called *Trans-Generation*.

When a heavily researched story I wrote about the subculture of death fetishists, people who make fake snuff films, was killed (heh) for being too controversial (despite being photographed by legendary photographer Stephen Shore), I decided I wanted to turn it into a documentary. I teamed up with a director and used my original resources and contacts in the death fetish community to create a fifteen-minute trailer that we shopped around, to no avail. It was deemed, pretty much all around, that the subject of sex and death together was just too dark. But on the basis of that trailer reel, I was hired as a field producer on *TransGeneration* by one of the production companies we had sent the project to. Basically, this meant that I collected raw footage of our subjects to send to the director in Los Angeles.

On December 23, 2004, I moved to Hudson, a small town about 120 miles north of New York, with the idea that I would drive to Northampton, Massachusetts, whenever we had to film. I slowly tapered myself off pills and went through minor withdrawal for about a week, but I drank heavily every night to get through.

I was also reeling from a brutal breakup with a guy named Joey whom I had fallen hard and fast for. He was best known in my circle of friends for burning his own initials into the inner thigh of a male fashion assistant at *Jane*. He was bearded, with a hairy chest and a penchant for wearing a raccoon tail from one boot. He was kind of evil, and I was insanely in love before finding out that he already had another boyfriend he had been keeping a secret from me. I was determined to use the isolation of a small town to clear my head and get over Joey.

I was 100 percent pill-free for the entire shoot. I was excited about getting to work on a documentary and I didn't want to mess it up. Without pills, my shyness had returned, but again I was able to fall back on the excuse that my subjects had to talk to me, since they had signed on for the project.

After we wrapped up shooting for the year, there was nothing left for me to do in Hudson. I suddenly found myself out of money and working as a landscaper, literally shoveling shit into the lush backyard gardens of mansions in Dutchess County. I actually really liked the hard labor, but loathed the class issues it was bringing up for me. Whenever some fabulously wealthy housewife would come out and yell at me that I'd accidentally ripped out all of her rare, hybrid perennials instead of the ragweed, I wanted to scream, "Fuck you, I've interviewed Patti Smith!"

It was time to get back into publishing.

My apartment on the Lower East Side was still being sublet by a friend of mine, so I ended up temporarily moving into a room in a house in Bushwick, Brooklyn, with a girl I knew named Zoe, a tattooed lesbian who worked at a sex shop. I didn't have a job lined up yet, but I'd been commuting down to the city from Hudson and going on interviews at various magazines. I had about enough money saved up to last me one month in New York.

I called the entrance to my new home the Tunnel of Terror. From the street, the row house looked like any other Bushwick building— wan yellow aluminum siding, bars over the windows, trash strewn among small patches of weeds trying to break through the concrete sidewalk. You had to avoid piles of feces, some of which looked disturbingly human.

Our place didn't have a typical front door; instead, a six-foot-high wooden box jutted out into the street, creating what looked like a small outhouse. You entered through that door, and found that the additional space where the sidewalk should be was an enclosed garbage room, the smell of which was your normal rotting food stench mixed with heavy top notes of baby diapers. There was another door four feet ahead, which led to a basement tunnel that stretched into darkness when the overhead lights were burned out. But sometimes the dim bulbs worked fine, providing enough light to watch four-inch cockroaches and rats the size of a cat part like the Red Sea as you walked through. The hardest part was getting to the end of the tunnel, where there were four concrete steps leading up to a heavy metal back door. The ceiling was so low that no matter how far down you stooped, the top of your head always grazed the exposed beams above. If you were lucky you'd just get a tiny bump. On bad days you ended up with a spider or a roach hitching a ride in your hair.

The door opened up onto a cement garden courtyard and a freestanding, three-story house smack in the center of the block. From the street, it was hidden from view. My new roommates had planted morning glories at the base of the fences that separated us from our neighbors' backyards, and several plant boxes held tomatoes, basil, and mint. There's no mistaking the industrial feel of a garden trying to grow in Bushwick, but the added green against the stark concrete ground made the journey through the Tunnel of Terror feel like a test of strength to reach Nirvana. There were two other people living in the house, along with two dogs who would constantly play in the cement garden. I wasn't worried about my cat Ollie getting along with the dogs, since he'd always been pretty dominant.

On my first night in the new apartment, I was feeling nervous after being gone so long from New York. I knew that Zoe had recently recovered from a nasty bout of stage 2 Hodgkin's lymphoma, so I asked her if she had any Vicodin or other painkillers left over.

"Sure," she said. She went into her room, came back, tossed me a half-full bottle, and walked out.

I sat on my bed, surrounded by unpacked boxes. It was the Fourth of July and booming explosions seemed to be coming from all directions, making Ollie freak out and cower with me on the bed. I emptied a few pills out of the bottle and rolled them around in my hand like dice. They were generic hydrocodone, 7.5/325 mg. I swallowed them and got to unpacking.

My new bedroom window gave me a view of the Chrysler building. It also looked out over the backyards of the neighbors on the other side of the block. I discovered the next morning that the yard just below my window was full of roosters. They started crowing at four thirty in the morning, and their piercing screeches sounded like they were in the room. Rage seared through me. I fantasized about picking them off one by one with a gun, but later felt guilty because Zoe told me they were being kept for cock fighting, so they were already on their way to a worse death.

While working on getting my room unpacked the next morning, Emily called. She'd made a point of coming to visit me while I'd been living in Hudson, something only one other friend ever did. But that was the point, I had needed to disappear for a while. She was the only one who understood just how badly I had been hurt by Joey and how much I had needed to get away.

She told me she had a surprise for me, and we made plans for her to come over later that evening.

When I hung up the phone I noticed Ollie sitting at the foot of my bed, scratching furiously at his neck. Shit. He'd only had fleas once before, when I'd taken him on a road trip with me down south with an ex-boyfriend. Along the way, we'd stopped overnight and stayed in the basement of a friend. We spent the whole night slapping our bodies every time we'd felt another flea jumping on us from the infested carpet.

I picked Ollie up and ran my fingers through his short curly hair and saw a black wormy-looking bug wiggle away from me. I jumped an inch ahead of it inside Ollie's fur and it bumped right into my waiting fingernails. I snatched it off him, pinching its head between my forefinger and the flat surface of my thumbnail. I used my other thumbnail to crush it until it made that horrifying, yet so satisfying "pop" as its body snapped. I knew that wasn't enough to kill it completely, so I went into the bathroom and poured liquid hand soap over its still squirming body. For some reason, fleas' bodies can't take soap, so I went down to the kitchen, filled up a bowl with warm soapy water, and headed back upstairs to my room. Ollie had been following me the whole time. When we got up to my room I put the bowl on the floor, leaned up against the bed, and scooped Ollie up and onto his back. The hair on his belly is sparse, and I saw about six different black dots swarm back into the safety of his longer fur.

I put him back down and grabbed the bottle of pills Zoe had given me, opened it up, took a few more, and got to work.

I scooped him back into my lap and made soothing little noises to keep him calm. He was purring—he thought he was just being held and scratched. I hunted the fleas like big game, stalking my prey, predicting their every twist and turn on his body. Each pop between my thumbnails was my reward. My fingers were covered in flea guts, the bowl floating with dying victims, still twitching as the soapy water finished the job.

My skin started to itch from the pills, a nasty side effect when you're pulling live bugs off your pet. I was convinced that I was covered with fleas too. I probably was. My sense of failure at protecting Ollie was crushing. Rationally I knew it wasn't my fault. The dogs must have brought them into the house, and the stairs were carpeted. But I couldn't shake the feeling that this infestation on my first day back in New York could only be a bad omen.

Emily arrived around 7:00 P.M. My bedroom was set up, and I'd given Ollie a break for the day after he'd lost patience and started squirming too much. I'd told my roommates about the fleas. They seemed nonplussed but agreed to treat all the pets and call the landlord to get the place fumigated. I didn't tell Emily. I figured she'd probably freak out and leave immediately.

I escorted her through the Tunnel of Terror and up to my bedroom, where she flopped on my bed, rolled over onto her back, up onto her elbows. "I've hit the mother lode," she announced with a certain mischievous pride.

She reached into her Marc Jacobs bag, pulled out a large bottle, and dumped about 150 tiny, oval yellow pills onto my bedspread. I flopped down next to her, careful not to disturb the pile.

"What are they?" I asked. They didn't look familiar. A dusting of yellow powder surrounded the pills, sinking into the fibers of my black bedspread.

"Norco," she said. "I asked an online pharmacist for Vicodin, but they sent me this instead. I love it. It's stronger. Here, take two."

I swallowed them, without telling her I'd already been on hydrocodone all day. (Even though she was being generous, I didn't want to share my own small stash.)

She'd found an online pharmacy that was selling her these but she was running low on cash. She wasn't sure if she could make her credit card payments that month, so she offered to sell half the pile to me. I reached for my wallet.

The high kicked in fast. My vision became blurred around the sides and I could barely breathe, but the warm tingling feeling all over my body canceled any fear of overdose. We caught up on New York gossip and sat on my bed all night watching movies, even though I kept having to force my eyes to focus. At one point we ordered food, but by the time it arrived I couldn't even swallow, and mine sat uneaten on the floor by the side of the bed.

Around one in the morning, Emily got up to leave. We stumbled through the Tunnel of Terror and I walked her down to Bushwick Avenue and hailed her a cab. We hugged good-bye and our skin stuck together in the July heat.

I stood on the corner for a long time after her cab drove off. I walked into the nearest bodega and bought a 7Up, then leaned up against the building outside to smoke a cigarette. Packs of roving kids would rush by, screaming and pushing each other into the street. I must have handed out about four cigarettes to people who'd stop and ask for one. I don't know how long I stood there in the middle of the night. I just knew I didn't want to go back through the Tunnel by myself.

Forty-eight hours later, two things happened. I got a call from *V Life* magazine, *Variety*'s monthly glossy. They hired me as their East Coast editor, which meant I would get to work by myself in the *Variety* offices, since the rest of the staff was located in Los Angeles. It was still an associate editor position, but because it was technically freelance, I'd be making more money than I'd ever made in my life.

The second thing was that Zoe popped her head into my room and said, "Hey, do you have that bottle? I need to give some pills to a friend who's got a migraine."

I'd finished the entire bottle off the day before.

"Um, there's nothing left," I said, reaching for the empty bottle that was sitting on my dresser. "I'm sorry, I thought you gave me the whole thing."

"I meant for you to take one or two, not the whole thing!" She seemed flustered and pissed, but reluctant to really ream me out. In retrospect, what I should have done is offered her a matching amount of Norco to replace the hydrocodone that I'd eaten. It's what I would have done normally. But for some reason, this time around the thought never even crossed my mind. It wasn't like me, but I implicitly understood now that once they were in my possession, any and all pills belonged to me and only me. I had become rewired. No one needed to know what I was holding. It marked the beginning of a greed I'd never known myself capable of.

I met back up with Zoe recently to ask her about that day, and her own experiences with painkillers as a cancer patient. The Tunnel of Terror had been renovated and was now brightly lit and had a real floor. We sat in the concrete garden and split a six-pack while her dog played at my feet. I tried not to get too close to him, no matter how cute he was. I didn't want to catch any fleas.

Zoe grew up in Beverly Hills and had gone to school there as

well. In the 1970s, her father had been the head of one of Hollywood's most successful studios and produced some of film history's
most loved and respected films. He was also a raging cocaine addict
with a small army of close friends who also happened to be doctors.

"A lot of other kids I went to school with had fathers who were
doctors," Zoe remembers. "Some had moms who were too, but honestly, in Beverly Hills, it was mostly the dads. The moms were at
home taking Valium and diet pills. In junior high, the girls I went
to school with were always stealing their moms' diet pills. By ninth
grade, they were dipping into the Valium, and by tenth grade they
started in on Vicodin and codeine."

Zoe's crowd wasn't so into painkillers. They liked pot and sometimes cocaine, and what they discovered was that the ever-present
drug dealers at their school would trade their wares for the Vicodin
the kids could steal from their parents. A bottle of Vicodin was good
for a quarter ounce of weed in trade.

"The kids who actually *did* the pharm drugs were the really fucking annoying popular kids who didn't want anyone to think they
were stoners," Zoe remembers. "The guys who did them were the
jock guys, and the girls, well, they were the girls who were stealing
their moms' diet pills in junior high."

Zoe wasn't exactly part of the popular crowd (she had become enemies with a classmate who was the daughter of a famous rock star),
but when the movie *Clueless* came out, she thought it was a fairly decent representation of her Beverly Hills high school and the rules of
its drug hierarchy. "The movie is obviously exaggerated," she says,
"but there's this part in it where they say something about how it's
okay to smoke a doobie once in a while, but if you do it every day you
should go hang out on the grassy lawn area with the kids playing
hacky-sack. But the fucked-up thing is, the girls who felt that way, the
Gucci-wearing bitches who would skip school to go to a Fred Segal
sale, felt it was fine to steal Daddy's prescription pain pills. And that's
because those drugs didn't have the same stigma attached to them.
We all saw our parents taking them."

Zoe's own parents were divorced, and when she was seventeen, her stepfather died from a blood clot during a routine surgical procedure. On the day of the funeral, Zoe's mother was having a meltdown and sent her to pick up her Valium prescription from the drugstore. On her way back home, Zoe was hit from behind by another car. Her car was totaled. An ambulance came, but Zoe refused to get in it because she needed to get her mom's Valium back to her and make it to the funeral.

When Zoe woke up the next day, she was in severe pain. She stopped by her dad's house and mentioned it to him. He handed her a Vicodin, but she waited to take it until she got back to her mom's house. Her body didn't react well to it, and twenty minutes later Zoe was passed out cold on her mother's kitchen floor.

It was the last time she had taken Vicodin before being diagnosed with cancer. She had just turned twenty-three and had what she thought was the flu, but after she got better, her lymph nodes remained swollen. After a few months and several misdiagnoses, she was diagnosed with Hodgkin's lymphoma. Her disease had progressed to stage 2, which means that the cancer is no longer confined to a single group of lymph nodes, such as those in the spleen, but has invaded two or more sites on one side of the diaphragm, the major muscle used for breathing.

Her first surgery involved cutting open her left shoulder above the clavicle to biopsy the lymph nodes. When the pathologist's report confirmed that cancer was present, she began five months of chemotherapy.

"The chemo was the worst for me," she says. "The nausea wasn't bad because they give you a ton of pills, but my sense of smell became so heightened, I could only eat really bland things that had no scent. My hair fell out almost immediately, but I took control over that myself and had a friend shave my head. What was horrible for me was this thing called a Port-a-Cath. It's this device that they have to surgically insert inside you to deliver the chemo. The chemo needle is incredibly thick, and I started having major panic attacks every time. I'd have to sit there with this giant needle sticking out of my chest for three hours. And then the last time I had chemo, the needle didn't go in far enough. It leaked and burned a hole through my chest."

Zoe didn't realize it had happened until she got home and took a shower. She had noticed that the area where the catheter had been was looking red and swollen, and after her morning shower, as she was drying herself off, a chunk of skin the size of a silver dollar came off in the towel, revealing the catheter underneath.

After that, Zoe switched to radiation treatments and eventually covered up the catheter scar on her chest with an orchid tattoo. You can barely see the chemo mark now.

Over the course of Zoe's cancer treatment she had several different surgeries. Besides the initial tumor removal and the insertion and removal of her catheter, she had to get part of her cervix removed because her doctors had discovered more cancerous cells there. She also had to have a bone marrow biopsy.

With all of these surgeries happening in a relatively short amount of time, Zoe racked up a big Vicodin and hydrocodone supply. Her body didn't react any better to the medicine than it did when her father gave her one as a teenager. She'd take extra-strength Tylenol instead, until one of her doctors finally gave her codeine instead of Vicodin.

"That was the one drug I got where I thought, 'Oh, I *like* this one,'" she says. "I definitely started taking it out of necessity, but I prolonged the prescription past the point of needing it. I had a pill form and a liquid form. But I still had tons and tons of Vicodin just sitting around. And everyone knew I had it. It was like, 'Oh, Zoe has cancer,' so my friends would ask me for it. And I would just give it away."

Zoe didn't mind giving out her pills to friends who she thought were just using them recreationally occasionally or needed one or two to treat cramps or a migraine. "But there was one person who kept asking me for it that I felt uncomfortable about," she says. "I knew he was having addiction problems—with heroin, I think. He seemed to be nodding off a lot at the time, and I knew he was having trouble at work because of it. I gave a few to him at first but cut him off pretty quickly. I think he might have been taking OxyContin too, and for some reason, Oxy scares me. I associate it with street drugs, like heroin. If I'd been given Oxy for my surgeries, I never would have just handed it out to people. Vicodin just seems more controlled somehow. When I'd give it out to people I'd assume they were responsible enough not to take it all at once and OD. But I guess that's a pretty dumb assumption."

Her fear of OxyContin may also stem from her father. When Zoe was nineteen, she and her brother had to take him off life support after he had succumbed completely to cancer and slipped into a coma. "This is a man who was addicted to cocaine for twenty-five years," Zoe says. "He had a very high tolerance for drugs. When we took him off life support, the nurse had been pumping him full of morphine, and before he died, she said she'd never seen someone have that much morphine in his system and not die from a drug overdose. She said he'd been given enough to kill an elephant. When my brother and I were cleaning out his house, we discovered a huge supply of OxyContin, about $15,000 worth, street value. We considered trying to sell it, but I threw it away because I could never live with myself if someone OD'd and died from something I'd given them."

I didn't have to deal with that fear, because I almost never shared my painkiller stash. Pot, coke, beer, even benzos, all those were meant for consuming with friends. But painkillers were mine, and initially Emily was the only one who knew when I was holding, since she was my original supplier after moving back to New York. But even when she ran out of her own stash early, and would call and ask if she could borrow some, I always lied and said I was out, too.

I hid my bottles in the bottom of my underwear drawer, and kept my daily dose in a small gold pillbox that I'd bought for ten cents at a garage sale in Tennessee when I was in the third grade. As a kid, I'd fill with it with tiny fake diamonds pulled off my sisters' costume jewelry and pretend it was my private fortune. For some reason I'd always kept the box, maybe anticipating its future use.

The top of the small box is layered in wood, with a gold four-leaf clover set in the center of it. For luck, I guess, that its user wouldn't mix the wrong pills and OD. I'd unimaginatively named it Clover. I could fit a lot of Norco inside, along with generous doses of the generic Valium I'd started buying online again. Whenever I came across hydrocodone from a friend or someone who was selling at a party, I'd have to swap a lot of Norco out of the box, since the hydrocodone pills were so much larger. Clover was small enough to slip into my pocket and go unnoticed anywhere I went. And I quickly realized that no one ever asks you questions if you pop open a pillbox and swallow something directly in front of them. When I'd been taking lots of Vicodin at *Jane*, I'd always go into the bathroom to swallow them, but my tiny box had an air of authority and old-world sophistication that made people, even family members, politely look away as I'd snap it shut with one hand and reach for a glass of water.

There was no one monitoring me at *V Life*. When I first started the job, I'd hoped I'd get to meet some of the *Variety* reporters. I'd always loved their film reviews and usually agreed with what they had to say. But they sat in high walled cubicles one row over and pretty much ignored me. The row of cubes I sat in was completely empty except for a lone sales rep. Since no one ever arrived at the LA office until at least 1:00 P.M. New York time, I could come in whenever I wanted.

At first it was a dream job. I reconnected with all of my old film publicity contacts from *Jane* and spent my afternoons going to screenings and my evenings covering parties and film premieres. And I was functionally high out of my mind.

My first month on the job, I flew out to LA to meet the rest of the magazine's staff. It was a sterile cubicle environment, and the vibe was completely different from what I had been used to at *Jane*. We'd had cubes as well, but they were always overflowing with free CDs, books, DVDs, and weird personal items like a giant stuffed Yeti or Post-it notes attached to computer monitors with random messages like, "This world is uninhabitable." At *V Life*, there were no thirty-minute gossip sessions on the floor outside the editor in chief's office, no group lunch breaks to McDonald's, no yelling questions across the office floor at someone when you needed to remember the name of some random person Paris Hilton had been sleeping with two months ago, and having four different people yell back four different names.

But the LA staff was nice to me. I was too nervous to take any pills while I was actually in the office there, so I'd wait until I got into the parking garage at the end of the day before popping anything. I'd only learned to drive a year earlier, when I was living up in Hudson. I'd always lived in small towns or large cities, and no one had ever taught me how: I'd always gotten by on public transportation and rides from friends. After work I'd get in my rental car, take three Norcos, leave the *Variety* offices, and drive the Pacific Coast highway to Malibu. I'd find parking lots that said they were closed, but no one ever seemed to be watching them, so I'd pull up as close to the sand as possible and sit on the beach by myself until it got dark. The ocean always smelled rank and rotting, nothing like the clean salty air of the Atlantic. I'd walk along the beach until it got too cold and then head back to my car and just drive around for hours, turning down side street after side street, trying to imagine the lives of the people who lived inside these suburban homes. I'd always accidentally run a few red lights or stop signs because I was too high and distracted by the houses that I thought might have been the filming location for the exterior shots of Buffy's house on *Buffy the Vampire Slayer*. None of them ever were, but luck was always with me as far as my driving indiscretions—there were never any cops around. Maybe it was Clover looking out for me.

It was lonely, but at that point in my life I'd come to embrace loneliness. It was all I knew after a year away from the city. And as long as I had pills, I had a friend. The only time I ever really cared was at night, when I'd want someone to hold while I was falling asleep.

V Life was putting me up at the Avalon Hotel in Beverly Hills, a midcentury modern building where all the rooms surrounded a swimming pool that was always empty. After I'd get back from my drive, I'd order a cocktail and lounge by the pool, with its flickering underwater lights, hoping someone would talk to me.

I'd finally go up to my room, fall asleep, wake up, and start the same day over again. I was becoming aware that the pills that had initially lowered my social inhibitions were now building a bubble of isolation around me. I was all right with that, though. As much as I craved human contact, I now craved someone who could share the isolation with me. I wanted someone to take pills with so that we could be alone together.

Emily and I started going out on Friday nights to Hot Pink, a party on Avenue B that was pretty much the exact same group of people I'd always seen out before I left New York, only in a new location. Everything was the same, right down to the shitty coke, the Joy Division songs followed by 1980s metal, and twenty-five-minute-long bathroom lines. At a certain point we gave up and just did bumps off the backs of our hands in the corner, rather then wait for the privacy of a stall.

Cocaine and Norco made for a nice, low-grade speedball. Emily and I would usually just lean against a wall and watch people. You could smoke in the basement, and we'd chain.

One night Emily had invited another one of her shaggy-haired musician guys. As soon as he mentioned something about a song he'd written in his journal that day I tuned out and scanned the crowd. It was more packed than usual, but the stairway was temporarily empty, so when a guy appeared on the landing and paused to survey the crowd, a spotlight shone down on him and only him. He had shaggy blond hair, bright blue eyes, and he was wearing some sort of shawl thing wrapped around his neck over a coat that looked as if it had been drawn onto his body. He stood there for a minute, just sort of staring out into space.

We were leaning against the poles near the bar instead of the wall that night, and I watched him head over to the bar and order a drink. He turned and saw me staring, and to my total shock he smiled at me.

Norco making me brave, I walked right over to him and said, "Hi," and he said, "Hi," and it was really just that easy. His name was Everett and he was just coming back from some party for the insanely expensive fashion label he worked for, and, weirdly, one that I had recently become obsessed with.

We shot the shit for a while about fashion. I'd always worn T-shirts and jeans exclusively, but when I'd been in Hudson I'd found an old leather Members Only coat with fur trim around the hood at a used-clothing store. I was really proud of it. I told Everett it was coyote, and he got this disgusted look on his face as he fingered the fur near my neck.

"You're wearing dog," he said.

"No, no, the label says it's made out of coyote!" I said. "I mean, I would never wear fur, but I felt like this poor coyote was trapped inside this coat, and I wanted to bring him back out into the world, so his spirit could, you know, see it . . . and stuff."

These sorts of ideas make perfect sense to me, but I realize I should keep them to myself.

"I wear fur," Everett said, shrugging. "Who gives a shit? We just made a bunch of coats out of Finnish raccoon. But this," he said, rolling my hood cuff through his fingers again, "is dog. I can tell."

I was mortified. So I ordered a shot of tequila. He paid for it.

"I'm going to choose to believe that this is a coyote," I told him after I put my glass back down on the bar. "And he is living around my neck and getting a second chance to see the world."

Everett gave me this weird smile that I couldn't read as pity or interest until he asked, "Want to come home with me?"

I shrugged and said sure.

We caught a cab outside, and as we were crossing the Williamsburg Bridge I suddenly remembered Emily and texted her that I'd left. The cab stopped at the Lorimer Street subway stop. Everett lived a few blocks away from it.

His place was empty of everything except clothes. There were four boxes in the living room and nothing else. His bedroom was tiny and faced the street, the walls were bare but there were piles of clothes everywhere and a big walk-in closet stuffed full of suits, sweaters, shirts, belts, shoes, boots, coats, bags. I'd never seen anything like it. In a guy's room, I mean.

We smoked in silence for a while, tossed the cigarettes out the window, and he leaned in and kissed me. Clothes came off.

"Wait," I said. "Do you have any condoms I can use?"

He rolled out of bed and rummaged around in his closet before coming back with some ancient-looking Lifestyles. I tried using one but it broke almost immediately.

"Are you clean?" he asked.

"Yeah, I just got tested as soon as I moved back here," I said. "What about you?"

"It's been a while, but I'm clean. I haven't been with anyone that way for a while. Just go for it," he said.

And so I did. The great and awful thing about opiates is that they make me stay hard forever, but it's usually nearly impossible to come. So I can go forever but eventually it just gets boring and I have to make sure the other guy gets off before I pull a muscle.

Looking back, I try to think what was going through my mind about not using a condom. I was drunk, obviously, but there was something more going on. This guy was from a world foreign to me, a glamorous fashion world I'd always pretended not to give a shit about but maybe secretly wanted to be a part of. Despite entering puberty at the late dawn of the AIDS epidemic and having condom use drilled into my brain since elementary school, I didn't want to disappoint him. The only answer I can come up with is that in some sick way I thought it would make us closer, and for some reason I badly wanted to impress him.

Eventually he came and we both passed out. I woke up at dawn as he was getting dressed. "I have a meeting with a buyer, but I'll be back in a few hours," he said. I nodded and dozed off again for a while but woke up when he sat back down on the bed to say good-bye.

He put his hand on my face and gently stroked my cheek.

"Listen," he said. "If you leave before I get back, and decide to steal my clothes, just don't take any of the stuff from the spring collection. They're samples, and the only ones we've got."

I nodded. It was a fair request. As soon as he left I got out of bed and wandered around his room. I couldn't remember his name until I found a stack of mail near the window. I sat cross-legged on his bed, smoked a cigarette, and looked around at the blank white walls. It looked like an asylum. The broken condom was still lying on the floor. I left it there. I looked at the pile of shopping bags and plastic-wrapped suits that made up much of his company's spring collection. I briefly considered grabbing it and running but told myself no, that's something I would have done years ago, when I was younger. This was my new life in New York City and I wasn't going to fuck it up by making enemies right out the door. I ground out my cigarette, dug Clover out of my pants pocket, popped a Norco to help with my hangover, and fell back asleep.

I woke up when Everett slid into bed beside me a few hours later.

"I can't believe you're still here," he said.

"How'd the meeting go?" I asked.

"They were late," he fumed.

I wrapped my arms around him and we fell back asleep.

When I woke up later he was still lying next to me, staring at my face.

"Want to get brunch?" he asked.

What I wanted was a shower and my own bedroom. I declined the offer, we swapped numbers, and I took off.

"Thanks for not stealing anything," he yelled down the stairs after me.

I decided to walk home instead of taking the subway. When I'd lived in New York before, I'd refused to ever come over to Williamsburg. I'd called it the Williamsburg Curse, because cab drivers never knew how to get to where I needed to go and the L train was constantly getting shut down, so I'd end up stuck in the freezing cold, waiting an hour for an overbooked car service to come pick me up. Or I'd wake up in some guy's house and drunkenly try to navigate my way back home to Manhattan without knowing where the nearest coffee shop or subway was.

But I was getting to know the neighborhood better. It was maybe a twenty-minute walk from Everett's place to mine. I still didn't know what to make of him, and as I walked home I tried to remember more details from the night before. He seemed to have the arrogance that I usually went for, but there was an underlying spite to it that went beyond the normal "I'm a badass who secretly has a heart of gold" type that I usually fixate on. I couldn't pinpoint exactly why I felt that way about him, though. A tiny residual pill wave rolled through my hangover and I forgot all about it. Pills could make me forgive and forget a lot of things. And if it hadn't been for that blind willingness to overlook what my instincts told me, Everett might have just remained a one-night stand.

CHAPTER 4

"I Couldn't Imagine Ever *Not* Doing Them"

AS A DRUG LOVER, I could (and frankly, still can) justify a million different reasons to start using. But I think a spontaneous lung collapse is up there with the best of them.

Heather grew up in a working-class family in Bay Ridge, Brooklyn, and has the accent to prove it. Her mother was fifteen when she had her and often Heather's needs would get pushed to the side. Heather came from a long line of addicts and alcoholics, and her grandmother was both an addict *and* bipolar. Heather was used to seeing psychotropic drugs lying around the house.

Because there was such a long history of drug abuse in Heather's family, her mom was reticent to even let her take NyQuil for severe colds. When Heather finally went off to college, she did her own share of drinking and partying, but, knowing her family's history, she never really got into the harder drugs. Heather had always suffered from panic attacks severe enough to make her vomit, but her mother just thought it was normal teenage adjustment. Heather's friends came up with the more creative excuse that she was possessed and had devils in her, like *The Exorcist*, because of the constant mood swings and vomiting.

After Heather graduated from college, she moved back to Bay

Ridge, with no job prospects in sight. Two weeks later, while she was taking a shower, her lung collapsed.

"It's called spontaneous pneumothorax," she says. "It was so random and weird. I couldn't breathe out. My solution was to just smoke another Newport."

Her mom, now a registered nurse, passed her breathing troubles off as allergies. But later, a friend of Heather's convinced her to go to the hospital, where she discovered that her lung was 80 percent collapsed.

"I had no insurance, and was just like, 'Fuck, I can't afford this,'" she says. "They had to put a chest tube in. They couldn't give me anything during that procedure because you need to tell them that you can feel it so they know it's in properly, but afterward they gave me a morphine drip. Look, basically, a collapsed lung isn't that big of a deal. It happens to a lot of people. But because I'd always been so anxiety-ridden, I was convinced I was dying. And once that morphine drip was in, for the first time in my entire life, I didn't feel any of that anxiety. It was a release. The colors were so bright, everything was prettier and more manageable. I watched a lot of TV, and *Seinfeld* had never seemed funnier to me. Obviously, I needed more right away."

The one unpleasant side effect of the morphine was that it made Heather nauseated, so the hospital began administering Demerol shots. Demerol is another narcotic drug that's similar to morphine. "Chemically or whatever, it just worked better for me," she says.

Every time the doctors tried to take Heather's chest tube out, her lung would collapse again. She remained in the hospital, high on her painkillers, for almost a month.

"The other nice side effect of the painkillers is that I lost a massive amount of weight," she says. "I had no appetite because of them and I lost about fifty pounds. For the first time in my entire life, I was skinny."

When Heather's lung was finally able to function properly on its own without the chest tube, she was psyched to get home and show off her new body. She also wanted to know what she was going to get to bring home with her. "It was the first time in my life when I had this fear that my drugs were being taken away from me, but I didn't recognize that I needed them. My mother had been tripping out that I'd been on so many painkillers to begin with, what with our family's history. Once I was home she said I could have Tylenol or Advil, but that was it. And I just knew that wasn't going to do it."

After Heather got home from the hospital, she fell into a deep depression. "I was detoxing from all the medicine I'd been given and I still had no job. I had quit smoking because I was terrified my lung was going to collapse again. I felt awful. Plus my anxiety came back, which really sucked because all the drugs in the hospital had quelled it while I was in there. So I started going out and drinking every night."

This self-medicating solution got Heather through the next few years, but in 2003, her panic attacks returned worse than ever, despite (or because of) getting engaged and scoring a great job as the national sales manager at Fresh, a major, high-end skin and body care company. "I was responsible for four hundred employees in thirty states and trying to plan my wedding at the same time, and I started having a nervous breakdown."

Heather, who now finally had great health insurance through her job, had been on Celexa, an antidepressant, for some time, but felt it did nothing for her panic attacks. A childhood friend named Tracy had the answer. "Go see my doctor," she said. "He's Dr. Feelgood. He'll give you whatever you want. Ask for Xanax. It'll calm you down and you'll feel so much better."

Xanax (alprazolam) is a benzodiazepine prescribed for the management of generalized anxiety disorder, anxiety associated with depression, short-term relief of symptoms of anxiety, and panic disorder. It can also be very addictive. Some people respond really well to it for panic attacks.

At first Heather avoided calling Tracy's doctor. "I was freaked out by the idea. For some reason I was a little scared of him." But a week before her wedding she put her back out. "I was literally walking like a hunchback and I had an event the next day that I had to look great and feel great for. So I went to see Dr. Feelgood. He gave me Xanax for stress and Vicodin for pain, and the combination was just magic. My anxiety was gone, the pain was gone, and everything felt awesome. I felt like I could do everything. I needed less sleep, I didn't need to eat, which was great for helping me get into my wedding dress. And I had more personality. Normally, I'm kind of a shy person. I'd think to myself, 'That person wouldn't want to talk to me anyway. I'm not going to bother.' Suddenly, I didn't care. I felt cuter, smarter, and funnier and I could talk to anyone. The night before my wedding, I had all my girls and my gays in a hotel room, and I just handed out Xanax and Vicodin left and right along with the champagne. It was a total pill-popping party."

At that point, Heather still had enough self-control not to take any pills on the actual day of her wedding. "I remember thinking, 'It's my wedding day and I want to be clearheaded.'"

After the wedding, Heather continued on her normally prescribed dosages, but after only a month or two she noticed that one of each pill wasn't working, so she began to take more. "That freaked me out a little. I hadn't really ever been abusing the pills before, except maybe the night before my wedding. So I let my prescriptions run out. And I woke up feeling like I had the flu. These were totally normal withdrawal symptoms at the time, but I didn't know it. I started having these emotional seizures. My body would be gripped by total anxiety and panic, followed by hysterical crying jags."

Heather called her husband home from work to take care of her. "He didn't know what was wrong with me. He was, like, 'I just married a mental patient.' I was crying nonstop, couldn't eat, but was vomiting, shitting . . . on myself at some points. I can't believe I didn't connect the dots at the time. That I had stopped taking all those pills too suddenly."

She finally called her grandmother, who had managed to stabilize her own bipolar disorder for years. She sent Heather to another psychiatrist, who prescribed more Xanax, but at *four times* the dosage. Heather's original Dr. Feelgood had given her 0.5 milligram pills to take as needed, but her new doctor put her on 2 milligram pills, three times a day. She didn't question a thing, figuring the doctor knew what was best for her.

But from there, everything started spiraling out of control. She had an unlimited supply of bricks (the 2 milligram tablets of Xanax come in little bars, commonly called "bricks," which can be broken into two 1 milligram segments or four 0.5 milligram segments). But Heather missed the combination of painkillers with her Xanax, so she began to doctor-shop.

Unfortunately for legitimate physicians, doctor shopping is incredibly easy now, thanks to the Internet. Before, crafty addicts had to rely on a hard copy of the *Physicians Desk Reference* to look up different pills and prescription info so they would know what to ask for. Now all they have to do is look up a pill online, see which symptoms match, and go to as many different doctors as they can until they find one who will prescribe what they want.

One of the biggest problems with dispensing pain medication is that there is no concrete way to measure pain in a patient. The closest thing doctors have now is the faces pain scale, an assessment tool originally designed for use with preverbal patients (that is, young children) and later used with non-English-speaking patients, the elderly, and just about everyone else. It's a chart of six simply drawn faces that range from happy to crying hysterically. You're supposed to tell your doctor which one best represents the intensity of the pain you are experiencing. Sometimes the doctor then correlates the face you choose with a number ranging from 0 to 10, with 0 meaning "no pain" and 10 meaning "the worst pain you can imagine" or "the worst pain you've ever had." It's an absurd practice, and one that is extremely easy to manipulate if you have even the most rudimentary acting skills. Heather, for example, used to walk into a doctor's office hunched over and use sciatica as an excuse to get painkillers. Some experts believe that such fakery is usually easy to spot. But pain is also an entirely subjective experience. Some people, especially men, may be feeling a lot of pain but downplay it in order to look tough, while someone who is really only in moderate pain may claim a higher number to get more drugs. Additionally, researchers at the Southern Illinois University School of Medicine studied the density of nerve fibers in women and men to investigate whether enhanced pain perception in some women has psychological, cultural, social, or anatomical roots. They found that women may have up to twice as many nerve fibers in the skin as men, so they feel some types of pain more intensely than men. Before I'd discovered pills, I'd always used pain as a secret, personal badge of honor. If I had cut myself on something or was sore from swimming, I just sucked it up. It made me feel strong, like I could get through anything.

Heather's doctor shopping went like this: she'd go onto her insurance company's website and go through the entire alphabet of doctors in New York that accepted her health coverage. "I didn't want to pay any more money out of pocket for pills because I needed to save money to buy pills online if I hit a dry spell," she says. "In worst-case scenarios, I would walk into an emergency room and say I'm on whatever drug, but I left my prescription in a hotel room in Boston on a business trip. But hospitals are the stingiest. They'll either give you one pill there or write you a prescription for, like, three pills. But I used the Boston excuse a lot in between prescriptions."

After a while, Heather's doctors started to get wise to her. "They weren't coming right out and saying, 'You're fucking addicted and you're sucking up all your pills,' but they were pretty much letting me know the jig was up and they weren't going to write me any more scrips."

That's when she started stealing prescription pads.

Unlike Heather, twenty-seven-year-old Jared fell into his painkiller addiction through nothing more serious than suburban ennui.

"I never like to trace my addiction to anything that was family-related," he says. "I had a normal upbringing, there was no abuse, no something where I could be, like, 'That's why I felt the need to do it!' The reason why I started snorting Percocet is because I just fucking loved it."

Jared grew up in an upper-middle-class suburb in Massachusetts, near Boston. He's tall and broad-shouldered with short, ever so slightly mussed brown hair. He looks like your standard handsome boy next door, maybe the one who played lacrosse and was always willing to pump the keg for you. High school was normal for him (beer blasts, Friday night dates, homework), up until his senior year when a close friend began working at a local mom-and-pop pharmacy. The owners had a few high school kids working there, illegally, since they had access to controlled substances in the back of the pharmacy and only licensed pharmacists are supposed to fill prescriptions.

"My friend started stealing all sorts of pills," Jared remembers. "At first it was just Xanax and stuff like that, which we would snort. I don't even know how we first thought to snort it, it just seemed like the thing to do. But one day he stole some Percocets. Snorting a Percocet is a lot of work. There's a lot of powder, a lot of acetaminophen, and it took forever to crush. There were three of us doing it together, and it was the best thing that had ever happened to us. It was almost like going back into the womb. I felt like I was in total control. I felt like all cylinders were pumping. It was a warm sensation where you felt like you could do whatever you wanted. I felt like I could talk to anyone, and I'd always been a little bit shy, socially. I'd even been to see psychiatrists about it, but this gave me more confidence than any shrink session. On Percocet, I thought this was how I was supposed to feel all the time, and the way I felt regularly wasn't right."

Jared would spend the whole night just hanging out at his friend's house. He had a huge place and his parents never came upstairs to his room. They could smoke cigarettes up there. Do whatever they wanted. Jared estimates that 95 percent of his high school pill snorting was done in that bedroom. They had a band and would play music, but they never actually wrote a song. After that first night on Percocet, his friend stopped stealing almost every other kind of pill besides Percocet. Whenever he'd fill a prescription or do inventory, he'd just grab handfuls of Percocets. "It was like the Wild West back then," Jared remembers. "No one noticed."

If I'd been as daring as Jared's friend, I'd probably be dead by now. When I was in high school, my best friend Amy's parents owned one of the town's drugstores, where she worked. She too had access to the back of the store where all the meds were kept, but we never even thought to steal pills. In the early 1990s the only pills you heard about were antidepressants like Prozac. We used Amy's access to the drugstore for more practical purposes, like scoring pregnancy tests for worried friends. Our town was so small that no kid dared just walk in and buy something like that under the watchful eyes of Amy's parents, who were prominent members of the community. So whenever someone needed something illicit, like condoms, they'd turn to us. We developed a strong nicotine addiction because the drugstore sold cigarettes, which Amy was able to buy for us when her parents weren't looking. But the best part had to be the access afforded us by the drugstore's computer. We could illegally find out who in our high school was on birth control, who was taking antibiotics for an STD, and who was on antidepressants, which back then, in our backwoods location, still carried a social stigma. Information like this about our classmates was crucial in a tiny high school, where petty rivalries between friends and cliques took on mythological qualities because of the sheer lack of anything else to do. It gave me a sense of power I'd never experienced, and even though I never did anything with the secrets we discovered, it was enough to know that I had ammunition should I ever need it.

Amy and I were also too concerned with finding a steady pot source to realize we had access to thousands of pills that would have made us feel a hundred times better. And looking back, I doubt Amy would have gone that far, had we known. Her parents were terrifyingly strict, and would have had us arrested.

"My entire senior year of high school was devoted to snorting Percocet," says Jared. His friend Tim, who was working at the drugstore, kept them in constant supply. "We were always telling ourselves, this is the best time we're ever going to have in our lives," he says. "We all had freshmen girlfriends. At that time we were really into Ecstasy, too. Me and three other guys all took our girlfriends to the prom, and on the way back we all took E. We had the limo drop us off at a park, and we were all just fucking in the grass."

Most of the other kids in Jared's high school were into drinking, dropping acid, and smoking pot. But he thinks there were probably other small pockets of kids doing pills too. There were always various people who would drop in and out of his crowd and snort Percocets with them.

One of the girls from prom night wrote about their Ecstasy experience in a journal. Her dad ended up reading her diary and called the parents of all the kids who had been involved. "My parents grilled me about all the drugs I'd been taking," Jared says. "I told them everything I'd been doing, except the pills. I wanted to keep that to myself. I didn't care about admitting to taking acid or anything else, but I didn't want them to know I was doing pills because I couldn't imagine ever *not* doing them. All the other stuff I could give up if I had to."

After graduation, Jared took a summer job as a counselor at a kids' camp. "I didn't have any pills up there," he says. "This was after we'd been snorting pills literally every day for the past year. Now I know I was going through withdrawal, but at the time I was miserable and didn't understand why. The symptoms were flulike, but the worst part was the mental stuff. I was in a constant state of horrible panic, and I was working with kids. I just wanted to get out of my body. By the end of the summer I finally felt all right, but I definitely wanted to get back to taking pills. I had no intention of stopping."

That fall, Jared started college at a school about an hour and a half from his hometown, studying English and literature. Tim ended up going to college several states away, but Jared's other main pill-snorting friend, Eric, got Tim's old job at the pharmacy. Eric picked up right where Tim had left off, stealing as many pills as he could get away with. He would drive to visit Jared at school and leave him with a bunch of pills. Jared would keep some for himself, sell the rest to other students, and give the money back to Eric.

"The haul always varied, depending on what he could get," Jared says. "Sometimes it would be hundreds and hundreds of pills. The students at my school were really into Valium and Xanax, so I could always sell those really easily. I'd keep the opiates for myself."

This went on for months, until Eric's bosses finally busted him. But since Eric was working in the pharmacy illegally to begin with, they couldn't exactly press charges. He never got arrested and the whole thing was settled out of court. But by the time that happened, Jared had been dealing on campus for so long that he had already developed other pill connections.

The first one was completely random. "I was walking down the street when some guy pulled up next to me in a car, rolled down his window, and said, 'Anyone want some Percocets?' It was the start of a long and fruitful relationship," Jared remembers. "He was an army vet who had his own prescriptions, which he sold to me. I'd also discovered a whole ring of people who were selling pills in town, and that's where I started getting OxyContin. I developed a very strict regimen. I'd snort Percocets throughout the day, just to give me a base high, and then spike that with a sixty- or eighty-milligram Oxy about three times a day."

Despite his heavy addiction, Jared ended up graduating college with a 3.7 GPA. "No one had any idea," he says. "I did well in school, but I looked bad. I had long hair, weighed about thirty or forty pounds less than I do now, and I had that sort of green, opiate look. The pills had stopped being fun since the middle of college. It just turned on me. There's a distinct point where it just flips around completely, and I was taking them just to function. I wasn't eating. I couldn't take a shit, and when I did, it was the radius of a baseball bat (constipation is a common opiate side effect). The drugs weren't fun anymore. They were horrible. But it was much worse without them."

CHAPTER 5

"Depression Hurts"

IN MY OWN CASE, and I think this is true for the majority of pill heads I've met, I was self-medicating for some form of depression. I say this because, well, not only did I know I was depressed, but there's a whole emerging field of study about depression manifesting itself as physical pain. Cymbalta, a popular antidepressant, has even incorporated this idea into its advertising campaigns. Depression *hurts*, the ads declare.

Dr. Carol Boyd's initial questions about painkiller use were developed back in 2003, and she is now developing new questions to address this theory linking depression and pain.

"All I was asking is, 'Why are you using it?' and they said, 'Because I have pain.' We didn't explore it enough," she says. "If I get funded again this time around, I'll be following kids around from the time they are eleven and specifically asking them why they are using and what kind of pain they have. I'll also be asking about any other health problems they have and what other pills they are on. Because one important thing we found is that if we controlled for antidepressant use in this group, that is, if they were already on antidepressants, they were not bigger nonmedical users of prescription opiates. In other words, it's possible that the kids who are using opiates are self-treating a mood disorder. We can't prove it yet, but my data is looking like that."

She isn't alone in this theory. As far back as 1995, an article was published in the *Journal of Clinical Psychopharmacology* by lead author J. Alexander Bodkin, now the director of the Clinical Psychopharmacology Research Program at Harvard University's McLean Hospital. The article was entitled, "Buprenorphine Treatment of Refractory Depression." First released in the United States in 1985, buprenorphine was a Schedule V narcotic analgesic in an injectable formulation marketed under the trade name Buprenex. Since 2002 it has been sold in the United States under the trade name Subutex, which is a sublingual (under the tongue) formulation, but federal regulations prohibit dispensing the drug for pain and have raised it to Schedule III. It may be used only to treat opiate withdrawal, much as methadone is used to treat heroin withdrawal. A special formulation of buprenorphine called Suboxone includes naloxone, a compound that immediately kicks narcotics off pain receptors. Naloxone is added specifically to prevent abuse, since it takes effect only if the tablets are crushed and injected, rather than taken orally. (Naloxone is commonly used for overdoses, and there's a growing movement to make it widely available to heroin and other opiate abusers through needle-exchange programs.)

The Bodkin study followed ten depressed patients who hadn't responded to other depression treatments and were given a small opiate dosage. Three dropped out because of side effects, but most of the other seven "showed striking improvement in both subjective and objective measures of depression." It should also be noted that two of the positive responders had had former opiate addictions or experiences in the past. (One of the former drug abusers actually deteriorated.)

Dr. Bodkin first became interested in buprenorphine while working on an entirely different class of drugs, monoamine oxidase inhibitors (MAOIs), a strong form of antidepressant, like Parnate (tranylcypromine) and Nardil (phenelzine). "The classic case with MAO inhibitors is that a person suffering from depression will go from being sluggish, unmotivated, and downhearted to being highly energized and ever so slightly euphoric. It's really striking when you see it the first few times. Prozac had just hit the market, and Prozac sure doesn't do that."

Prozac is in the family of SSRIs, or selective serotonin reuptake inhibitors. In the simplest of explanations, messages are passed between nerve cells in the brain via a *synapse*, a small gap between the cells. The cell that is releasing information does so by sending neurotransmitters into the gap. Neurotransmitters called monoamines (serotonin, norepinephrine, and dopamine) are recognized by receptors on the surface of the receiving cell, which then relays the signal. Around 10 percent of the neurotransmitters are lost in this process and the other 90 percent are released from the surface of the receiving cell to be taken up again by the sending cell, a process called reuptake. Some theories believe that depression is linked to the lack of stimulation by the receiving cell. SSRIs work by keeping the neurotransmitter serotonin in the gap between the cells longer, so that the receiving cell can be stimulated longer. Besides Prozac, other common brands of SSRIs include Zoloft, Paxil, Lexapro, and Celexa.

MAOIs work differently. Remember the 10 percent of neurotransmitters lost in the process of relaying a signal? They're not technically lost, they get burned up by an enzyme called monoamine oxidase, which is also found in the lining of the gut and other body tissues. Most of the relevant antidepressant-related MAO in the brain is in the pre-synaptic neuron (the sending cell), and inhibiting it with MAOIs allows a build-up of monoamine stores to be released as needed, thus easing depression symptoms. MAO is also responsible for the breakdown of monoamines such as serotonin. MAOIs block this breakdown process in the brain, making more neurotransmitters available.

"There were a lot of cokeheads at the time in the business class," Dr. Bodkin says. "I thought that maybe at least some of these people might be unknowingly self-treating an otherwise MAO-responsive condition with cocaine. I did a little more research and discovered that some cocaine addicts were responding well to a new opioid, buprenorphine."

Dr. Bodkin knew that opioids had been used to treat mood

disorders at the turn of the century before becoming widely stigmatized because of their abuse potential. But researchers were now presenting buprenorphine as a safe opiate because not only did the high feeling disappear after a day or two, it also didn't have the same withdrawal symptoms associated with other opioids. Laboratory testing showed a long delay before the drug disassociated from the neuron: it bound tenaciously to the receptor, reducing withdrawal problems. Another positive feature: as the dosage rises, respiratory depression only reaches a certain point, levels out, and then actually reverses itself a bit, so there was little danger of overdose. It had been used by urologists for postsurgery treatment since the 1980s because it was thought to have less effect on urinary retention than other commonly used opiates. (I can attest to the fact that opiates cause urinary retention—all in all, I've probably spent about two entire weeks of my life staring at the porcelain tiles above a urinal, trying to pee while high out of my mind.)

"Back in those days," Dr. Bodkin explains, "it wasn't a tremendously complicated thing to get permission to carry out an open trial. I was finishing up my residency and doing a fellowship here at McLean, and it was really quite exciting to see that some previously treatment-unresponsive depressed people had a fabulously good response to buprenorphine."

In the trial, all patients were taken off their previously prescribed psychotropic medications, except for benzodiazepines. They were given 0.15 milligram of buprenorphine every morning, and the dosage was titrated (meaning that more is added as one's body becomes used to a certain dose and it stops being effective) throughout the trial depending on each patient's tolerance and the clinical benefit they were receiving from the drug. The maximum daily dosage ended up being 1.8 milligrams.

At the end of the trial, Dr. Bodkin tried to raise money for more studies. "I'm not terribly enthusiastic about the application process," he admits, "so I didn't go absolutely to the mat with it, but I sent out several proposals and got nowhere with them. I ran into another group who were trying to raise money for a similar study. They had gotten stuck at the level of the institutional review board at one of the major medical centers. I realized, 'Jesus, opiates are so stigmatized that they aren't going to give this a shot,' although it remains in my armamentarium, as it did then, for treating people who really need it. You've really got to get informed consent, and you've got to be careful. When I first published that article, I had an awful lot of people showing up for treatment, and I was a little too young and naïve to realize that a fair number of them were drug abusers who thought they'd found a doctor who was cool enough to prescribe to them. That's one of the things that made me less of a passionate advocate than I otherwise would have been."

After Dr. Bodkin realized he had been prescribing to drug abusers, he took them off the medication and they sued him for injury. "It was really ugly," he sighs. "It took years to get it over with, and it was the nightmare of my life at the time. I was a fool. I should have been able to see at the door that there were personality problems. I started out with the position that people were just trying to make themselves feel normal and well, but I quickly discovered that there are several other groups of people with motivations to specifically seek out opiates who are very self-destructive, and destructive to others."

Like me.

Dr. Bodkin knows of one doctor who prescribes oxycodone to treat depression. "He thinks it's sensible to go with the most euphoriant of the pills. For a period of time he needed other doctors to cover his patients for him for various personal reasons, and I was one of them. In those situations I made every effort to switch people over to standard antidepressants or buprenorphine because I didn't want to be involved with prescribing oxycodone."

Dr. Bodkin believes it's usually unwise to prescribe oxycodone or other strong opiates for depression. "People who do it tend to get in trouble," he says. "Even if it were a lifesaver for a patient—and who knows? it might be in some patients—prison isn't a nice place to spend your adulthood. And although oxycodone is an extremely useful pain medication, even very respected physicians can get investigated by the DEA and occasionally go to jail, and the sentences can be bloodcurdlingly long. It's almost a religious matter in some circles, in the same way that there is a kind of religious opposition to the use of marijuana for people getting chemotherapy. People are dying and there are organizations out there saying, 'Don't spoil their souls—they won't get into heaven!'"

These days Dr. Bodkin is focusing more research on MAO inhibitors. I'm biased against these antidepressants, because I had a bad experience with one when I was a teenager.

The main problem with MAOIs is that monoamines don't just burn up neurotransmitters; they also burn up a molecule called tyramine, which affects blood pressure. So when monamine oxidase is blocked, tyramine levels rise too.

I was prescribed Parnate when I was eighteen. It was for depression, which at the time was manifesting itself in me as hatred for my parents—pretty much like any other teenager. According to the newly revised twelfth edition of *The Pill Book: The Illustrated Guide to the Most Prescribed Drugs in the United States* (now includes self-injectables!), Parnate is prescribed for major depression that doesn't respond to other drugs. It is also prescribed for a variety of conditions, including "bulimia, cocaine addiction, night terrors, post-traumatic stress disorder, and symptoms of multiple sclerosis."

I'd never been on any other antidepressants before. All I knew is that Parnate got me high. It was a speedy, sleepless high that I quickly grew addicted to. During the few months I was on Parnate my diet consisted solely of Coca-Cola and Ritz crackers. There were bizarre side effects, like brown semen and tremors.

The sleeplessness was the worst. I felt an unexplainable need for pressure on top of me, so I'd sleep between the box spring and the mattress, like a bed sandwich. And all I could think about was waiting until morning so I could take another one of my pills. No one was monitoring my use of this drug. I was simply handed a prescription from our family therapist/psychiatrist (who the family only saw five times since that was all that was covered by our insurance), with a list of strict instructions, which included a long list of foods I couldn't eat, like cheese and soy sauce, because they contained an excess of tyramine. But I barely had an appetite, so it hardly mattered.

I began taking Parnate during the summer after my senior year of high school and continued into my first year of community college. During that time, my older sister got married. The wedding was to take place at my grandmother's house in Tennessee, and I took a bus down to Philadelphia, where my father was living with his new wife. The plan was for all of us to drive down to Tennessee together from there. I arrived giddy and restless from having to sit still for so long on the bus. And I was hungry. They didn't have any Ritz crackers at my dad's house, but my stepmother offered me ramen noodles.

I didn't know that she liked to spice them up with soy sauce.

Halfway through the bowl, I put my spoon down and said, "Something's wrong."

My stepmother glanced up at me from across the room where she was packing for the trip and asked, "You okay?" before looking back down at her suitcase.

A terrifying feeling was starting at the base of my spine, a sharp stabbing pain right above my butt, and my body filled with adrenaline. I couldn't breathe.

"Something's wrong," I repeated, pushing back the chair and trying to stand up. I leaned forward over the table, knocking aside the bowl of ramen. The pain that had started at the bottom of my spine was traveling upward. The stabbing sensation had reached the middle of my back, and I realized it was crawling straight up toward my head.

The taste in my mouth suddenly became vividly familiar. "Is there soy sauce in this?" I yelled.

My stepmother nodded, a scared look on her face.

"Oh god, get Dad," I said. She ran to the door and shouted his name out toward the parking lot, where he had been loading up the car for our trip.

"Please god please god please god," I whispered. The pain had reached my neck. I ran to my bag and grabbed the bottle of Parnate. My dad came running into the room, and I shoved the bottle of pills into his hand just as the pain exploded into my head, like a fountain of churning acid that had been traveling through a narrow tube, finding its pool of release.

I went blind, everything turned into a whitewashed nothing. My head felt like my brain was swelling ten times its size and straining against my skull, ready to burst it open. I think I was screaming or crying, I don't remember. The next thing I knew I was in the front seat of my father's car, head between my legs, repeating "Make it stop." I passed out. When I came to again I was on a stretcher, surrounded by doctors who were yelling something at me, trying to stick a needle in my arm. I sat up and vomited everywhere, spewing ramen across the room, hitting a nurse. Puke filled my lap. I just remember crying and apologizing over and over before lying back down and passing out cold.

I slept for about six hours. When I woke up, it took me a minute to realize where I was. I was exhausted and realized there were needles attached to my arm. A doctor came in after a while, holding my bottle of Parnate.

"We've called your prescribing doctor," he said. "He says you should go off them immediately. You're going to be fine."

I was released a few hours later. Our trip to the wedding was delayed by one day but we continued. I felt weak and out of it for the entire drive down, but by the time we arrived in Tennessee the incident was pretty much behind me. I was happy that I was finally able to drink at the wedding, since alcohol was also on my prohibited list of items I couldn't ingest while on Parnate. I laughed when family members asked me about it, playing it off like it was no big deal.

In retrospect, what pisses me off the most is not the fact that the doctor prescribed it to me, but that there was no one following up on my intake to see how I had been reacting to it simply because of an insurance cap. Even after the hospital called our prescribing doctor to tell him I'd experienced a reaction, I never received any kind of follow-up phone call. I swore off antidepressants for years. Alcohol, pot, acid, and coke would work just fine for my problems. And I could eat whatever I wanted on them.

I recently tried to track down my medical record from the hospital my father had taken me to, to find out exactly what had happened to my body during the reaction, but they only keep records for ten years. According to Dr. Bodkin, though, I went into hypertensive crisis, and my blood pressure probably shot up to somewhere around

290 over 210. "Some people die of that," he told me. What happens is that blood pressure gets so high that it can burst blood vessels in the brain, which is why, when MAOIs were first introduced in the 1950s, there was a wave of deaths from brain hemorrhages before scientists figured out the tyramine connection. To this day, I refuse to eat anything with soy sauce.

My other horrific antidepressant experience came from a case of off-label prescribing, where doctors prescribe medications for uses other than their intended, FDA-approved purpose. At least, I'm pretty sure it did. Right before I had quit *Jane* magazine and was planning on moving away, I was feeling a lot of heightened anxiety and depression, so I went to a doctor near our offices and asked for a therapist recommendation. I'd had to find a new doctor, instead of going to my normal guy, since our company's insurance policy had changed.

"You're depressed?" she asked. "I can take care of that." She opened up a cabinet stacked with samples of a drug called Zyprexa. She actually told me not to look it up on the Internet. "There have been some really good studies about how this drug is actually great for depression. But there are a lot of whack jobs on the Internet saying it's dangerous. But trust me."

Of course I immediately went home and looked up the drug online. It turned out it was an antipsychotic medication for bipolar disorder and schizophrenia, but there were some testimonies saying it was found to be good for "normal" depression as well. I stupidly gave it a shot. One week after I started on it, I found myself in front of my bedroom mirror with an X-Acto knife stolen from the magazine's art department, hacking away at my arm and chest. I'd never had any cutting issues in my life, and I'm permanently scarred now from the experience. I stopped taking the pills the next day.

CHAPTER 6

"Remember *Valley of the Dolls*?"

HERE'S A LITTLE-KNOWN SECRET about Washington, D.C. The DEA building has, hands down, the best museum in the entire city. Forget the Smithsonian—next time you're in D.C., make sure to get over to the DEA Museum and Visitors Center. It contains a timeline of drug abuse in American history, starting with vintage bottles of Mrs. Winslow's Soothing Syrup. The label reads: "For children teething. Greatly facilitates the process of Teething, by softening the gums, reducing all inflammation; will allay all pain and spasmodic action, and is sure to regulate the bowels. Depend on it, Mothers, it will give rest to yourselves and relief and health to your infants."

Each bottle was *loaded* with morphine. The product finally got pulled off the market around the turn of the century after babies kept mysteriously dying. I bet there were more than a few moms who were pretty bummed about the recall, because, let's face it, if anything is going to effectively silence a screaming baby, it's morphine. The museum covers all the basic stuff you learn in antidrug seminars in school, but what sets it apart is the amazing amount of paraphernalia on display—things like antique syringe kits found in the pages of the Sears & Roebuck catalog (some drugs with the worst reputations, like heroin and cocaine, were once entirely legal in the United

States); a rabbit-and-fox fur coat worn by a former DEA agent to "blend in" with Cleveland drug traffickers in the 1980s; and an entire fake head shop storefront called Jimmy's Joint, with its name lit up in blue neon letters.

The newest addition to the museum is an entire wing devoted specifically to the DEA's efforts at diversion control. The exhibit is part of its Good Medicine, Bad Behavior campaign, and it's pretty dramatic. The pharmaceutical wing leads with an enormous medicine cabinet, opened to reveal two-foot-high bottles filled with brightly colored pills the size of English muffins. They include the most common illegally diverted pharmaceuticals, including hydrocodone, Oxy-Contin, and amphetamines. One side of the medicine cabinet is filled with giant fake prescriptions for each drug and a list of their intended uses. The other side lists each drug's bad side effects. The weird thing is that the fake prescriptions that list the *good* qualities of the drug are all written out to "John Doe II," as if already predicting the death of anyone taking these drugs, even for the right reasons. I'm being glib—there's also a sobering slide show of young people who have died from overdoses of various forms of drug combinations and some really informative exhibits on how all these different drugs interact in the body.

I ended up at the museum because I had a meeting with Chief Mark Caverly, who works for the DEA's Liaison and Policy Section. He agreed to meet with me to discuss the DEA's work on combating prescription painkiller diversion. His office is located near the Pentagon (and, more importantly since I arrived early for our meeting, directly across the street from the Pentagon City Mall food court).

The security for getting into the actual offices of the DEA building is pretty intense. There are at least four security guards at the main entrance, and you have to put your bags through an X-ray machine and be escorted inside by someone who works there. My contact was a member of the DEA's press office who had been extremely helpful in setting up the interview. When we got in the elevator, there were several other people in it dressed in nearly identical dark blue suits, including a man and a woman who had obviously worked together before, but hadn't seen each other in some time. The conversation went like this:

WOMAN: Oh, how *are* you? I haven't seen you in forever! It's like you just disappeared! We miss you!
MAN: Ha-ha, I miss you ladies too. I was transferred.
WOMAN: To what department?
MAN: I can't tell you.
WOMAN (*SYMPATHETIC, UNDERSTANDING NOD*): Got it.
MAN: I mean, I could, but I'd have to kill you.

There was nervous laughter all around, followed by uncomfortable silence for the rest of the elevator ride.

When we got to our floor I was ushered into a plain conference room. The press agent sat down too, and I realized he wasn't going to be leaving. Mark Caverly came in and sat down and I got this nervous feeling that I was being secretly videotaped. Caverly looked like he'd come straight from central casting for a DEA agent in a bureaucratic position, with his set-in-stone facial expression, blank eyes peering through wire-rimmed glasses, and perfectly pressed suit.

"So," I asked, "why now? How did prescription painkillers get so huge?"

"I think there were some societal influences," he said. "And I'll give you my personal opinion. As a society, we turn to pharmaceutical drugs for everything. If you have a common cold, if you want to grow hair, whatever the medical condition is, we, as Americans, turn to pills to solve the problem. If you go to a doctor's office and don't get a prescription, most people feel shortchanged. They want medicine. And beyond that general acceptance of pills and pharmaceuticals, I think there's a perception of safety with pharmaceutical drugs. When you talk to people about heroin or cocaine, they know there's a danger to it. You don't know what it's been cut with, so you don't know how strong it is. You don't know what your reaction is going to be. And with pharmaceutical drugs, for the most part, they are FDA-approved and created under sterile circumstances. Add to that the fact that you get some of the same physical responses taking pharmaceuticals as you would with any opiate, like heroin. People taking Vicodin or hydrocodone, which is probably the most popular pharmaceutical drug in the United States, get the same rush as they would taking heroin, but you're taking something that people perceive to be safe."

Caverly was partially responsible for one of the nation's currently most successful prescription-monitoring programs, called KASPER (Kentucky All Schedule Prescription Electronic Reporting). A prescription-monitoring program, or PMP, is exactly what it sounds like—a method of tracking an individual's entire history of prescriptions, regardless of the doctor who had prescribed it. Kentucky was one of the earlier states to be hit with a particularly large Oxy-Contin abuse epidemic. "When I was working in Kentucky, we were seeing OxyContin being traded for services. It became a coin in trade. People who needed their car repaired would pay the mechanic in OxyContin instead of cash. I can remember working cases in eastern Kentucky where a whole family would go to a doctor—literally, you'd have the mother, father, and maybe two or three kids—and they'd all jump in the car and drive down to the doctor on the same day at the same time, and they'd all walk out with their own prescriptions for the same drugs, typically oxocodone or hydrocodone."

I found Caverly's surprise about trading pharmaceuticals for favors rather quaint. I'd been doing that ever since I'd first gotten into pills, and not just with opiates. On one occasion, a bartender I knew at Mars Bar, a famously filthy dive on Second Avenue, contracted gonorrhea. I had a particularly sexually active friend who kept a stockpile of the antibiotics used to cure it (procured from the Internet), so I traded Valium with my friend for the antibiotics and then traded the antibiotics to the bartender for a night of free drinks.

Anyway, Caverly doesn't have any theories as to why Kentucky became such an epidemic state, but he does believe it goes back to our general culture of pharmaceutical abuse and believes that PMPs can help curb that problem.

"I think there are thirty-six states with active prescription-monitoring services right now. These are state programs; they're not operated by the federal government. I was part of a group that worked to get KASPER through the state legislature. The resistance we primarily got was from the privacy level, the concern was, 'Big Brother is going to know what prescriptions I'm getting,' and people didn't like it on that basis. The success of the prescription-monitoring programs is that they don't authorize anyone that doesn't *already* have the authority to look at the information (i.e., the DEA). To me, that addresses the privacy issue. And from a law enforcement perspective, it just saves a tremendous amount of time."

The privacy issue still isn't exactly resolved though. Yes, the DEA can already gain access to your complete medical records, but doctors in states that don't currently have PMPs only have access to the files made under their *own* care, not any other doctors you may have been seeing.

In the past, when the DEA was working on a case where a complaint was filed against a particular physician, the only way to find out what the doctor was prescribing was for the officers to go to each pharmacy within a several-mile radius of the doctor's office and get copies of computer records.

"It was very time-consuming. And then you had to put all the information together to see if there were any suspicious prescribing patterns. With a PMP you just make a request for a report."

The DEA claims that over 90 percent of the PMP reports in Kentucky and other states are actually being requested by doctors themselves. They want to know if their patients are abusing drugs. It's a tool that helps them weed out potential drug abusers from people who are in legitimate pain and need access to these powerful meds. And doctors need to watch their backs now, since many are being thrown in jail for their often-legitimate prescribing practices. But that's a whole other story.

After my meeting at the DEA I drove over to the Substance Abuse and Mental Health Services Administration (SAMHSA) to meet with its esteemed director, Dr. Wesley Clark. According to his official bio he has led the agency's national effort to provide effective and accessible treatment to all Americans with addictive disorders. SAMHSA works closely with DAWN, the Drug Abuse Warning Network, to compile the National Survey on Drug Use and Health. These stats are considered the gold standard when it comes to tracking abuse trends, and they're what the DEA relies on for its numbers.

"You want to know how long we've had a problem with pills?" he asks me when we sit down in a small conference room. "Remember *Valley of the Dolls*?"

Again, as with the DEA, my interview was being monitored by a media rep. I was slightly offended. In the magazine world, it's considered the ultimate in bad form for a publicist to sit in on an interview. I was quickly learning it was different for book research. Or maybe it's just standard government practice.

"If you want to track trends," he continues, "then you're relying on data streams, and the data streams show that indeed there has been an increase in prescription drug abuse. But I am fond of saying if it *can* be abused, it *will* be abused. Look at 'cheese heroin' in Texas. Adolescents discovered that if they mixed Tylenol PM with low-grade heroin and snorted it, it accentuates the high." Cheese heroin has killed at least twenty-one kids in the Dallas area since 2005. Writer Jack Shafer wrote in *Slate* that the stuff looks like finely grated parmesan cheese, and this may be the source of the term. Or it could be a bastardized version of the Mexican slang word for heroin, *chiva*. Of course there's always *South Park*'s version—that it's fon-to-due.

"We think we have a pain problem now," Dr. Clark says, "but we haven't seen anything yet. What happens when all the baby boomers turn sixty-five? Baby boomers are more active than their predecessors. Exercise is promoted as an essential function of cardiovascular health, but as this generation gets older, problems like degenerative joint disease are going to start to develop, so they become more prone to injury." Which means more and more painkillers out there to be illegally diverted.

It's the same theory that Dr. Carol Boyd had, and it makes a lot of sense. Think about it: the baby boomers were notorious for their drug experimentation, and they aren't going to question for an instant if a doctor hands them a prescription. My own mother, the quintessential baby boomer (ex-hippy, now firmly ensconced in academia), has had a series of small surgeries over the past few years. When I first confessed to her that I had a problem with painkillers she said, "Well, they do feel *awfully* good."

Dr. Clark and SAMHSA don't work on supply reduction of drugs, like the DEA. What they are interested in is demand reduction. "What you are getting into is a whole philosophical thing," Dr. Clark says. "What is the philosophical imperative to want to change one's mind about drug use? The National Institute on Drug Abuse argues that people want to change their mood because they want to feel good or feel better. People who have depression do seem to get some beneficial effects from the mild euphoria, but they will do better with cognitive behavioral therapy or with antidepressants, which have their own side effects but aren't nearly as problematic."

Unless you eat soy sauce.

I ask him who he thinks should be responsible for spreading that message.

"I think it's multiple sources," he says. "We think parents need to begin the message, the faith community needs to articulate the message, peer groups need to articulate the message. People who have bad experiences need to tell other people. If you want to feel good, there are a wide range of less toxic activities that can make you feel good about yourself, whether it's a ballgame, or a hobby, or a church or temple, even meditation."

The problem is, I *still* can't imagine doing any of those things without taking a few opiates first.

Joseph Califano Jr. is the chair and president of the National Center on Addiction and Substance Abuse (CASA) at Columbia University. Under the Carter Administration, he was also secretary of Health, Education and Welfare from 1977 to 1979. He recently came out with a book called *High Society: How Substance Abuse Ravages America and What to Do About It.* He shares my doubts about the effectiveness of current antidrug programs. In his book, he particularly takes the Drug Abuse Resistance Education program to task. DARE was founded in 1983 and is now found in 75 percent of the U.S. school districts. It's taught by policemen "who are paid to show kids how drugs are used and describe the experience of those who use them, and has repeatedly been found worthless," he wrote. "Extensive research led by Steve West at Virginia Commonwealth University, and published in the *American Journal of Public Health*, concluded that DARE was 'ineffective' as a prevention method and 'a huge waste of time and money.'"

Califano asserts that this is because the reasons kids turn to drugs have almost nothing to do with being informed about the dangers of using them. "The presentation on the dangers of drug use will have little impact on the likelihood that a child who is experiencing depression, anxiety, learning disabilities, eating or conduct disorders, low self-esteem, or sexual or physical abuse, neglect, or who has no hope for the future, will self-medicate with drugs and alcohol," he states.

And he's right.

When I was in fourth grade, my mother brought home one of those Nancy Reagan Just Say No pledge cards and asked me to sign it, making me promise that I would never do drugs. I did, and she hung it on the refrigerator. But even at age nine, as I was signing my name, I clearly remember thinking to myself, *This is total bullshit.*

Califano believes that an effective antidrug program in the schools would need to be tailored to suit the individual needs and concerns of different communities. "School curricula should be scientifically validated," he writes. "The best programs—and there are several— provide realistic information to kids in school. They're tailored to the types of schools; recognize gender, age, ethnic, and racial differences; and cover all substances, alcohol and tobacco as well as illegal and prescription drugs."

It sounds ideal, but I still doubt that anything could have cured me of my innate curiosity about drugs as a teenager. It was something that seemed to be an inevitable part of my life, as necessary and commonplace as homework and the household chores. It was the same situation with both Jared and Caleb. And by the time Heather was hooked, she could have cared less about any sort of antidrug program she'd attended in school.

But Califano is determined to keep fighting. As of October 2007, CASA filed a petition with the FDA to stop direct-to-consumer advertising of controlled substances. DTC ads for controlled substances had been banned for years, but they had been brought back during the Reagan administration.

The petition asks for two things. One, that in certifying new drug approval applications, the FDA makes every effort to minimize the drug's potential for abuse without compromising its therapeutic effectiveness. It doesn't do that now, as evidenced by the whole Oxy-Contin debacle. Two, that before the FDA approves any of these potentially abusable drugs, it has a risk management plan in place. "Today, they don't really have a risk management plan until we're already in trouble," Califano told me. "We've filed the petition, but so far there haven't been any comments on it. We'll keep pushing."

CHAPTER 7

"It Was the Worst Week of My Life"

CALEB HAS A YOUNGER sister named Sarah, who is diabetic and used to using needles to inject her insulin. "She became a heroin addict at sixteen," he says. "When we were thirteen and fifteen we used to smoke pot together all the time. We'd get high, drop acid, the usual. But at around age sixteen she started doing speed, and it really drove a wedge between us. She became this monster, totally awful and unknowable, the family member from hell. And then she went from speed to heroin. I caught her shooting up one night, and I said, 'Listen, you tell our parents tonight or I will.' They ended up putting her in rehab."

I find Caleb's strong negative reaction to heroin surprising, considering the chemical similarities between heroin and OxyContin. The two seem linked in so many people's minds.

"Having done both, I'd just say that OC is a lot better," Caleb explains. "First of all, you know exactly how many milligrams you're doing. It's really hard to overdose unless you're totally retarded, because you can control exactly how much you're doing and the strength of it every time."

This logic blows my mind. The public perception of OxyContin among opiate users seems to fall into two distinct categories: people like Caleb, who think it's totally safe because it came from a doctor; and people like Zoe, who are freaked out by it because they perceive it to be so closely linked to heroin. The fact is that although some physiologic effects, such as respiratory depression, are predictable and should be taken seriously, everybody's body chemistry is different and is going to react in a different way to any type of drug. You have to factor in whether other drugs are being used with it, be they more typical prescription drugs or illegal ones. Also, OxyContin is different from hydrocodone in that the dosage equivalents are usually higher because of the controlled-release formula, and Oxy doesn't contain acetaminophen, which means you are getting a pure high of the opiate ingredient.

"When I first started doing OC, I was really into the trifecta of a little beer, a little pot, a little bit of pill," Caleb says. "All three together just put me in the perfect zone."

Sure, the combo sounds awesome, but mixing pills with alcohol, marijuana, other opioids, or opiates like heroin and morphine is extremely dangerous because all of them are central nervous system depressants. When used together, they have an additive effect on respiratory depression, a condition in which the muscles used in breathing, such as the diaphragm, fail to respond as carbon dioxide levels in the blood increase. Again, look at the case of Heath Ledger, who was taking medications in their recommended doses, but the combination proved fatal. And when you combine a prescription narcotic with alcohol or pot, both of which already depress the central nervous system on their own, you are vastly increasing your chance of an overdose.

Caleb's sister eventually got out of rehab with a methadone prescription. Both of them were still living in their parents' house. Sarah tried several times to help Caleb get off pills, but he kept slipping up, and eventually she just caved and gave him the number of one of her former dealers. "I'd heard from some of my friends that she might have been using crack at the time, but I don't know that for sure," Caleb remembers. "But she got me in touch with one of her people, this messed-up junkie who said that she knew people who had OC. This lady was so off her shit, she was like a forty-year-old baby. She'd been doing crack and heroin for so long she couldn't keep a cell phone for three days without losing it. She couldn't have $100 in her pocket without it immediately getting stolen from her in the street. She was a mess. She took me to another guy who told me, 'Listen, this bitch is crazy. Let me be your hookup.' And from then on I had a steady hookup for OC without having to drive to Tijuana."

Caleb's new dealer would drive from motel to motel as a liaison. He never held the pills himself. He just knew every single person in Los Angeles who was holding. Caleb would pick him up, he would give Caleb directions, and he'd take him to the people who were selling.

"At one point he got locked up for something for a couple of weeks," Caleb says. "He left his phone with a guy who *does* keep pills on him all the time, so then I just started going directly to him. Which was great, because that other guy could get really paranoid and weird, and it was such a pain in the ass having to pick him up in the heart of the ghetto to find some other person who he has to hassle with to get them."

By this time, Caleb had given up on almost every other kind of drug for getting high. "Everything else has such a downside. Ecstasy leaves you all shaken and awful, coke keeps you up all night, pot makes you sleepy, and alcohol makes you act like an asshole. But on pills, I'm still me. I'm just happy. You just have a lovely sort of buzz to everything you do. Pills have a big downside to them, but it's not in the high itself. They're just too expensive for me to do them all the time, and the comedown is hell. So now I've started taking methadone when I get cravings."

Caleb's level of denial is terrifying, given his own sister's drug use. But it's an easy denial to slip into, because even though he still lives at home with his parents, and goes out to dinner with them all the time, they never know he is high. If the people he lives with can't even see the problem, there's no way he can see it for himself.

Heather's attempts at writing her own prescriptions by stealing prescription pads weren't always successful. "One time I stole a page out of my medical records, because I noticed the nurse was photo-copying my prescriptions," she says. "Since they always write in this crazy language that no one understands, I could now see exactly how they were being written. But it didn't work. Thank god nothing major happened," she says. "I'm sure the pharmacies could have called the police or something if they wanted, but most of them would just refuse to fill them, or would end up calling the doctor to check and see if it was legitimate."

William is a Los Angeles–based pharmacist at one of the major national chains. He sees people trying to fake prescriptions at his drugstore all the time, but he backs up Heather's assertions that the police don't usually get called. Even if they do, often little happens.

"There are a couple of ways that people forge prescriptions," he says. "If someone steals a prescription pad from a doctor's office, we usually get some sort of email blast about it, but only if it's a doctor's office we work with a lot. That way we can keep an eye out for prescriptions from that particular office, and call to verify that they're legitimate if a scrip comes in. But if someone steals a pad and we don't get notified, it's really hard to verify those prescriptions, because the pads are legitimate and we're not required to confirm every prescription that comes in. I'm pretty flexible about what I'll fill, but there are some definite tip-offs when I can tell something is out of the ordinary."

The first for him is someone who doesn't have insurance, but is willing to pay cash for an opiate prescription. Another one is a customer who specifically requests a brand name as opposed to a generic, and is willing to pay for the difference. "It's my understanding that the street value for the brand medications is a lot more than for the generics," he says. (For someone without insurance, in New York State, a prescription for thirty Vicodin costs around $70, versus $20 for generic hydrocodone.)

One day William was working when a customer came in with a preprinted prescription for OxyContin, but it still had a doctor's signature on it. It was from a doctor's office in Nevada.

"We just weren't comfortable with it," William says. "So we told the customer that we were going to have to verify it, and they were fine with it, almost as if they'd been expecting us to say that. They told us the doctor's office was closed but to call the doctor's cell number, which was on the prescription. I looked up the doctor's office, faxed it to them anyway, and they were open. They looked at the cell number that supposedly belonged to the doctor, and it was actually the number of another patient, who must have been waiting for a call from us so he could pretend to be the doctor. The doctor wanted us to press charges, so we called the LAPD and they weren't exactly helpful. If you tell them, 'This person was just trying to forge a prescription,' their response is, 'If we come right now, are we going to be able to arrest them? Are they still there?' And of course they aren't, this guy had already hightailed it out of there. The cops usually tell us to forget it and then get mad at us for making the system so easy for people to manipulate."

Another way that people can forge prescriptions is by simply impersonating a physician and calling one in to a pharmacy. But in order to do this, you need to know the doctor's DEA number. A DEA number is a specific code given by the DEA to anyone who is permitted to prescribe or distribute scheduled drugs. The idea is that it helps track controlled substances. Every physician and pharmacy has one and there is a general pattern to the numbers and letters.

At William's particular pharmacy, which was formerly another chain entirely until his current company took it over, the DEA number never changed. So it's hardly a foolproof tracking system. Also, depending on what schedule the drug is, a doctor doesn't always have to be the one phoning in a prescription. It can be a nurse or an assistant or anyone pretending to be any of the three, as long as he or she has access to the right DEA number.

"For phoned-in prescriptions, it all depends on how they deliver the information," William says. "If they're hurrying and just want to give out the information, nine times out of ten I would believe that. Not that most physicians or nurses are rude, it's just more believable."

Here's another interesting fact. You know how you always have to go way in the back to find the pharmacy in a drugstore? It's designed as a theft deterrent, since it's far away from the exit. "My pharmacy is a little different," William says. "The space is an older design. Pretty much anyone could come in, hop over the counter, take what they want, and run out before anyone could even react."

"The other thing is that if someone works in a pharmacy, and they're brave enough to do it, they can get away with a lot." We've already seen this with Jared's friends, but William tells me a story about a bigger heist.

A lot of the neighboring pharmacies within William's chain know each other well. They do relief shifts if someone calls in sick, and they go to other pharmacies if they're out of stock on a particular medication. One day, at one of the neighboring pharmacies, a guy walked in wearing the customary uniform and said he was from the nearby branch and needed to pick up some supplies for his store. He knew the system and no one even questioned him—they just let him right into the back. He got away with $20,000 worth of OxyContin. "I would never let something like that happen at my pharmacy, though," William says. "This robbery took place at a twenty-four-hour one where everyone was busy and didn't really have time to focus on anything."

Heather was always really bummed out when a pharmacy would call a doctor to verify a prescription she'd stolen, because it meant that she could never go back to that particular doctor. The times that it did work for her was when she would steal a blank prescription, then trace the wording directly from a legitimate scrip onto it, just changing the date. This is pretty much impossible to do now, since no doctor in his or her right mind would ever leave a patient in a room alone with a prescription pad. But any doctor can make a mistake and leave a pad out, especially in a busy hospital.

At that point in her life, pills, and the search for them, were all Heather cared about. "I wound up losing my job at Fresh," she says. "I was taking days off or just not showing up. I wasn't the same person who had started out at that job. I wasn't the same person who had been promoted three times in quick succession. They were just, like, 'What the hell happened to this girl?' If I woke up and didn't have any pills, my priority for the day was not a company event at Bergdorf Goodman; it was getting to whatever doctor was going to give me pills right away."

Because of her senior title, Heather found another job pretty quickly, at Nars, another huge cosmetics company, but she lost the job almost immediately. "I don't remember a minute of it," she says. "And they fired me quick. I deserved it. I maybe worked five hours in a month before they canned me."

I wasn't quite at the point in my painkiller use where I'd just not show up to work in order to find pills. But a large part of the day in my cube was usually spent hunting on the computer for more sources.

Upon graduation from college, Jared was still such a highly functioning addict that he managed to score a coveted job as the assistant to a major book publisher in Boston, about an hour away from his school. He met a few people in Boston who were selling pills, but they weren't coming in as frequently as he needed to keep up his habit, so he ended up traveling back to campus all the time to score.

At this point, Jared was snorting thirty to forty Percocets a day and still topping that off with a few Oxy.

"I always had shit in my nose, and about a year into my job I was just, like, 'I can't do this anymore.' Obviously, for my job, I was supposed to read a lot of manuscripts to see if they were good enough to pass on to the publisher or one of the other editors. I literally did not read a single thing. I'd just say, 'Yeah, I read it, it's not good.' I'd reject everything, because what if I lied and said I'd liked something, and then one of the editors read it and said, 'This sucks, what the fuck is wrong with you?' It was just safer to say everything was bad."

"I knew I needed to try and get off the pills," he says. "My friend who had originally started stealing pills from the pharmacy for us back in high school was in a similar place, so we decided to just go to his parents' house for a week while they were out of town and quit cold turkey. I used the vacation time I'd built up, and it was the worst week of my life. It was like living in a nightmare. I couldn't sleep, I couldn't eat, I was shitting all over the place every five minutes. I was crawling out of my skin. We took benzos, but that never really helped. I was just burning for an opiate so badly that taking anything else was like a slap in the face. And the worst part is that I knew the opiates were one phone call away; it could make all of this terror disappear.

"But we got through it. A week later I was beginning to feel a little bit better, but still crazy. So I went back to work. And even after that week of pure hell, my whole mentality was, 'That didn't kill me, so whatever. I can start right back up again now. I got through it, and it will never be any worse than that. So I might as well just go back to snorting my pills.'"

Jared's friend went right back to pills again, too. The pills had become such an integral part of their lives that they had no idea what else to do with their time. All they knew was work, the hunt for pills, and the high. "What the fuck was I going to do if I didn't do pills?" Jared says. "It was a completely empty existence without them. I thought that at least the first time I did them again after going clean for a week they would be amazing, I'd be able to get a good high, like when I'd first started using. But no, it went right back to that level of general bodily maintenance."

This is why most long-term drug abusers eventually just stop getting high from whatever they are hooked on and are only using to stave off withdrawal symptoms. In someone who is not physically dependent, when the body experiences some form of stress, such as vigorous exercise, epinephrine is released to transmit signals of pain or discomfort to the brain. To keep this response in check, naturally produced endorphins kick in and bind to the neurons responsible for pain transmission, thereby limiting the amount of norepinephrine released in the brain. Think of endorphins as the body's own morphine.

Since opioid drugs like Percocet fool the body by attaching to these same endorphin receptors, flooding them with an artificial surplus first causes not just pain relief, but euphoria as well. But over time, the body produces fewer and fewer endorphins. If the drug is then withdrawn, the body has neither its own painkillers nor an external supply of artificial ones to occupy the receptors. Thus, the horrors of withdrawal.

CHAPTER 8

"Are We Being Irresponsible?"

EVERETT CAME OVER TO watch movies the night after we first hooked up. I went and met him at the subway stop so he didn't have to find the place alone. I was high, wearing a sleeveless shirt, loose jeans, and flip-flops. It was already October but warm out that day. I leaned over the railing at the top of the subway stairs, waiting for him to come out, but he exited across the street and came up behind me instead.

We eyed each other in that way that you do after you see someone you've drunkenly hooked up with, trying to figure out if he is actually cute or if you were just wasted. He acted a little gayer than I remembered, but other than that he seemed cool. We walked back to my place, stopping to get sodas.

"What the fuck," he said when we got to the Tunnel of Terror.

"Ignore it," I said.

We got upstairs and into my room and flopped down on the bed.

"Um, I have to tell you something," I said.

He got this scared look in his eyes.

"No, nothing bad, it's just that I took a bunch of pills today, so if I act kind of spacey, that's all it is."

"Oh," he said, sounding relieved. "What kind?" he asked.

"Vicodin," I said. I didn't feel like explaining the difference between Vicodin and Norco, and figured Vicodin sounded safer, less drug addict-ish.

"Got any more?" he asked.

Yesssss! I thought to myself. My selfishness about hoarding pills had some flexibility when it came to cute guys draped across my bed.

"Sure," I said. I got up and picked Clover up off my dresser.

"How many do you want?" I asked.

"How many did *you* take?" he asked, narrowing his eyes.

"That doesn't count," I said. "I've got a tolerance. Start with one, you can have more later if you want."

He swallowed his pill, and we curled up against each other and turned on the movie. I think it was some blockbuster action film I'd gotten from Netflix. I can't remember which one because we made out for most of it.

After that night, Everett pretty much moved into my room. The relationship developed fast; we decided to become boyfriends within two weeks. I didn't know much about him, except that he grew up wealthy in the South and had gone to private school. He could be very arrogant and bitchy, and one night at dinner I told him that if that was the real him, I really wasn't interested in getting to know him better. Almost overnight he softened up whenever he was around me.

I was so psyched to have what seemed like a normal life. Normal, I guess, as far as bourgeois New York City life goes. He would come over to my house every night after work, we'd order food, watch TV, fall asleep. I took pills every night. He'd join me occasionally and never said anything to me about my intake. On the weekends we'd go out, do coke, come home, and stay up all night talking and fucking. He told me he'd had to go to rehab when he was in high school for coke use, and I was too high on pills to think that the fact that he was doing coke again was a problem.

At the time, I had a really, really bad tattoo on my left arm. It was a cover-up of an even worse tattoo. I'd gotten the original one when I was seventeen, fresh out of the closet, out and proud and going to ACT UP protests. One hungover morning my friends and I went to a strip mall outside of Syracuse, and I got two male symbols inter-twined at the top of my inner forearm. The tattoo artist was this huge, burly, homophobic biker guy who was clearly disgusted, but happy to take my $50. I'm pretty sure it was out of spite that he dug the needle deep, deep into my skin, so the tattoo, when healed, was raised up as if it was in 3-D. I was happy with it for about a month before I realized how incredibly lame it was. For the next seven sum-mers I wore Band-Aids on my arm whenever I went out in short sleeves. The skin around it was always red and irritated from ban-dage glue. When I graduated from college and got my first job at *Interview* magazine, I finally had enough money to get it removed. I went through three rounds of laser zapping, but all that managed to do was lower the ink content so that the tattoo was finally flush with my skin. The procedures were insanely expensive, so I decided that I would just get a new one over it now that the tattoo was flat.

Tattoo number two was done in 1997, which is way too late in that decade to excuse its tribal, Lollapalooza-esque design. I'd tried for years to come up with a design to cover up the second one, but now that I was making real money at *V Life*, I decided to just go to a pro-fessional. I found the best tattoo artist I could, a Russian woman who worked out of a boutique store in Williamsburg. I knew I wanted a raven, and when I told her, she laughed and showed me her card. It had a huge raven on it. Fate! She designed a new one for me, with large spread wings, that covered the old tattoos up entirely.

Everett came with me to hold my hand during the first round. I didn't take any pills, I wanted to feel this pain—maybe as punishment for having such bad tattoo judgment in the past. The pain was unreal; the flesh inside the crook of your arm is incredibly tender. I went someplace dark in my head. It took four hours, and Everett stayed and held my hand the whole time. By the end I was a quivering mess. I felt like I was in first grade and the world was new and raw and scary all over again. I know it sounds like I was being a total wuss, but damn it, it *hurt*. It was worth it, though. The raven looked wise and incredibly strong. I felt like it was my protector against the world: it would keep me from harm.

Everett got me in a cab and took me home and we fell asleep

early, my arm wrapped in plastic wrap, slippery with vitamin E gel. That night, Everett had a nightmare that woke us both up early in the morning when he kicked me, thrashing around.

"Fuck," he said, after opening his eyes. "I just dreamt that your raven came up out of your body and attacked me. It was trying to peck my eyes out and its wings were beating all over my face." He looked scared.

"I told you," I said. "He's my protector. Are you secretly evil?"

"No," he said, tickling me.

But for the next few days he kept bringing the dream up, and he looked nervous every time he did.

I had to go back to the tattoo parlor a few weeks later for some re-touching. This time, Emily came with me and we were adequately prepared with pills. I was too embarrassed to ask her to hold my hand, and she kept wandering out into the store section to look at clothes, or out onto the sidewalk to smoke. The pills helped the pain this time, but it was still there. The combo of pain *and* being high felt exquisite. Emily had told me once about having to have a colonoscopy when she was twenty-one because her family had a history of early colon cancer. She had been awake for the procedure and had been given an IV drip of Demerol. "It was so strange," she had told me. "It was like I knew that *someone* was in pain, but I didn't know who it was."

The feeling was similar, but slightly different for me. The pain was there, but far away, removed. As if I'd floated out of my body but was tethered by a few last nerve endings, just to keep me rooted to the flesh I'd come wrapped in.

When it was over we walked down the street to a nearby café we loved. The trees were changing color and we were wrapped in scarves. We walked slowly, taking in the silence that was rare for this part of Brooklyn. Every time we walked past a particularly beautifully hued tree we'd stop in front of it, my one good arm wrapped around hers, and stare up at it in silence until she'd get impatient and say, "This is gay."

We spent the rest of the afternoon at the café, sipping coffee, discreetly taking more pills, sitting mostly in silence and listening to the music playing. It was a steady stream of music like American Analog Set and José González—all mellow, relaxing stuff that replaced any need for conversation. At the time, we thought that was what was so great about pills. We never needed to talk. Emily and I could sit for hours on end and not say a word except for the occasional "Pass the sugar," and yet we'd feel so connected to each other through the shared physical sensations. We felt sorry for the overcaffeinated patrons around us, who couldn't feel the steady, slow warmth coursing through our veins. Pills made it hard to swallow, so we'd order small things, like toast with jam and lots of butter to lubricate our throats.

Eventually, inevitably, I ran into Joey, the guy I had broken up with right before I left New York to move upstate. Everett was out of town visiting his family, and I was at Hot Pink getting drunk by myself when he walked in. Joey froze when he saw me.

"Hey, Tiger," he said. "When did you get back in town?"

There were multiple chills coursing through my body, but I forced my face to stay steady.

"A while ago," I told him. He looked terrified.

"Why didn't you call me?" he asked. "I thought you had disappeared forever."

"I tried to, but I got bored," I said. "Why would I have called you?"

"I feel terrible about what happened," he started, but I cut him off.

"I don't care. I'm over it now. We can be friends. I don't want to make a big deal out of it."

On stage, some girl had taken off her shirt and was shaking her breasts all over the place while the MC poured a beer over them.

"I feel really weird," Joey said.

"Don't," I said.

"No, I treated you like shit. And I'm really sorry, I mean it."

We leaned against the bar in silence, watching the antics onstage.

He kept buying me beers and repeating the phrase, "I feel really weird."

I told him that he shouldn't because I was dating Everett now and I was happy.

"I know Everett," he said.

"I know," I said back.

"He's really sweet. And cute."

"I know," I said again.

He just frowned and made a sort of "Hmph" sound.

I don't know why I stood there with him for so long. It felt like we were both waiting for something. I had sworn off Joey forever, and yet the pill and booze combination dissolved all of my former convictions.

I eventually got drunk, which is hard for me to do on pills. For me, the opiate high usually cuts a swath through the haze of alcohol, much like coke wakes your ass back up when you start getting too sloppy. "I gotta go," I finally said after Joey's fifteenth "I feel really weird."

"Can we hang out sometime?" he asked.

"I don't know," I said. "Maybe. My number is still the same."

Joey texted me the next day, and despite my hesitations I agreed to go see a horror movie with him later that week. That had been our thing when we were dating. We'd sneak a bottle of champagne and some cocaine into the movie theater at Kips Bay and get trashed while watching horror movies, then troll from bar to bar and eventually end up back at my house.

I didn't tell Everett I was meeting Joey. I told him I had to work late. It wasn't because I thought I was going to cheat on Everett—there was no way I was going to hook back up with Joey—I just wanted to see how it went. Joey had held such fascination for me for so long, and I wanted to rid myself of that. I needed to make him human. In a way I think it was an effort to make me feel better about myself. I needed to prove my feelings were really over.

I saw him waiting outside the theater. He'd grown more of a

beard and was wearing a huge coat with giant fur trim. When he saw me coming he did a funny little tap dance and waved. I laughed, relaxed. The pills probably helped, but I didn't feel anything romantic for him the whole time we were in the movie. I can't remember which one we saw—I think it was either the remake of *The Fog* or *Slither*. There was a little bit of sexual tension during the jumpy parts, when we'd grab each other's arms, but other than that he was a gentleman. He had bought the tickets, he bought soda and popcorn, and he was on his best behavior. Afterward he asked me if I wanted to go get drunk.

"No, I've got to get home to Everett," I said.

He looked sad and we hugged good-bye. I jumped in a taxi, elated. The Joey I'd just spent time with wasn't the Joey I had known. He had grown up some, and the sleazy, bad-boy thing about him that I had been so attracted to before seemed to have dissipated. Besides, Everett was such a safe harbor, and he represented everything I'd never had in a boyfriend before. He was stable, had a great job, and was seemingly deeply in love with me. There were warning signs, though. I found out four months into our relationship that he had been lying to me about his age. He had always told me he was twenty-eight, but it turned out he was twenty-four. He casually yelled this fact out to me on the dance floor at Misshapes one night when we were both high on coke. I freaked out; he didn't see what the big deal was. The next day I cut my hangover short by taking extra pills and had to explain to him through my haze just why this was so wrong. "I'm trying to build a real relationship with you," I told him. "And you can't lie to me."

He was still an unrepentant snob. He definitely toned it down when he was around me, but he was one of those people who would openly make fun of other people's style or looks. I've never had patience for this; it's one of my biggest pet peeves. It's such a transparent form of insecurity. He'd turn the tables on me when we'd fight about him being too caustic, telling me that I was overly sensitive—which is true. I know this about myself. I'm abnormally sentient. Every time I heard Everett making fun of people I put myself in their place, imagining how they would feel if they overheard him. Which happened, a lot. It's another big reason why pills were such a crutch for me. They dulled my overly sensitive feelings to a point where they were manageable.

My own weakness for drugs began at such a young age. It makes me even more certain that I'm just genetically programmed for addiction. Back when I was fourteen, I found myself driving around one night with some punk kids I'd recently met. I was sitting in the backseat, and the guy in front of me was freaking out because he was scared that he was doing too much cocaine and it was taking over his life. It was a really heartfelt conversation. The driver was trying to calm him down and telling him that he was going to help him get clean. The other kid was near tears. He suddenly reached into his pocket, rolled down his window, and said, "I'm throwing this shit out right now."

I'd never even done cocaine, and I knew next to nothing about it. All I'd done up to that point was drink and smoke cigarettes and pot. But before I even knew what I was doing I leaned forward and caught his hand as it was outside the window. The wind snapped both of our arms back. I cupped the bag of coke out of his hand before he could let it go flying down the highway and pulled it back into the car, into the backseat, into my pocket.

"I'll take it," was all I said.

On Emily's birthday I met up with her during my lunch break for a pill handoff and to give her a gift. It was a tiny, leather Smythson of Bond Street pouch on a key chain. The pouch, which was shaped liked an envelope and had a button snap, had the word *Pills* embossed in gold letters on it. She loved it. She'd been having a rough time lately: her boyfriend had been sleeping with another girl. "Are we being irresponsible?" she asked as she took several pills out of her bottle and loaded them into the Smythson envelope. "I mean, should we be worried?"

"I'm not worried," I said. "I feel fine. I'm not addicted."

"My problem is that it's medicine," she said. "I can always justify it. I mean, I've got pain. I can't believe David is fucking that bitch."

"I can't believe you're still fucking him," I said. "You need to stop."

"The thing about it is that pills make it so much easier, even if it means I can't have an orgasm. They make me feel more in love with him. They coat loneliness with loveliness."

I rolled my eyes and laughed, but I knew I was enabling her. I wanted her to stop putting herself in the bad situations that the pills brought her to, but she was still my one steady hookup at that point.

Until the following week when she received a letter from the FDA.

I was working from home, and she called me in a state of sheer panic.

"It says that Customs found a FedEx package at JFK with my name on it, full of a controlled substance," she whispered. "It's got my work address on it! What the fuck am I going to do?"

"What exactly does it say?" I asked.

"'Please read the enclosed notice of Detention and Hearing carefully, since it explains why the package addressed to you violates U.S. law.' I think I need to get a lawyer. There's a number here that says I can call if I have any questions."

"Don't panic yet," I said. "Call the number, find out what exactly this all means for you."

"What if I get fired?" she said, near hysterics. "What if police show up here? I just got the corner office!"

"Just call," I said and hung up. I wish I could say I was concerned for her—her future, her career—but I was pissed and panicked about where the hell we were going to get our pills now.

Emily didn't call back until the end of the day.

"Sorry," she said. "It took me a while to get up the courage. A woman answered and I said, 'I just got a scary letter,' and she said, 'Did you order a prescription online?' and I said yes. She said, 'Don't ever do that again.' I asked if I had to make a court appearance, and she told me no, and to ignore the paperwork and just never do it again, because it means they have my name and they'll be watching me."

"Fuck," I whispered. "What are we gonna do?"

I only had about thirty Norco left.

"Not order online," she said. "One of us needs to start sleeping with a doctor."

"Not it," I called out, as if it was all just a game of tag, and hung up the phone. But her comment gave me an idea. I went onto Craigslist, under the M4M section, and searched "Doctor." The Craigslist sex postings generally creeped me out, but they could be fun for a laugh or for free porn if I was alone and feeling uninspired, imagination-wise, since there were so many amateur pictures that came along with the posts. About fifteen posts came up. Most were from guys looking to play out doctor fantasies, but two were from supposed actual closeted doctors looking to hook up. I sat there staring at the computer for a long time, wondering how I could work out a trade for a prescription in exchange for something besides sex. Maybe I could start an email exchange until I discovered their identities. Hopefully, they would be married and I could blackmail them for pills. Or maybe I could even just threaten to expose their sex cruising to their hospital staff. Finally, thankfully, a little voice inside my head said, *You are acting craaaaazy*, and I quickly clicked off the page.

In the end the solution was much easier. I just posted a bulletin on my MySpace page, asking if anyone had any Vicodin they wanted to sell. By the next day I had three different offers.

I brought Emily along for the first deal. It was from a club promoter who threw parties I'd been going to for years. We met at a Starbucks near Union Square.

"I just bought this bottle off a friend," he explained to me. "But I need money. I want to keep some for myself, though. I have to go visit my family soon, and I would never be able to do that without these."

It was a bottle of sixty. We divided it up between the three of us in the Starbucks, then left to smoke cigarettes. We handed off the money while walking west on 13th Street, in front of a stretch of gorgeous brownstones, and parted ways on Sixth Avenue.

"That was easy," said Emily as she swallowed two, dry. "But how often can we keep this up? This is only going to last me about three days."

"I'll keep working on it," I said. I didn't tell her I had two other deals already set up.

Emily and I were returning from an evening press screening of *Shopgirl*, both high, when my cell phone rang. It was my boss in LA, and I debated letting it go to voice mail for a second before answering. We were near the office anyway, so if it was an emergency I could get to it quickly.

I ducked into a doorway on 34th Street, motioning for Emily to wait for me. She was staring up at the Empire State Building, slowly exhaling smoke.

"Hey, what's up?" I asked.

"Hey," he said. "Sorry to call so late for you."

"What's wrong?" I asked. I could hear it in his voice and racked my brain for something I might have forgotten to do, a deadline I might have missed.

"The magazine is folding," he said. "I'm so, so sorry."

"Shit," I said. "What happened?"

"It was a business decision on the company's part. We're going to put out one last issue," he said. "I feel terrible for hiring you and then having this happen."

"I'll be fine," I said. And truthfully, I did feel fine. There was an uncomfortable thought trying to work its way into my mind about not having much money saved up, but the pills pushed that fact right back down. "What about all of you?" I asked. "How's everyone taking it?" I asked.

"We're all pretty upset," he said. "But we don't want to just slack off now, we want to go out strong, put out the best last issue we can."

"Deal," I said. He apologized some more, which was really sweet of him. I knew it wasn't his fault. We agreed to talk more the next day and figure out an exit payment strategy.

I stepped out of the doorway and looked around for Emily. She was standing near the curb, still staring skyward.

"Claire Danes should, like, get an Oscar for that movie," she said.

"I'm out of a job," I said. "The magazine is folding."

"Oh no!" she said. "What are you going to do?"

"Try and get my job at *Jane* back?" I offered.

It took two months, but that's what happened.

I was still in contact with all my old friends from the magazine. When I told them I was out of a job, many of them recommended me to Brandon Holley, the new editor in chief.

I landed an interview with her, which I felt went well. She seemed grounded and down to earth. I had slowly tapered off taking as many pills as I had been, mainly out of fear of running out of money, so by the time we met I was pretty much sober. I hoarded what I had left for special occasions or stressful situations, one of which arose as I was leaving the new building *Jane* was located in. (It had recently been absorbed into Condé Nast and the offices had been moved to a much more corporate headquarters in midtown east.) I was feeling great about the interview and psyched about the possibility of working again with a group of people I adored. When I got out of the elevators on the ground floor, I was a little turned around and lost. It was already early evening and when I started down one hallway a large security guard appeared out of nowhere and told me that particular exit was closed.

"Sorry," I said. "Can you tell me how to get out of here?"

"Follow me," he said and we turned a corner. He pointed down another hallway and said, "Just follow that one."

"Thanks," I said and started walking away.

"Hey," he yelled after me.

I turned around and he came right up to me, so close that I could smell the sharp, rancid scent of his aftershave.

"Do you mess around?" he asked, under his breath.

"What?" I asked, totally confused.

"Do you fool around?" he repeated, and stepped even closer.

"Oh, um, no, thanks," I stammered, then ducked around him and practically ran down the hallway.

I know there are guys out there in the world who probably jerk off to fantasies like that. Or more likely, would have taken the guy up on his offer. I'm not one of them. I just felt creeped out. That night I laughed about the incident to my friends. But I'd been feeling so excited about the idea of getting my professional life back, and something about the interaction was bringing up a dark feeling in the pit of my heart. I felt like I was six years old and I'd just wet my pants during class. I felt ashamed.

I dipped back into Clover that night before starting to work on my story pitch ideas for Brandon.

Everett had been nothing but supportive since I'd lost my job. Every trace of his arrogance was gone and most nights we slept face-to-face, with Ollie on top of one or both of our heads. He loved Ollie as much as I did, which made me trust him even more. We hadn't slept a single night apart in months, and my bedroom was filled with his clothes and $5,000 samples from his company's clothing line. I was going on different job interviews while waiting to hear back from Brandon, and for the first time in my life, thanks to Everett, I looked the part of a real magazine editor. I knew I had great experience, but I'd never really cared about clothes. Everett taught me how to dress. He threw out most of my closet and replaced it with a small fortune in shirts, pants, shoes, jeans, and coats from his work.

The one thing bothering me about our relationship was that we'd been together long enough that condoms had totally gone by the way-side. I get tested for HIV religiously, but he still hadn't been tested since we'd met. But he was healthy, we were monogamous, and most of the time I was too high on pills to really care if either of us was wearing anything. I had a hard enough time finishing as it was be-cause of all the pills I was on, and the last thing I wanted to deal with was another barrier between us. But I trusted Everett. For the first time in forever I felt protected, taken care of.

On Valentine's Day we met at Moto, our favorite Brooklyn res-taurant, directly underneath the elevated JMZ subway line. They had a prix fixe Valentine's Day dinner that I'd made a reservation for. I was in a particularly good mood because I'd just scored a huge bottle of hydrocodone from a MySpace friend. Everett and I exchanged gifts over the table. He bought me a T-shirt from Opening Ceremony. I bought him a Smythson of Bond Street foldout photo case with room for two small pictures inside. I didn't have any good photos of us to use, so I'd drawn pictures of each of us inside on small pieces of paper.

The first course was a single, cooked quail heart pierced by a spear on a plate. I should have taken that as a warning.

We polished off a bottle of wine, ordered more, and by the end of dinner had decided to find our own place and move in together.

I was ecstatic. I'd never officially lived with a boyfriend before. It was a new step toward adulthood, and I knew it was just a matter of time before I found a new job. With his urging, I even agreed to stay in Brooklyn and give up my Manhattan apartment.

We spent all the next day emailing each other listings of apartments in Williamsburg, and found a large one-bedroom with room for a home office right next to McCarren Park. I called the Realtor and made an appointment for us to look at it together the next day.

Everett called around six.

"I've got to go out to dinner with the boss and some clients," he said. "We're going to be out late, you probably shouldn't wait up."

"Okay," I said. "We're on for 9:00 A.M. with the Realtor though, so don't get too drunk!"

"I won't," he laughed. "And don't you take too many pills! I love you."

"Love you too," I answered.

I watched TV for a while and started to get sleepy, but I was horny with excitement about the next day. Since I wasn't going to get laid that night, I decided to take care of things myself. I'd taken two pills earlier and was having a hard time getting my body to work properly on its own, so I flipped open my laptop to look at some porn. Everything I could find was too clean-cut, too muscled and hairless for my taste, so I went to the Craigslist postings for some real-people shots. I clicked on anything that said it had a picture attached. That's when I saw Everett.

The flash of the camera he was holding out toward a mirror obscured his face, but his tattoo and the bracelet he always wore were clearly shown. He was standing up, his jeans and underwear pulled down to his thighs, his cock out and shirt lifted with his other hand.

I stared and stared, not wanting to believe.

I read the post.

"5'11', 145. Bottom but love it all, mild to wild. Need to travel during day. Meatpacking District, Chelsea or West Village is best."

I felt a scream rising up inside me. My entire body was trembling and I couldn't breathe. All of those neighborhoods were within easy travel distance of his office. I realized a low moan was escaping from my mouth. I tried to stand but quickly had to sit back down because the room was spinning.

Trust. It is all there is to believe in. Not love, but trust. At times you can temporarily fall out of love with your partner. It's normal. You work through it. But without trust, there's nothing.

I fumbled for Clover and swallowed four more pills. They did nothing to stop my racing heart. Adrenaline coursed through me, and in a blind fury I grabbed everything I could find that belonged to him and threw it into a huge pile in one corner. I didn't even realize I was crying until I stopped and sat down on the bed, hyperventilating.

My phone rang. It was Everett.

I answered it and said, "I know everything."

"Huh?"

"Craigslist. I saw it."

"What are you talking about?" he asked, but I could hear panic in his voice.

"The pictures, the posting."

"Someone must have stolen a picture of me," he stammered. "It's not me."

I started laughing loudly, scarily, then abruptly stopped. "Don't," I said.

"Let me explain," he said, and I could hear him crying. "I love you. I never did anything."

I hung up.

He called back about four times. I let them all go to voice mail.

I paced. I ran up and down the stairs four times. I still couldn't breathe, so I sat down on the edge of my bed and tried to focus on air going in and out of my lungs. There was no anger, just an actual pain in my heart. I was itching from pills. Convinced I had caught crabs from him, I ran into the bathroom and pulled down my pants and furiously combed through my pubic hair until my back hurt from leaning forward. There was nothing there. In the back of my head I knew that crabs were the least of my worries, but I suppressed that thought. Beat it down. I dropped to my knees and tried to throw up but nothing happened.

As manic as I was, though, there was a rational voice inside me that knew my reaction to his betrayal had to do with more than just our relationship. This was a grief brought on by the fallibility of humans, particularly men. They (we) cheat. And I hated myself for thinking that. Half the time now I was so high on pills I passed out before Everett and I could have sex at night. Even through my shock, I didn't blame him for looking elsewhere. I just couldn't understand why he had wanted to move in with me. I guess because then he could have it all. He could fuck who he wanted and then always have someone to come home to and hold at night. How many other halves of couples did the same thing?

That night I drank. I met some other friends in the city at a bar and got blind wasted. They dutifully offered support, but in situations like this, everyone involved knows that nothing can change the hopelessness, that feeling of being so desperately alone. I appreciated the effort but I was still in shock. The only thing that could get through to me was the sharp, medicinal taste of rotgut, bottom-shelf whiskey on my tongue. It helped to just maintain at least one of my senses.

Three days went by. On the second night I think I came close to overdosing. I don't even remember how many pills I took, I just remember lying on one of my roommates' beds with a hoodie over my face. He had a friend over and we were listening to Type O Negative, and every time I put my head down I would black out for a few seconds, then come to as a different guitar chord or key change ripped through the room.

Everett had been calling and texting several times a day. I still had the mountain of his clothing sitting on my bedroom floor, and I wanted it out so I finally texted him back, telling him to come by and pick up his stuff.

When he arrived, he texted me to let me know he was outside the Tunnel of Terror. I told him to just use his set of keys to let himself in. I curled up in bed and braced myself.

But when he entered the room, I couldn't even look him in the eye. He had two enormous, army-sized duffel bags with him. He dropped them to the floor and sat down at the foot of my bed.

"I never did anything," he said.

"Right," I answered.

"It was fantasy," he said. "I'd get pictures from guys. I just liked the thrill. I'd delete them immediately."

It sounded like bullshit, but I understood it. I'd been looking at the pictures myself just for the thrill. It's how we'd gotten here in the first place.

I sat up and looked at him. "If that was true," I asked, "why post in New York? Why be so specific in your wording about needing to 'travel during the day'? Why choose neighborhoods that are right where you work? If you just wanted naked pictures of strangers or had some sort of exhibitionist thing going on, you could have posted in any other city and gotten the same responses."

"I don't know," he said and he started to cry. "I love you, I never would have done anything."

I wanted to believe him but I didn't, couldn't. I lay back down and hugged a pillow, Ollie nestled up against me.

"We didn't use condoms," I said.

"That was your idea," he said.

"I know," I said. "I trusted you. I'm a fucking idiot."

He started crying again. "What can I do?" he asked. "This can't be over."

"Go get tested," I said. "Bring me the results, printed on paper. Then we'll talk."

He packed up his things in silence, but his mood had seemed to improve. "I'll go tomorrow," he said. "I promise."

I could tell he was excited, and it was unfair of me to give him false hope. I knew that no matter what the results ended up being, we were through.

He texted me the next morning to tell me that he had a three thirty appointment at a testing center that would give results back in twenty minutes. He promised to call as soon as he got out.

Five o'clock came and went. I'd been tested for HIV enough times to know that the waiting lines were ridiculously long and you usually had to wait at least an hour before you even got in to see someone. I finally called him around six to check in. The call went straight to voice mail.

I called Emily. "Everett isn't calling me back," I told her.

"He probably didn't even go," she said. "I bet he chickened out and is too scared to tell you because he knows how pissed you'd be."

By eight o'clock I was in a frenzy, calling and texting Everett every three minutes. I called his best friend to see if he knew where he was, but those calls went to voice mail too.

It didn't feel real. I'd spent my entire life being so careful. But I should have known better. My younger sister's lifelong best friend, Katie, had been in a committed, monogamous relationship for years, when one day out of the blue she got a phone call from the police, telling her that her boyfriend had tried to rob a KFC at gunpoint and was in jail. Two days later Katie got a call from a strange girl who just said, "You'd better go get tested." It turned out that her boyfriend had been HIV-positive the entire time they'd been together and he'd never told her. He was monogamous, but still knowingly passed the virus to her, as well as to the mysterious caller, who had been his girlfriend before Katie.

Pills. I swallowed handfuls, mixing the hydrocodone with online

Valium but sleep never came. They did nothing to curb my anxiety, my worry for Everett and for myself. I watched my pulse beat under the skin of my wrist. Was it inside me?

I don't remember falling asleep but my cell rang at 8:00 A.M. It was Everett.

"Where have you been?" I asked, still trying to open my eyes.

"I'm positive," he said.

I started to cry.

"The testing center is expecting you today, get there as soon as you can and ask for Laura. She'll get you in ahead of everyone else and do the test." He was calm, his voice maddeningly even.

"Why didn't you call last night?" I choked.

"I couldn't, I'm sorry," he said. "I know it must have been awful for you, but you know, sorry, I had my own shit to deal with."

"No, I understand," I said. I was still crying. "I'm so sorry. How are you holding up?"

"I don't care about myself," he said, totally monotone. "But if I gave it to you . . ."

His voice trailed off.

"I'll go now," I said. "Will you come with me?"

"I have to get to the showroom. It's a huge day for us."

"I'll call you as soon as I'm out," I said. "I love you."

I got out of bed and made it to the bathroom before I sank in the doorway.

Emily met me at the center. She clutched my arm and said, "Everything is going to be fine."

"We never used condoms," I said. "I don't think ever."

"Everything is going to be fine," she repeated. "Are you ready to go in?"

"I need a cigarette first," I said. "If I'm positive, this will probably have to be my last."

"Stop it," she said. We smoked in silence on a bench outside the center.

"It's funny," she said, exhaling and waving her hand toward the center. "Getting tested, it's like our generation's version of the draft. We're all just waiting for our number to get called."

"Grim, Em," I said.

We ditched our cigarettes and walked inside. It was cold and medicinal, with dirty floors. A security guard directed us to an elevator. When we exited upstairs we were met by a receptionist in front of a room packed with people nervously avoiding eye contact with each other, except for the occasional couples, both gay and straight.

"Shit," Emily muttered. "Thank god you've got VIP access."

I asked the receptionist for Laura, and a few minutes later a woman came and collected me and ushered me to a back room. "You're Everett's friend, right?" she asked. I just nodded. I couldn't even speak.

She had me wait outside a door where someone else was getting blood drawn. "Do this one next," she told him and handed him some paperwork.

She waited while he drew the blood and took it from him. "Just wait out there," she said. "Give me twenty minutes."

I went back out to the waiting room. Emily looked ridiculously glamorous. She was wearing a Chloé dress, with a vintage shawl thrown around her shoulders. I was hiding underneath the same gray hoodie I'd been wearing for the past few days. I sat down in the seat she'd been saving for me, resting my head in her lap. She stroked my shoulders while we both stared at the clock in silence.

Laura finally came out and beckoned me. Emily squeezed my hand as I stood up and I followed Laura to her office. All I could think in my mind was *My life is about to change.* I tried to read her body language but she had a great poker face until we were finally behind closed doors. I sat down in the chair and she finally turned around and beamed at me.

"Oh, thank god," I said. I started shaking.

"Completely negative," she said. "Do you want to see for yourself?"

"Yes, please," I said.

"Don't tell anyone I'm doing this, we're not allowed to do it legally. Give me your finger," she instructed as she slapped on some plastic gloves.

She pricked my finger and added the blood to a small vial with some other liquid, then stuck a rectangular piece of paper in it with tiny measured marks on it.

"See, watch," she said excitedly, as capillary action drew the liquid mixture up the piece of paper. "If it rises above this line, you are positive. But as long as it stays below here, there are no antibodies present."

It felt like a game show, watching my blood creep slowly up the marker and praying it wouldn't go farther. I wanted to shout "No whammies!"

"See?" she said. "Not a trace. But we're not out of the woods yet. When was the last time you and Everett had unprotected sex?"

"I think a month ago," I said. "Maybe six weeks?" *Jesus, no wonder he was cheating on me*, I thought. "I mean we were doing other stuff, but not, you know, the really unsafe stuff."

"You need to come back once a month for the next six months and get retested," she said. "Honestly, it usually would have presented itself by now, but six months is still our safety mark."

I stood up and hugged her.

When I got back out to the waiting room I could see terror on Emily's face. I realized I'd been gone much longer than a usual negative response would have taken, so I flashed her a discreet thumbs-up sign. She jumped up and we got out of the building as fast as we could.

"Can we please never do that again?" she asked.

"I have to go back once a month for the next six months," I said.

"Holy fuck," she said.

"I can do those on my own," I said. "She seemed pretty sure that I was safe. It's just in case. But this basically means I have to be celibate for the next six months."

"Big fucking deal," she said. "I have to get to the office."

We embraced and I thanked her again. But I knew I didn't need to.

I called Everett and told him the news. "Oh, thank god," he whispered. "I can't talk now but can I come over tonight to talk?" he asked.

Yes.

When he arrived we spooned in silence in my bed for what felt like hours. I think I even fell asleep for a while. He was so fucking young. I couldn't be angry with him. It wasn't his fault that this disease exists. But I know it was also so easy for me to think this, knowing I was the one who was negative after both of us fully participated in unsafe sex.

"Do you think you know when you got it?" I finally asked.

"I have an idea," he said.

"Was it before or after I met you?" I asked.

"I *never* cheated on you," he said.

"You sort of knew, though, didn't you?" I asked. "That's why you never went and got tested earlier when I asked you to."

He didn't say anything and I knew I was right. I didn't have it in my heart to be angry at him for putting me at risk. It was just as much my fault for being so high that I hadn't trusted my instincts and thrown out all caution. I'd wanted so badly to believe that I'd found love, I had been so happy to exist in my bedroom pill cloud—lights out, TV flickering, two naked bodies, and no cares.

I tried to figure out why I had tested negative. Maybe it was the pills that had saved me. My sex drive had begun to dwindle so low that at times I'd force myself to give him head to hold up what I felt was my end of the relationship. Always high, always with one eye on the TV.

I looked into his eyes. I wanted so badly to believe that he had never cheated, that his "exhibitionist" story was true. In a way I did believe him. But I knew that the relationship was over, regardless. Even if he wasn't lying, the image of him online had cast too large a shadow on us.

"I can't be your boyfriend," I told him. "But I won't leave your side."

"Do you have any pills?" he asked.

I got up and picked Clover up off my dresser, handed him two hydrocodones, took three for myself.

"We need to find you a doctor," I said. I knew he didn't have health insurance, since he was technically a freelancer at his company.

"Laura told me Callen-Lorde has free services I can use," he said, referring to a GLBT community health center in Chelsea.

"Are you going to have to start on medications already?" I asked.

"No, no. My T-cell count is still high enough that I don't have to start on any cocktails yet. I just need to stay healthy."

I immediately regretted giving him the pills. "My old doctor from when I had insurance is an HIV expert," I said. "You should go see him. He'll take care of you. We'll figure out the money."

We drifted off to sleep, holding each other tight.

The next few days were a continuous cycle of sleep, pills, television, and tears. Everett didn't take any time off work. We didn't talk about HIV or health care or therapy or any of the things one should in that situation. I didn't spend any time on the computer, researching what new drugs were available for him. I avoided all the normal caretaking duties that should come with a situation like this. All I wanted was to stay inside my pill bubble, where nothing could get to me.

Then, Brandon Holley called to tell me I'd gotten a senior editor job at *Jane*. I was ecstatic. I'd get my old life back, and I'd be working with all the same people I loved. Even better, I'd now have health insurance, so I wouldn't have to continue my HIV tests at the public health office. I'd be in the hands of my old doctor, an expert who I knew would take care of me in case the virus showed up at a later test.

I took Everett out to celebrate that night. He was happy for me but seemed sad too. "Everything is working out for you," he said. "Things like that don't happen to me. I've always had bad luck."

I didn't know what to say. Of course I was happy I'd tested negative so far. But that happiness was completely overshadowed by my sadness for him. Things had basically returned to normal for us. He was sleeping over every night; we talked or texted multiple times throughout the day. The only difference was, we weren't having any kind of sex.

I threw myself into work. I was so grateful to have my old job back, but with a better title and a much higher salary. As soon as my health benefits kicked in I made an appointment with my old doctor, whom I loved. He is one of those rare New York City doctors who actually genuinely cares about his patients and remembers their history on sight.

We caught up on everything in his office, and I explained the Everett situation. He was sympathetic yet stern about always using condoms. "It's sad," he told me, "but you really can't ever be too safe." I knew it was true, but it depressed the hell out of me. Was there really *no one* I could trust?

He did an RNA viral load test on me, explaining that it was a more intensive kind of HIV test than the kind the community health centers used. "If there is *any* trace of HIV in you right now, it should show up on this test," he said.

"We'll have the results back in a week." He also tested for every other STD known to exist. I wondered if he would find opiates in my system, too. I kept my mouth shut about that part of my life.

It was a torturous week, waiting for the results, but luckily we were closing an issue, so I was swamped at work. It felt so good to be back in the game. I stayed until at least eleven o'clock every night, grateful for the distraction. And I was having fun. It was definitely a cleaner version of the magazine I used to work for now that there was a new editor in chief; I could no longer use the word *fuck* in my text, but it was a minuscule price to pay for the job security.

The ultimate perk was reconnecting with my old friends from the magazine, in particular Stephanie. We'd been best friends when I'd worked at the magazine before, but during the time I'd been gone her career had been on the fast track and we didn't have as much time to talk. She was now executive editor at *Jane* and had her own office, which became my safe haven whenever I started to freak about my potential HIV status. There is no better job in the world than one where you can go into your boss's office, have a good cry in front of her, and then hand in an edited story about how female porn stars were finally starting to grow their pubic hair back in.

The following week I went back to my doctor's office, preparing for the worst. Everything came back negative. "At this point I think you're in the clear," he said. "Enough time has passed that something would have shown up on these tests. You should still come in every few months for another test, but I don't think you need to get tested once a month for the next five months. It might be a bit too much for you to handle, psychologically. Just *always* use a condom."

"Don't worry," I said. "I'm never having sex again."

I kept my pill use down to evenings now that I was working full-time again. I'd take enough at night that I wouldn't feel any strong withdrawal symptoms until late afternoon. I'd usually take some as I was leaving work, so they'd be kicking in just as I hit the subway station in Grand Central. It made the rush-hour commute a gentle hub of dreamy yet determined activity. There was no stress among the masses. I'd bump from person to person like a slow-motion pinball. I'd study people's faces with no anxiety about staring boldly at them. Humans at the end of the workday are so beaten down, but I wasn't one of them.

Everett had started spending more nights at his own house. I knew he still hadn't told his family. "It would break my brother's heart and my mom would just think, 'I told you so' or something," he said.

"But you have to tell them eventually," I said. "You're going to need financial help when you do have to go on medications. They're expensive."

He just got irritated with me and told me he didn't want to talk about it. Our relationship was in limbo, I think he felt I no longer had the right to say things like that to him. One night, over sushi, he finally told me that he needed to move on.

"I'm not going to sit around waiting for you, hoping you will take me back," he said. By the time dinner was over he'd given me the day he wanted to come get the rest of his stuff out of my house.

Emily and I used my HIV-negative status as an excuse to embrace our new celibacy. Weekend nights, we'd curl up in her bed, take celebratory pills, drink champagne, and cement the dark times. I'd go to the movies with Stephanie after work or spend time with friends from college I hadn't seen in years, but I'd never let on that I was high. The short-term memory loss that had taken over my brain because of the pills was a positive side effect as I waited out the months, with regular tests to make absolutely sure I was negative. The relief one would expect never came though. I felt a certain amount of freedom now that Everett was no longer in my life, but I didn't quite believe that the virus wasn't still hiding somewhere deep inside me, waiting to reveal itself at some unexpected moment. I recognized this as paranoia and decided that it was time for me to enter into therapy. I didn't want to see a psychiatrist, because I wanted to avoid being put on antidepressants: What if they interacted badly with my painkillers? I just needed someone with experience to talk to, someone who would help me get the inside of my brain to match the enthusiasm I threw into my work at the magazine. Emily had been in therapy for years. Her doctor referred me to a man who practiced in the same office. He was ridiculously attractive, with a boyish face and a soft southern accent. We clicked immediately, but his soothing tone was the same balm that my pills provided me. He never challenged me; instead, once a week I would fall into his couch, open my mouth, and just spill out words. He'd nod, agree, and laugh softly. I could say anything I wanted with no consequences, and meeting with him became as addictive as my opiates. But I didn't tell him about those, instead choosing to just process what had happened with Everett. There were never any breakthroughs, but I depended on this therapist and his nonjudgmental way with me.

9

Heather Hits Rehab

HEATHER WAS FAR FROM realizing she needed any sort of therapy. She was still ordering her combo of hydrocodone and Xanax online, even after she'd lost her job at Nars. "The painkillers prevented me from eating, which I loved," she says. She never strayed from her perfect combo.

Like me, Heather also never got into snorting her pills. "It's not like I'd never snorted anything in my life," she says. "I'd definitely done my share of cocaine and K, but it just never occurred to me to crush them up and snort them. I'd just put them under my tongue and let them dissolve. That was my ritual. It tasted awful, very metallic and bitter, and I'd get this sensation very similar to coke drip."

Heather was oblivious to the fact that her marriage was falling apart. Her husband's father had been a heroin addict when he was growing up, so watching Heather spiral out of control brought up all of Derek's childhood issues. "He was upset all the time," Heather remembers. "He was crying constantly, having to leave work early to come take care of me because I was such a mess, physically. He had to become such a caretaker that he didn't even have time to get pissed off at me."

But Heather's own rage was starting to spiral out of control. "I've never been an angry person," she says. "I was the oldest child, and our house was always so chaotic. My needs were pushed to the side. I never felt like my emotions were that important, so I always stuffed them inside. And now, for the first time in my life, all that anger was finally coming out. All my anxiety in life stemmed from the fact that I was molested when I was five and never told anyone about it."

Heather blurted this fact out to her mother during an intense phone conversation. "She was saying, 'I don't know why you're so fucked up,' and I was, like, 'Here's why! You left me with X and he molested me. Take it and deal with it.' And I hung up on her and proceeded to take out all my anger on her. I knew her Social Security number, and I went to Barneys and opened up a line of credit in her name and spent a massive amount of money. I also decided I wanted porcelain veneers on my teeth, so I opened up another credit account in her name and headed off to the dentist. I didn't really want any of that shit, it was just a 'fuck you.' I'd never dealt with that much rage, but even at the time there was a voice inside me wondering if this was real emotion or just a by-product of the chemicals being moved around in my brain. Or maybe the pills were just the catalyst I needed to finally get that rage out of me. I still don't know."

Heather's final personal low took place when her pills were accidentally delivered to the wrong address, and she held her neighbor's mail ransom.

"I was out of pills and had been waiting desperately for my delivery and they hadn't arrived. I finally got the tracking number and called FedEx. It turns out they had delivered them to a house two blocks away, and some Arabic guy who lived there had signed for them. I went absolutely crazy."

Heather made Derek drive her to the neighbor's house. She climbed up his front steps and started banging on his door, but there was no answer. "So I took all of *his* mail," she says, "including another package he had waiting for him, and brought it all back to the car. Derek started freaking out, he was, like, 'You can't steal someone's mail! That's illegal!' He tried to get me to put it all back. But I didn't care. I went home, Googled the guy's address, and was able to get his telephone number. I kept calling until I finally got him on the phone."

Heather told him that if he didn't come over to her house immediately she was going to call the police. "Which is just crazy," she sighs. "I'd already stolen his mail, and what was I going to say? 'Police, he's got my drugs that I ordered through the mail!'

"The whole experience was hitting rock bottom for me. I ended up hearing much worse stories when I finally went to rehab, but that was bad enough for me. This was a perfectly nice neighbor who I had to sit next to on the train every day."

At this point Heather was unemployable. Derek wasn't making much money. "It became clear to me that I had to do something or we were going to end up in a homeless shelter," she says.

So she called her grandmother, the former addict. She'd been a bartender in the 1960s and had gotten hooked on Black Beauties (a popular form of trucker speed from that time period, a mix of amphetamine and dextroamphetamine, one of the ingredients found in Adderall), but had been sober now for over twenty years. She told Heather she had no choice but to go to detox and start a twelve-step program.

"I was like, there is no way I'm going to a twelve-step program," Heather says. "It's God-centered and I don't believe in any of that shit."

But she knew she had to at least go to detox. "It was that addict mentality of all or nothing," she says. Just like Jared's first attempt at getting clean. "I told myself I was going to get clean tomorrow and everything is going to be taken care of."

Heather spent the night before she went into rehab taking every single last one of her pills. They were still too precious to her to just flush them away. The next morning Derek drove her to the closest hospital. Since he knew he couldn't have contact with her while she was detoxing, he gave her a little notebook in which he'd written down all the things he missed about the old Heather and everything that she'd be getting back in her life. He included a picture of her taken when she was five and wrote, "Take care of this girl and love her."

"It broke my heart," she says. "I knew I had to do it for Derek, even if I couldn't do it for myself."

Derek took her to a hospital in Sunset Park, Brooklyn. "It's a great trauma center," she says. "It's where anyone in Brooklyn who gets their arm chopped off would go. But the neighborhood has its share of prostitution and drug trafficking. And the detox center admission process was a joke. It's basically like a lotto system. There are only a certain number of beds, so if you show up and they are all taken, you have to come back the next day and try all over again. When I spoke to them on the phone before coming in, the woman on the line told me to show up really early. I had to sign a ton of papers and then give them a urine sample so they could assess how many meds I was going to need. You could go in there and say, 'I take sixty milligrams of Xanax a day,' but if you only have a certain level in your urine, they base your cocktail on that."

Heather was admitted and given a drug cocktail that included an antiseizure medication and sleeping pills. There was no treatment aspect to her detox except medication.

Every four hours everyone would shuffle up to the front desk and get their pills, just like in *One Flew Over the Cuckoo's Nest*. Heather found it cold and impersonal. It had nothing to do with her emotional health and well-being; it was strictly about flushing out her system. And some people weren't even taking that seriously. There was one girl in detox at the same time as Heather who was seven months pregnant, and her boyfriend checked himself in and smuggled dope in for her so she could shoot up. There was another kid there who Heather thought was a really sweet, innocent guy. Turned out he was a pimp with a twenty-girl roster. He'd only checked himself into rehab because heat from the cops had been really intense that week and he needed to get off the street.

"Honestly," Heather said, "I was probably the only person in there who had even set foot in a college. The education level was appalling. But I felt like I could identify with these people, even if they felt there was no way in hell I could identify with them."

The detox program really pushed the twelve steps. By day 7, Heather's time was up and she was sent home. "I still didn't want to do the twelve steps, so I came up with this whole plan how I was going to do yoga and start chanting. And for the first three days home, I felt awesome. I was in the 'pink cloud,' which is a rehab term for how you feel when you first get out, and everything seems brand-new again. I could hear birds chirping and food tasted incredible and everything smelled better. And then I hit a wall."

Heather later learned she was experiencing post-acute withdrawal symptoms, which is a series of withdrawal symptoms that can still manifest even after you've cleared the drugs from your system. For Heather, one of these symptoms was panic attacks—the very reason she'd gotten into pills in the first place.

She went back to her original doctor and explained her symptoms, and he wrote her another prescription for Xanax, even though she admitted to him that she had just gotten out of detox.

After that bottle ran out, she went to her friend Jen, who was working as a stripper at one of New York City's most popular strip clubs.

"Apparently there's a massive pill culture in strip clubs," Heather says. "Just huge. There are a lot of doctors who frequent them and keep the girls amply supplied, so Jen always had some. She hated seeing me go through any sort of withdrawal and would share what she had with me. After a while she started to resist, so I'd just tell her that I thought I was about to have a seizure. I'd whip that line out and manipulate her into giving me more. She was one of my oldest childhood friends."

One evening, Derek watched as she discreetly tried to put something in her mouth. She claimed it was an aspirin, that she had a headache, but he forced her to open her mouth and saw several pills under her tongue. Heather broke down, saying, "I have to stay on it."

Derek had no clue how to help her and felt like he was starting to go crazy himself. He felt terrible about getting in her face and being angry, because he could see just how bad it was for her. She was shitting and vomiting constantly, and sometimes not making it to the bathroom in time for either. "I'd be hot, then cold, then hot again, coupled with the blackest depression I'd ever had, times a thousand. I felt like I'd be better off dead, that killing myself would be easier than going through it. More than anything, it made me understand why people stay drug addicts."

Derek started doing research online about real rehabilitation facilities, and checking with his work insurance to see if it would cover any of the costs. Luckily it did, except for the copay.

Six weeks had gone by since Heather had gotten out of detox. They went to Derek's family's home in Long Island for Thanksgiving dinner; by noon Heather was sleeping while Derek was in the kitchen talking with his family.

"My sister was pregnant at the time," he says, "and my mother was asking me why I hadn't been around much to support her when the rest of the family was so excited. I just started crying and saying, 'You have no idea what's going on in my life.'"

But Derek had forgotten that his mother had spent years watching her husband suffer as a heroin addict. She recognized a lot of the same symptoms in Heather and told him, "I think I have an idea."

Derek told his parents about the different rehab centers he'd looked up online and how much money he had to come up with, and his father simply said, "I'll pay for it."

Derek and Heather selected a facility in Miami, Florida, because of their emphasis on a painless detox. "When I spoke to them on the phone, they really catered to my fear of withdrawal. They promised that I would have a cocktail of drugs to slowly wean me off, and that I would feel no pain whatsoever. And the pictures on their website showed a beautiful beach. I was so excited, I thought I was going to a yoga spa retreat. I brought all of my yoga clothes, chanting CDs, Saki bath soak and perfume."

Except for the yoga clothes, it was all immediately confiscated upon her arrival. "The center was actually located in a strip mall that sat on a canal filled with Budweiser cans and alligators," Heather sighs. "There was one enormous room with a huge television and about eighty zombies in various states of withdrawal. There was a back patio overlooking the canal. It was the social nexus of the place. People who were starting to get their feistiness back would sit out there smoking from 8:00 A.M. until 1:00 A.M."

Heather's cocktail consisted of various painkillers, the muscle relaxant Soma, sleeping aids, but no benzodiazepines. "There was a lot more pill addiction in this detox center than what I had experienced in Brooklyn. In fact almost everyone there had some sort of pill issue, even if they were mainly there for something else, like alcohol or heroin. There was one nurse who was coming off an insane amount of morphine. She was doing a *six-month* detox program in order to get off it."

In fact, Heather quickly discovered that there were a lot of nurses in her detox program, most of whom had become addicted to painkillers they were stealing from the hospitals they worked in. And through them, Heather learned how to manipulate the system to get more painkillers.

"There was one who was going through her tenth detox program. She told me to tell the nurse on duty that my foot hurt, and specifically that it was a shooting pain up my leg," she says. And it worked, she got additional handouts. Heather quickly came up with her own stories, such as migraines and her tried-and-true sciatica that worked to get her more painkillers.

"I think I was able to get away with so much because I was the only one who seemed normal there," she says. Unlike some programs, "there was no scheduled time to get up in the morning, because a lot of people were on meds that made them sleep a lot. There were some people there who I never once saw open their eyes. I was one of the only people who got up early every morning, showered, dressed, and put on makeup, instead of walking around in my pajamas with a blanket, screaming and wailing."

Heather was the good girl, and because of that none of the staff suspected her of abusing the system. But even though Heather was putting on a brave face, she was still tortured inside. "My body was just demented," she says. "I'd gone from shitting constantly to not being able to poop for three days because of all the painkillers I was on and additionally scamming. I just remember lying on the bathroom floor and thinking to myself, 'I'm in Miami, trying to shove a suppository up my butt. What the hell am I doing here?'"

Every night, members of the local AA chapters would show up to lead group sessions. "One of them kept hitting on me in this really pervy way. I was in fucking detox—I couldn't believe he didn't have any other available choices," she says.

Heather was also seeing a therapist every day, one she was initially distrustful of, mainly because she didn't feel like she could trust anyone. But about halfway through the detox, she started to connect with her therapist. At this point she had met so many people who had been inside the detox system and knew how to manipulate it that she realized she didn't want to be that person.

"This was already my second time in, and it just hit me that if I kept it up I'd be back again and again and again, just like the rest of the people in there. I knew my family didn't have the money to help me out, and Derek's family certainly wasn't going to pay for me to go again. I knew that Derek would leave me if I didn't start taking this seriously, and then I'd have no one."

So Heather admitted to her therapist that she had been lying to the nurses. The therapist warned the nurses not to give Heather anything else, but it was a moot point because she stopped trying to get anything else besides what was already being prescribed for her.

At the end of her detox, Heather had the choice either to go back home or to go to a rehab center. Many of the people whom she'd befriended told her she should just go home. "They'd say, 'Come on, look at all these other people in here. You're so much better than them,'" she says. "But that was the game I'd been playing my whole life. I knew I wasn't."

Heather met with "ambassadors" from rehab centers around the state and selected one that offered morning meditation and yoga. "I was like, that's the one for me, that's the stuff that's going to keep me sober."

The center was located in Fort Pierce, Florida. "It should have been called Fort Piss," Heather says, "because it was seriously the armpit of Florida. There should have been an old blues man on every corner, wailing about how horrible life is there. Maybe there are some parts of upstate New York that *might* compare to how shitty and rundown and left behind this town was. The rehab center was in another strip mall, but the living quarters were in an apartment complex called Virginia Gator Park. It was a gated complex, but also a disgusting nightmare. There was a pool you'd never want to even put a toe into and rows of apartments for the rehab people, right next door to apartments inhabited by drug dealers."

The yoga and meditation that Heather had been so looking forward to consisted of rising at 6:00 A.M., making her way down to the beach with the other patients, and standing in a circle while praising Jesus. "I was furious," she says. "There was a Jewish guy in the program and he and I just clung to each other."

Heather resisted the program's twelve-step leanings every step of the way. But she knew she had to figure out a way to make rehab a positive experience for herself, especially since Derek was begging her over the phone to stay. But her experiences at this particular facility were pretty horrifying, starting with the brutal gang rape of a new patient whom Heather had befriended.

"It was her first day at rehab," Heather remembers, "and she was being admitted for heroin addiction. There was something about her that reminded me of Janis Joplin and I was just drawn to her. While she was checking into the apartment complex, we started talking and getting along and I invited her over for coffee. I wanted to take her under my wing."

The apartments in the complex designated for the rehabbers were monitored by what Heather describes as "a group of awesome big fat sassy black ladies, who were really sweet but had no real training." Their job was to get people settled in their rooms, wake them up in the morning, ferry them back and forth between the complex and the strip mall rehab center, and do random room checks for contraband material.

Heather said good-bye to the new girl, Tina, as she finished her check-in. She noticed some of the local drug dealers hanging out nearby, but didn't think anything of it. They were always around. After Tina had checked in and was waiting for her room assignment, she was left alone on the porch.

Heather came back after a while to see if Tina had finished check-in so they could hang out, but she was nowhere to be found. Heather asked Missy, the woman who had admitted her, if she had seen Tina, but she hadn't. After a few hours had passed and there was still no sign of her, Heather became frantic. She forced Missy to come with her to knock on the apartment door of the dealers she had seen lingering nearby.

The door opened and there were several men inside who claimed not to speak English and shut the door in their faces. They were on the second story of the apartment complex and were standing outside the door when a wayward, flea-ridden, three-legged Chihuahua hobbled up the stairs toward them. The dog's owner ran up after it and whispered to Heather and Missy that he had heard through the grapevine that the men had a girl inside their apartment. Missy pounded on the door again and yelled that she was calling the police. She and Heather ran to the office to make the call, when the apartment door opened and all the men ran outside, hopped into a van, and drove off. The apartment door locked behind them. When the police arrived, they knocked it down and found Tina cowering naked in the bathroom. She had been raped repeatedly after being lured inside with the promise of a fix.

"It was just this awful, horrible realization that even though we were in rehab, we weren't safe," Heather says. "When I got upset about it, one of the counselors made some crack to me about how I must have seen worse on the streets. I was, like, 'I've never been on the fucking streets. My streets were carpeted doctors' offices with old copies of *Parenting* magazine on the coffee tables.'"

Heather wasn't learning the skills she needed to live. She began to develop relationships with other patients and tried to help them through their recovery, but she kept getting called out on it from the therapists because she wasn't focusing enough on herself. She also never got used to the common AA mantra about working the twelve steps: "It works if you work it, so work it, you're worth it."

"It was just this dumb cheerleading chant we had to do every morning before going into group therapy, which never even really focused on addiction issues," she says. "It was more about resolving really fucked-up high school issues, like one patient getting upset that two other patients were sleeping together, because everyone was suddenly discovering their sex drives again after getting clean."

To make matters worse, the main therapist with whom Heather

had been working, with whom she was just beginning to develop a bond, suddenly had to leave because her son died.

By the time her twenty-eight days were over, Heather was more than ready to go home. Derek flew to Florida to pick her up, but it wasn't the happy reunion they'd both imagined. Derek was furious to discover that the rehab center was still keeping her medicated. She was taking Cymbalta, an antidepressant, Lyrica for anxiety (which was being prescribed off-label), trazodone to help her sleep (an antidepressant, also being prescribed off-label), and Seroquel to ward off panic attacks (an antipsychotic, once again, being prescribed off-label). She was on more medications coming out than she had been on going in. This is fairly standard with rehab because of the anxiety, depression, or sleeping issues that can arise with newfound "sobriety." But Derek hadn't been expecting all these new medications. He associated Heather's problems with pills, and now she was taking more than ever.

In *High Society* Joseph Califano discusses the biggest problem with rehab facilities: The twenty-eight-day cycle that almost every residential treatment program functions on is not determined by any sort of medical need; it is simply the reimbursement cap set up by commercial insurers. He claims that even higher-end facilities like Betty Ford and Hazelden only have success rates of around 30 percent. Both centers refute that claim and boast much higher success rates, but they also only monitor their patients for one year after leaving.

Heather arrived home with no follow-up therapist. Her rehab center advised her to get a low-stress job ("moron job," as Heather puts it) when she returned home. "It actually makes sense," she says. "If I had taken on a stressful job I would have slipped up for sure. I needed to take it easy for a while, let myself be a dummy, because I couldn't think straight. I couldn't form sentences, and I had tremors in my hands from the combination of pills I was on. I slowly tapered off all of them over the course of about six months." During this time, she was under the care of an osteopathic doctor who was monitoring her decrease.

When she was feeling stronger, Heather took a job helping to run a high-end spa in Manhattan. It was the last time she would slip up. She was stressed and tried to order Xanax online, but Derek had been monitoring her email and busted her. She canceled the order. "I'd been thinking to myself, if I just had one Xanax, I can get through this week. But in reality there is no way: one would quickly become ten. Getting busted by Derek was the best wake-up call, because even after rehab, I don't think you're ever out of the woods. Especially with pills."

She isn't even sure she would have taken the pills if Derek hadn't caught her. "I might have gotten freaked out and thrown them away. I might have gotten them and done them all at once. But I think I'm too scared to go back to that lifestyle again, because I know there would be no coming back. Derek would leave, my family wouldn't help me again, and I would just be alone with my drugs. That's where any addiction is going to take you."

For people who don't want to deal with rehab, or even just a week-long detox, there are many different companies in the United States that offer anesthesia-assisted rapid detoxification, AARD, more commonly known as ultra-rapid detox. The person is put under anesthesia and given a medication like naloxone, which strips opiates off the brain's receptors by shoving them aside and taking their place. Because naloxone is an antagonist, it is drawn to these receptors, but can't do anything once it gets there. It's kind of like the situation of a drunken stud who does everything he can to get someone in bed, but is too wasted to perform once he's actually in the sack.

Patients usually wake up feeling groggy and hungover, but the cravings are gone. The procedure isn't covered by insurance and can cost anywhere from $10,000 to $20,000. Detractors of AARD argue that patients need a much longer amount of aftercare and therapy, since many are simply released back to their homes after just a few days. And on July 8, 2008, a popular medication used in ultra-rapid detox called Revex (nalmefene) was discontinued by its manufacturer with no explanation. AARD can seem like an easy solution for people who can afford the process and don't believe they have the time to go to rehab, but anyone who chooses this method should make sure to have proper aftercare set up, for example, a therapist or regular attendance at NA or AA meetings. Otherwise, AARD seems like an expensive and ineffective way of dealing with the problem. Sure, you won't suffer the same amount of withdrawal pain, but there is virtually nothing stopping you from going right back to taking whatever it was you were taking before you went under anesthesia.

Caleb eventually cut down on his daily OxyContin use and saved the pills for special occasions. "They're just too expensive," he says. "I can't afford them." Now he takes illegally obtained methadone to stave off his cravings. According to the DEA, prescriptions for methadone have increased by 700 percent from 1998 to 2006—just another example of more pharmaceuticals being out there to be diverted. Caleb eventually stopped using the drug dealer who made him drive around to different places to pick up drugs. "If he's not on crack, then there's something seriously wrong with him," Caleb says. "He's just crazy as hell, and it got to be such a pain in the ass picking him up in the heart of the ghetto, then driving around to find some other person that he has to hassle with. The guy I use now is just a godsend."

And, apparently, the dealer believes that himself. "He comes to town three times a week," Caleb says. "He drives around in this giant old green Cadillac convertible, blasting this Christian gospel sermon out of the radio. You know the kind: 'And the Lord will strike down his enemies,' blah blah blah. He usually has methadone, OxyContin, and Valium, and he just drives around all day making his deliveries. He's always glad to see me, and he gives me a preferred-customer status. He'll let me hold a few of whatever I'm buying until next week, or work with me on pay, or give me an extra pill for free."

But the Christian hookup doesn't always work out to Caleb's advantage, because product availability fluctuates. "Recently he was out of methadone, and I couldn't find it anywhere else," Caleb says.

"So I had to take OCs every day just to maintain and not get withdrawals. I wasn't very happy about it. It cost way too much."

If I were an enterprising drug dealer with a regular customer like Caleb, I would make *sure* I consistently ran out of methadone and only had OxyContin available. It just makes sense from a business standpoint, especially if you were having a slow week in your other drug arenas. I'm just saying.

Caleb has been on methadone for well over a year now. "There's absolutely no high to it," he says. "It just delays my withdrawal symptoms."

But at this point going off methadone would be almost as bad as going off OxyContin. "It's just that I never wanted to go through withdrawal in the first place," he says. "The 'dones are really cheap, it's been relatively easy to maintain a steady supply, and I've been able to delay taking everything out of my system. It's hard to say, 'Okay, I'm going to set aside a week when I feel worse than I've ever felt in my entire life. I'm going to put aside my friends, my family, my job, everything—just to check out. It's just so much easier to keep saying, 'Oh, next week, next week.'"

CHAPTER 10

Fight or Flight

MY FATHER CALLED. THERE was something wrong with my grandmother in Tennessee. I have a hard time paying attention to him, my mind shuts down a little whenever he, or even his voice, is in proximity. All I heard were the words *infection, necrotic tissue, surgery.* He asked me to come down to take care of her in the weeks after she was released from the hospital. "She'll need help around the house," I was told. The rest of the family would take turns once I left. My grandmother, Bobby, had been the only member of my family besides my two sisters who had ever showed a consistent interest in my personal life or my career. I'd even put Bobby in *Jane* once, describing a trip we took to Alaska together to see the glaciers and look at whales. She was the only family member who subscribed to and actually read every issue of *Jane.* (My mother once described it as a magazine "utterly without substance.")

During high school, I had spent every summer with Bobby in Tennessee. I'd sneak booze from her liquor cabinet, and we played card games for dimes on a large, round green marble table she'd had custom-built. Her house had been designed by her and my long dead grandfather. It has glass walls that stretch the entire length of the back of the house, looking out over a long, curved stone porch and a sloping lawn that leads down to dark woods, teeming with birds and deer. When I was a teenager, she was the only member of my family who ever made me feel like I could do something productive with my life. When I had first gotten my job at *Jane* my father had congratulated me, but what stuck out the most in my mind was him laughing and saying, "I'd always thought you'd be in jail by now." But Bobby, who had worked as an editor for years, told me about the Kennedy side of my family, which ran a small newspaper dynasty in Michigan. "It's in your blood," she said, and raised her glass of bourbon in salute.

I didn't know what to expect when I arrived in Oak Ridge, but I knew that I was going to do the caretaking sober. I didn't bring a single pill with me. I wanted all my faculties if I was going to be taking care of the one woman who had made me feel worthwhile. As for her injury, all I knew was that she had fallen a few months ago and developed a small cut on her left calf. Over time it had become red and infected, and then it became seriously infected. The tissue in her leg had become necrotic.

When I arrived I ran straight up to Bobby's bedroom. She had the blankets pulled up to her chest. One of my cousins was sitting on the edge of the bed. We all hugged hello and Bobby said, "Do you want to see it?"

I nodded. There was a strange slurping sound coming from the other side of the bed. She pulled down the blankets to reveal a foot-long, four-inch-wide trench dug into her calf. The inside of the trench was stuffed with foam, vacuum-sealed with some sort of clear plastic wrap, and hooked up to a clear tube that ran down her leg, onto the floor, and into a Medi-Vac, the source of the sucking sound. It was a large, whirring machine that constantly siphoned pale pink goo out of her leg with a wet, straw-at-the-bottom-of-a-milkshake sound.

None of this did anything good for my sudden onset of pill withdrawal.

The next morning I woke up early, snot pouring out of my nose and onto my pillow. I was freezing cold and my legs had the shakes, but I forced myself downstairs to prepare breakfast and coffee. I'd had minor bouts of withdrawal before, in between pill hookups and when I'd moved up to Hudson, but those were nothing compared to how I was feeling now. While I was trying to make toast my arms began to shake and my bones felt as if they were being clawed apart. I fought the sensations, took deep breaths, brought everything up to Bobby on a tray, and set it on a card table my cousin had set up in the room. I helped her to the bathroom and sat on the bed with her while she ate, trying not to look too sick, but I kept blowing my nose. She, of course, went into grandmother mode, but I convinced her it was just a mild cold.

"I'll run out and get some DayQuil when I get groceries," I said.

She listed a bunch of items she wanted me to pick up, and as she was talking she reached over to her bedside table and picked up a bottle, opened it, and swallowed two pills. The act itself caused a Pavlovian response in me. When she put the bottle down, I saw that it was Percocet and felt a tremor course through my entire body. I couldn't hear anything she was saying. I just stared at the bottle, fighting with myself not to devise a plan to get inside of it. I refused to let myself fall that low, to steal pills from my sick grandmother.

I had to ask her to repeat some of the grocery items she was craving and took off for the store. I drove the long way, wondering what would have happened to me if my mother hadn't remarried and moved us away from this town when I was in the fourth grade. I'd probably still be stuck here.

Oak Ridge, Tennessee, was one of three towns built to complete the Manhattan Project. The farmers who originally lived there had all been kicked out under eminent domain, the law that allows the government to seize private property for its own use. It was called The Secret City, and lived up to its name. I remember very little about my childhood in Oak Ridge, and what I do remember is always cloaked in shadow.

The town is filled with sirens built onto the telephone poles, and a few times a year they go off as a test, in case anything goes wrong at the laboratory. Our teachers taught us to crawl under our desks with our arms covering our heads.

Besides its nuclear history, Oak Ridge is different from most suburban towns in that most of the houses were built up in the ridges, so they can't be seen by aircraft. All of the winding roads make it sort of like driving through a low-rent, prefab government housing version of the Hollywood Hills. All the houses look the same; there were only seven different versions of the same model with a few sub-models thrown in as well. The town's residents were later granted land at a cheap price to build their own homes.

Bobby didn't find out what my grandfather was doing at the lab until after the bombs were dropped in Japan. One morning in August 1945, she turned on the radio and learned what her husband had been working on. He called her almost immediately after to explain. After she hung up, she sat by the phone and wept.

On my way to the store I drove past the children's museum. It was housed in a building that had been an elementary school in the 1950s and then, when I was a child, converted to a day-care center on one side and a day facility for mentally disabled elderly people on the other. The school's decaying gymnasium in the center of the two wings separated life and death. The bathrooms were located on the old people's side of the building, and twice a day, we kids would march down the hallway until we hit the stench of prepared food from the cafeteria. The old people weren't allowed in the bathrooms while we kids were inside, but if you had to go anytime that wasn't designated, you had to make your way alone down the old school's hallway through the safety zone of the gymnasium. Past the old men with rotten teeth, drooling and grinning as they wandered the hallway. Sometimes one of them would follow you inside the bathroom.

On several occasions when my father or mother would pick me up from day care, I would have shit or pissed my pants rather than go inside that bathroom on my own.

When I got back to the house from the grocery store I swallowed three DayQuil, then fixed lunch for Bobby and brought it upstairs.

She was dozing and the goo tube had become wrapped around her leg. The Medi-Vac was making a scary buzzing sound, so I quickly unraveled the tube until the sound stopped and I saw another glob of pink jelly get sucked through the plastic.

She woke up and told me that the home health care nurse had called and would be coming by soon to change the foam in her leg trench. I watched as she ate her lunch. And after I had cleaned up the dishes I came back upstairs to her bedroom.

"I just hate that you're seeing me like this," she told me. She loathed not being in control, and so did I. I was feeling worse and worse and was beating myself up inside. I knew that I needed to be entirely present in order to properly take care of her. We were two invalids, but I had to keep my sickness secret. I lay down on the bed next to her. The back wall of her bedroom, like the rest of the house, was one huge window that looked out over the lawn and into the forest beyond. We sat there together quietly for a while, just staring at the woods, when my fingertips suddenly went numb and I wasn't able to catch my breath. The light in the trees suddenly looked strange, disorienting.

"I'll be right back," I said and ran outside, grabbing the cordless phone in the kitchen to call my older sister, Erica. We'd always been close. She pretty much raised my younger sister and me until she went away to college when I was in seventh grade. But she'd become increasingly busy raising her own two kids, so much so that our adult friendship seemed to be taking a backseat. I understood this completely, but sometimes I couldn't help but feel jealous.

She was completely unaware that I had an issue with pills, but as far as I was concerned, I hid that fact from everyone.

"I think I'm having a panic attack," I said, when she answered.

"Just breathe slowly," she said. "Concentrate on the air going in and out of your lungs."

"I can't even breathe," I said, laughing to make it sound like I wasn't scared, but my voice cracked and shook. "My fingers are numb."

"You've got a lot of responsibility down there," she said, her voice maddeningly soothing. "It makes sense that you'd be nervous and scared."

I got angry. She had no idea what I was going through. I briefly considered telling her the truth, that I was going through withdrawal, but when I played out that scenario in my head, my anger softened. She'd want to fly down, she'd have to find someone to take care of the kids and her business—I couldn't do that to her. I was alone in this, and that thought distracted me enough to snap me out of my panic attack. I knew I could take care of my grandmother, and suddenly I was pissed that Erica thought I was too weak to do it, when she had no idea what I was actually going through. I held onto that anger to get me through.

"I'm feeling better now," I told her, suddenly. "Thanks, I can handle it."

I went inside, made some tea, and went back upstairs.

"Who were you talking to?" Bobby asked. "I thought I heard voices."

"Erica," I said. "I had to ask her something. Want to play cards?"

Bobby smiled and sat up in bed as I maneuvered the goo tube so it wouldn't get stuck under her. I sat cross-legged next to her and began to shuffle. Just over her shoulder, on the bedside table, I could see the giant bottle of Percocet. I kept shuffling the cards over and over, staring at it, until Bobby dryly said, "I think they're done."

The home health care nurse showed up later that afternoon. She had the east Tennessee twang that no one I knew growing up had: most of the families I knew had been imported to the town to work at one of the labs. Her hair was dark and crisp from hair spray, and she wore way too much eyeliner and Payless sneakers. I loved her.

I sat on the bed and watched as she pulled a chair up to the side of Bobby's bed, turned the machine off, and began to unwrap the wound. I trusted her implicitly, because Bobby had told me she was the one who first realized something was wrong with her leg. She had sent her to the hospital after dressing the wound one day, and the hospital had sent Bobby home, saying nothing was wrong. But the nurse knew necrotic tissue when she saw it and sent Bobby to another doctor, who immediately admitted her to the ER.

As the nurse removed the foam from the trench I felt my stomach lurch. Bobby winced and grabbed my hand. I was feeling dizzy, but I refused to leave her side. The nurse gently cleaned the wound, and Bobby gripped my hand tighter while I babbled about what Netflix movies we should order next. She went along with the conversation and never once said a word about the pain she must have been feeling, but my hand quickly grew numb from her grip.

The nurse removed a large new piece of foam from her bag and held it up to the wound, then she cut it into a matching smaller piece. As she stuffed the foam inside the trench, pulling the flesh back so it would fit inside, Bobby cried out. I could feel tears welling up in my eyes, but I held them in. I just rubbed her shoulder and arm and said, "It's going to be over soon." She looked at me and laughed, but I recognized the sound, it was the same scared, cracking laughter I'd spat out when I was talking to Erica.

It was over, finally.

The nurse turned the machine on and I watched as the plastic vacuum-sealed the wound shut, like a late-night infomercial for a machine that sealed up meat for freezing. The sucking sound started immediately, and after a few seconds we all watched as the first glob made its way down the tube.

"Your surgery is set for the end of the week?" the nurse asked.

Bobby nodded. As long as the machine was able to get rid of all the necrotic tissue, she was set to have the foam removed and a large flap of skin cut from her abdomen to seal up her leg. I had no idea how they were going to fill the hollow space inside. The nurse left and Bobby fell back asleep.

I went into my room, which was my father's old bedroom. The ceilings were high and slanted, with exposed crossbeams. I'd always stayed in this bedroom as a kid, and my cousins would sleep in the adjoining bedroom, which had belonged to their father. I'd also lived in this room for a few summers as a teenager. It had always given me night terrors. When I was a child I would wake up in the night and see a dark figure standing over the bed next to me. Sometimes it would sit down beside me. And once it left, I was convinced it was hiding in the closet next to the bed, waiting for me to fall back asleep.

This bedroom still haunted me. I could never get a good night's sleep in it. Now, as an adult going through withdrawal, I felt even worse in there.

The next day, when I got out of the shower and walked to my bedroom, I smelled a strong odor, as if the cat had defecated right outside the bathroom door. I heard Bobby calling weakly for me. I grabbed a pair of jeans and ran to her room. She was standing just inside her bathroom leaning over the sink, trying to slip her nightgown over her head. Her back and legs were covered in runny feces.

"I've had an accident," she said quietly.

"It's okay, don't worry about it. I'll take care of it," I said, as soothingly as I could.

It was this moment that snapped me physically out of my withdrawal. It was the power of seeing someone need me so badly, knowing how she must have felt in that situation, the machine dragging along behind her and the bathroom floor covered with the mess, that made every physical symptom in my body disappear. Maybe it was the adrenaline rush of knowing I needed to go into emergency mode and make her feel safe at the same time.

I gently lifted her nightgown over her head and tossed it into the bathtub. She'd had a mastectomy about ten years earlier.

I'd never seen the result. She wouldn't make eye contact. I helped her into the tub, making sure we kept the machine outside of it and the tube running smoothly into her leg, and I began to sponge her off as she leaned on me for support. I made jokes about how I'd seen much worse in college, that everything was going to be okay, that this was most likely a result of the many antibiotics she was on. She stayed quiet the whole time, except for the occasionally whispered "I'm sorry." I told her this was nothing, that she had supported me my whole life, this was the least I could ever do for her.

I continually rinsed and added more soap to the washcloth, got new clean ones out of the utility closet, and started over. I couldn't give her a full shower because of the Medi-Vac. I had to ask her to bend over to clean the worst of it and she made a tiny whimpering sound but quickly choked it back. I concentrated solely on the task at hand. It was almost meditative. I blocked every thought from my brain except the goal of getting her clean and comfortable. I'd process the eventuality of the human body later.

I finally got her completely clean, into a pair of adult protective underwear I found at the bottom of her closet, into a clean nightgown, and back into bed. She was fatigued from having to stand for so long and quickly passed out. I spent the next hour cleaning the floor of her bathroom, disinfecting, and making sure everything was spotless. I went back into my bathroom and into the shower, crying under scalding hot water. I wanted, *needed* her pills. But there was no way in hell I was going to take them.

CHAPTER 11

How to Destroy a Doctor

BOBBY'S SURGERY WAS A success, and my younger sister showed up to take over so I could get back to work in New York. I was proud of myself for not stealing any of her pills, and ashamed of myself for feeling proud about something that should just come naturally to a person. But it helped to know that I was not alone in my desire. Sadly, stealing pills from elderly relatives is pretty common.

Diversion of pills takes many forms. In most cases, doctors are legitimately prescribing medication for people who are in chronic pain. Some doctors are less than scrupulous, but they are the minority. It's quite possible that early refills for people in chronic pain, especially for the elderly, are needed because someone has been pilfering some of the pills, either for personal use (like I almost did) or to sell. Unfortunately, it's the doctors who are being prosecuted, when, in most cases, they were just trying to help a patient suffering from intolerable pain. There's a huge difference between the doctor who helps operate an Internet pill mill and the doctor who gets busted for legitimately prescribing painkillers to people who need them for their intended purpose.

In February 2002, a doctor in Florida, James Graves, was convicted of manslaughter in the deaths of four patients for whom he had prescribed OxyContin. He was sentenced to sixty-three years in prison. This was at the height of the OxyContin panic, when the media was collectively ejaculating over the idea of hillbilly heroin. Dr. Graves argued that he had been prescribing the medication legitimately; he even made his patients sign "pain contracts" promising to follow his instructions. Michael Gibson, Dr. Graves's lawyer, was quoted as saying, "If a patient lied, there was little Dr. Graves could do about it. Addicts are not dumb. They lie, they make things up and exaggerate things."

This is absolutely true. I know that toward the end of my abuse I could have walked into any doctor's office and walked out with a prescription for some sort of opiate. (That is, other than my *real* doctor. He's too smart for that.) I had researched all the right things to say, knew all the problems, such as migraines, that could manifest real pain without showing any physical symptoms.

In January 2002, Barry Meier, a reporter for the *New York Times*, interviewed Dr. William Hurwitz, a pain management specialist and lawyer located in McLean, Virginia, in connection with the Graves trial. Hurwitz stated that "many doctors like himself believe that large daily doses of narcotics such as OxyContin are an acceptable way to treat chronic pain. But he says his own experience has shown him that such practices can quickly bring a doctor to the attention of law enforcement; in the past decade his medical license has been suspended and revoked over narcotics prescriptions; it has since been reinstated."

Dr. Hurwitz went on: "When [the DEA] sees anybody prescribing these meds they think the worst and presume the worse, and if there is a bad outcome they act as aggressively as they can."

Dr. Hurwitz had clearly already caught the eye of the DEA, so I wasn't too surprised to see his name pop up again two years later. Dr. Hurwitz, the man who had been going to bat for other doctors, was now on trial himself for "drug trafficking."

The DEA had recently realized it needed to create a "principle of balance" to determine the guidelines of access to pain medications and the approaches to containing abuse, addiction, and diversion. It published a report on its website: "Prescription Pain Medications:

Frequently Asked Questions and Answers for Health Care Profes-
sionals and Law Enforcement Personnel." It outlined succinct de-
scriptions of the circumstances under which a doctor could be
persecuted. But suddenly the report was pulled from the DEA website
with no explanation except that it had contained "misstatements."
Some doctors believe it was pulled because it contained language that
would have cleared Dr. Hurwitz of all charges. Instead, Dr. Hurwitz
was initially convicted of more than fifty counts of narcotics distribution. He was sentenced to twenty-five years in prison. Thankfully,
two years later his sentence was reduced to five years because of errors
by the judge. After Dr. Hurwitz's practice was shut down, two of his
patients committed suicide because of their debilitating and chronic
pain.

Doctors can cut patients off medications if they believe their patients are abusing them, but it's absurd for a doctor to have to act as
a policing agent with every single patient. Obviously there are many
red flags a doctor can watch for, but there seems to be a witch hunt
going on in the United States for doctors prescribing pain medication. This problem was expertly detailed in the *New York Times Magazine* cover story from June 17, 2007, "When Is a Pain Doctor a Drug
Pusher?" I'll tell you when. It's when a shady doctor is working in
tandem with a pharmacist to set up an online pharmacy, or an un-
ethical doctor is doling out prescriptions to a wealthy client or a celebrity because he's getting paid to do so. I know of one ridiculously
famous musician who travels on tour with his own personal doctor,
who writes him prescriptions for whatever he wants. Except for extreme situations like this, doctors should be treated as medical experts
who are using these drugs for their intended purposes. But the sad
fact is, many doctors are now terrified to prescribe these drugs, even
if their patient is suffering horribly.

Siobhan Reynolds, the founder of the Pain Relief Network, is one
of the nation's biggest activists for pain relief and support for doctors who are being prosecuted. She started the network when her own
husband, Sean Greenwood, died of a rare congenital connective tissue disorder called Ehlers-Danlos syndrome. Sean's body didn't
produce enough collagen, a chief component of connective tissue,

so his joints were too loose (the medical term is "hypermobile") and he experienced severe arthritic pain and horrific headaches. There is no cure for this disease. Sleep disturbances are common, and those affected can develop heart disease and diabetes from inactivity.

Siobhan and Sean eventually found Dr. Hurwitz, who was willing to prescribe the levels of OxyContin Sean needed to live something resembling a normal life. He was finally walking around, actively partaking in their son's childhood. For the first time ever, Sean was taking his son to school and helping him with his homework.

Dr. Hurwitz knew that he was taking a huge risk by prescribing the amounts of Oxy that he was for Sean. But he still had faith in the government. After six months, however, he was arrested, and Siobhan had to scour the country for doctors willing to treat Sean's pain. Most kept him at a "safe for them" dosage, which actually did nothing for Sean's pain. Every now and then she would find someone who would give Sean the doses he needed, but then, like clockwork, they too would get arrested for "overprescribing" and Sean would suffer with his pain.

One symptom of Ehlers-Danlos syndrome is a weak vascular system. Siobhan believes that because of all the untreated pain Sean was experiencing, he couldn't sustain the blood pressure rise. One day Siobhan had finally found a doctor who was willing to mail a powerful liquid form of an opiate to them, and while they were waiting for it to arrive, Sean died of a cerebral hemorrhage in front of Siobhan and their son.

Siobhan has since shared her experience with doctors all across the country and has testified on behalf of those who are being prosecuted. Her main issue is that "The vast majority of meds that are on the street that are actual pharmaceuticals are not from doctors at all. They're from hijacked trucks and other forms of diversion way up in the supply chain, and that is the DEA's fault. They want to cover that up by prosecuting doctors."

It's a strong accusation, but one that theoretically makes a lot of sense. Think of Caleb's first major Oxy hookup, from the truck robbery. Or Heather and her theft of prescription pads, or Jared's friend who was stealing from the pharmacy. And then there are my postings on MySpace. With the exception of Heather's first visit to Dr. Feelgood, none of us were getting the drugs that we were abusing from doctors.

But it's much easier for the DEA to follow a simple path of prescriptions from a prescription monitoring program than to get inside the mind of an actual criminal. Remember when I interviewed Mark Caverly at the DEA and I was put through a rigorous screening process? All of my belongings were x-rayed, my bag was opened and checked, and I had to walk through a metal detector. After the interview, I was sitting in my car in the DEA parking lot rummaging through my bag for the car keys, when I noticed Clover down at the bottom of my bag. I hadn't looked inside Clover in months, and when I did, I discovered four 4-milligram Dilaudids, half a hydrocodone, and an 80-milligram morphine pill. I couldn't believe my luck at not getting busted, and I still wonder if I hold the dubious award for being the first person to successfully smuggle illegally obtained drugs directly into—and out of—DEA headquarters. Even if it was an accident.

The DEA is so successful at prosecuting doctors on murder charges for "overprescribing" when accidental deaths occur because the Controlled Substances Act states that as long as a doctor writes a prescription in the course of his or her professional practice for *a legitimate medical purpose*, he is exempt from prosecution. This means that juries with limited to no medical background decide whether a woman suffering from severe pain with a very large dose of morphine in her system is being "overprescribed" by her doctor. The fact is, even the CDC admits most opiate overdoses happen in combination with some other form of drug.

The DEA has now created an environment of fear, where doctors are terrified to prescribe opioids to patients who desperately need them. But they need to step up their efforts at controlling diversion higher up on the distribution scale. Mark Caverly told me that while the DEA is allowed to conduct unannounced, on-site inspections of anyone who has a license to distribute controlled substances, these inspections happen only every two or three years. The auditors count bottles and check inventory histories, but they don't look inside all the bottles. Schedule II narcotics are required to be kept in a vault, but Schedule III narcotics like Vicodin and Percocet are only required to be kept inside a cage. I was once able to pick the industrial-strength lock to the front door of my apartment building, with minimal previous breaking and entering experience. How hard can it be to pick the lock on a cage?

According to the DEA, the safeguarding regulations are detailed and stringent, but they have remained basically the same since the 1970s. Now that the illegal market is so extremely strong for these drugs, it might be time for a safety update.

Dr. Alexander DeLuca is a skinny man with lots of energy who tends to pull at his hair when he's frustrated. He's another vocal advocate from the Pain Relief Network, but he came to find himself in that position by surprise. During the 1990s he had been chief of the Smithers Addiction Treatment and Research Center at St. Luke's Hospital in New York. During his tenure there he built a research institute into the clinical fabric of the center, writing a new computer program to easily track all of the center's patients through their treatment. "Nobody did that in addiction medicine, and we were finding out all sorts of fascinating stuff about our treatment programs," he told me over tea in his apartment on Central Park West. "In some of our programs, there was a zero success rate! What I realized is that it literally meant there was no way to leave! The treatment wasn't adequate, and I wanted more. So I worked on getting grants to generate academic quality research. I brought in over $3 million in just a couple of years."

He shakes his head sadly as he takes a sip of the coffee he made for himself. "My wife was smarter than me," he says. "When I got the job, she told me, 'Alex, your career life expectancy is now measured in years.' I didn't believe it. It was my home. I built it!"

Dr. DeLuca's eventual downfall was his sense of compassion. He believed in "harm reduction," which is a set of public-health practices that help reduce the negative effects of substance abuse by providing, among other things, counseling, needle exchange programs, and HIV testing. He wouldn't turn away a patient who wasn't willing to sign on to abstinence on the first day, knowing that relapse was almost certain. Dr. DeLuca always allowed Alcoholics Anonymous to hold meetings at his facility, but he also allowed Moderation Management to hold meetings. This organization, which is essentially a support group for people who recognize that they have a problem but aren't ready to commit to full sobriety yet, focuses on harm reduction, reducing, for example, the amount a person drinks, sometimes to the point of complete sobriety, sometimes not. (It's worth noting that Audrey Kishline, the woman who created Moderation Management, left it, went back to AA, then got into a drunk-driving accident that killed a twelve-year-old girl and her father.)

The press got wind of it and suddenly there was a media firestorm about how Dr. DeLuca had turned the Smithers Center into a Moderation Management program. He was fired on the grounds of no longer supporting the "program philosophy of total abstinence."

Dr. DeLuca quickly released his own press statement on the matter: "I have been surprised to find myself cast as a speaker for the harm reduction movement," he wrote. "I have received hate mail, solicitations to write books, and multiple requests for interviews to discuss whether abstinence or moderation is the best treatment for alcoholism. This is about as rational as asking whether coronary bypass surgery or medication is the best treatment for heart disease."

He believes the problem lies in a clash of cultures. "On the one hand we have a tradition of 'tough love,' 'hitting bottom,' 'confronting denial,' and avoidance of psychotropic medications. On the other hand, a more modern and medical approach works directly with ambivalence and motivation, and is often accompanied by pharmacotherapy for the craving, anxiety, depression, and insomnia so common in early recovery."

He goes on to dispel the myth that harm reduction promotes permissiveness by comparing it to its other more accepted uses in all other fields of medicine. "If a person is overweight and has an elevated blood sugar and is at risk of developing adult onset diabetes," he says, "a physician might recommend a strict diet and exercise program. But if the patient cannot or will not comply with the recommendations, the physician doesn't send him away to return when he is ready to accept the diagnosis and be compliant. Rather, the physician might start drug therapy while continuing to work with the patient on his resistance to, or problems with, the diet and exercise regimen. This is harm reduction. We accept the refusal or inability of the patient to do the best thing, and try our hardest to do the next best thing."

Dr. DeLuca believes that this distortion of medicine works into all medical fields, particularly pain medication, because of all the recent prosecutions. "Most doctors will use more toxic meds for way too long at way too high doses before they go to opioids. And even if you do get to opioids, the doses will be so controlled that you won't get titration to analgesic effect. You'll be undermedicated."

Dr. DeLuca came to know Dr. William Hurwitz through various conferences. "He ran the Peace Corps in Brazil," he tells me. "He was this really idealistic, extremely bright man. I always enjoyed his company, but I think juries found him a little cold, or maybe arrogant."

Since Dr. DeLuca was the addiction medicine specialist and Dr. Hurwitz was the pain medicine specialist, Dr. Hurwitz wanted them to join forces. "You have to understand," DeLuca says, "in 2000 we were coming off a decade of revelation in pain medicine."

He's right—for all the media attention about the dangers of Oxy-Contin, it was a revolutionary form of pain relief for chronic sufferers. And doctors were learning more about titration and how the body really could grow to withstand higher doses of all forms of opioids that could cure pain. When used correctly, OxyContin was a wonder drug that could actually cure debilitating pain that other drugs had been unresponsive to.

But they never joined up. Over the next year Dr. DeLuca ended up at a public-health school, got sick with hepatitis C, and became a father. Dr. Hurwitz came under investigation by the state for drug trafficking and was sent to prison.

After Dr. Hurwitz was arrested, Dr. DeLuca joined a closed list-serv of doctors who were also facing charges. "I thought, this is just crazy! These guys are facing *murder* charges. I started to see patients differently, and I became scared to treat them."

So Dr. DeLuca quit medicine in order to testify on behalf of his colleagues. He was going into high-profile federal court cases where doctors' assets had been seized and they'd already spent a year and a half in jail, and frankly, he didn't want the feds coming after him, too. In order to safely defend his fellow doctors, he had to give up his own career.

He also questions the extremely high numbers being released by the Drug Abuse Warning Network about prescription drug abuse. "Couldn't they have done one lousy prospective study?" he asks. "Actually follow a cohort of high school students? We could have had a twenty-year prospective study by now, but for all the billions of dollars they spend, all they get are raw numbers without denominators."

What he means is that these numbers reflect one moment in a person's life, not use over the course of a lifetime.

"They could have mounted a public-health study," DeLuca says. "We'd know a lot more about addiction, what actually happens to people who use drugs. But the government isn't interested in that. They don't actually care about abusers. They think they're criminal scum. If they wanted to understand you better and treat you better, they would have studied it."

Opioids now have such a criminal stigma attached to them that they aren't even available in countries that desperately need them. An article from the September 10, 2007, *New York Times* described in detail a woman from Sierra Leone who had breast cancer. Her tumor had burst through her skin, "looking like a putrid head of a cauliflower weeping small amounts of blood at its edges." The cancer had also spread to her lymph glands and ribs. She was going to die, and she was going to die in extreme pain because her country refuses to import morphine for fear of encouraging addiction. The article quotes David E. Joranson, director of the Pain Policy Study Group at the University of Wisconsin's medical school: "Doctors in developing countries have beliefs about narcotics that prevailed in Western medical schools decades ago, that they are inevitably addictive, carry high risks of killing patients, and must be used sparingly, even if patients suffer."

And the DEA's very public prosecution of so many American doctors can't be helping matters internationally.

CHAPTER 12

Jared's Turn

JARED WAS BACK TO using again daily, and it came to define everything about him. "Honestly, I just didn't know what to do with my time," he says. "My entire existence was occupied with going to get them, doing them, worrying about how I was going to get my next batch, worrying about where the money would come from. It consumed my entire life."

It's a common reaction for anyone who initially tries to stop a negative behavior, whether it's drinking too much, or drugs, or even anorexia. The disease becomes you, and without it, you feel lost. So Jared started using again, at the same dosage he'd been on originally. "I thought at least since I had gotten off them, I'd be able to get a good high again, like the first time I'd used. But that didn't happen. It went right back to the level I'd ended at within a week. My girlfriend dumped me and I moved in with a roommate."

His new roommate wasn't an idiot. He could hear Jared crushing up pills and snorting them every morning before work. He began to make some phone calls to Jared's friends, asking them if there was a problem. Finally a close friend of Jared's who had gotten out of the drug scene after high school came to visit him.

"He said 'Dude, you look like shit,'" Jared remembers.

Jared didn't say anything to him about his condition, but while they were catching up, his friend mentioned that he needed to hit up a drugstore to fill a Percocet prescription for a recent sports injury.

"I became manic," Jared says. "I was, like, 'Let's go get the Percocets, let's go get them now,' and my friend was, like, 'What is *wrong* with you?'"

Jared kept on raving about how they had to go to the drugstore immediately to fill the prescription, even though it was 10:00 P.M. And then something inside him switched. He heard himself. He heard how insane he sounded. He thought about the time his mother had gotten home from surgery with a bottle of Percocets, and he spent three hours in the bathroom, shaving off the markings and ridges on Tylenol pills and shaping them to look similar to Percocets, and then switching her bottle out with his fakes.

"I just laid everything out to my friend," he says. "No one had ever told me that what I was doing was fucked up in such an accusatory way. I'd had girlfriends who called me out on my use before, but I'd always lie and just say I'd only done one pill. Or I'd just flat-out deny it. Money was another big issue for me at the time. What had started out as such an easy thing—my friends giving me pills—had turned into serious debt. I'd been given $30,000 as a graduation present, and it was all gone. I was $15,000 in credit card debt. I couldn't pay my rent. I thought I was going to have to start stealing."

Jared's friend listened to his entire story and said two simple words. "Tell someone."

Jared called his brother, a doctor. He initially wanted to find a way to quit without having to go to rehab. He also lied to his brother about his use, telling him that he was only snorting about ten pills a day, when at this point he was actually up to forty pills, with three to five 80-milligram OxyContin chasers spread throughout the day.

"He pretty much told me that I had to tell my parents. So I did. I called them and laid the whole thing out to them. They drove to Boston to get me."

Jared knew he was going to be away for a while, but he didn't want to lose his job. "So I went into my boss's office and told her I had nut cancer and needed testicle surgery," he says. "I figured she wouldn't ask any questions."

He was right.

Jared's parents made all of the arrangements and found a facility nearby. But he could feel the panic setting in. He had just run out of the last of his pill stash. So he went to a regular doctor and confessed his addiction.

"I told him, 'Look, I'm going to rehab. I've got a problem. Either give me some pills now or I'm going to go out on the street and get them. I just need something to tide me over until the withdrawal treatment starts.'"

The doctor wrote him a prescription for ninety Percocets.

"So now it was a day before I was supposed to go into rehab, and I had this huge bottle of Percocets, so I began to just inhale them," he says. "I was freaking out. I literally could not picture getting through a single day without them. I couldn't understand how the rest of the world was walking around without them. I had lost touch with how you could possibly talk to someone or do your laundry or even watch TV. My parents knew I had the Percocets, so they were crying hysterically and I didn't care, I just kept crushing and snorting them because I knew, 'Last chance.' I'd gotten so good at this point, I could crush and snort an entire pill in under a minute."

Jared's parents were terrified he was going to run away, so they kept a vigil by the front door of his apartment. But he didn't, and before he got in the car with them the next morning, he stuffed as many pills as he could inside his shoes.

"I was smoking cigarettes in their car, which I wasn't allowed to do, swallowing pills at every chance I could," he says. "Once it came out that I was using, and everyone knew, I just didn't care. It all roared out. I'd been trying to hide in a suit and pretend I had a normal life for so long, and now that the secret was out I just didn't give a fuck anymore. We pulled into a 7-Eleven, and I just took off, running into the bathroom and shutting the door. I was crushing up pills on the back of the toilet seat when my dad burst in, picked me up, and threw me back down on the ground, like a raving maniac."

Jared's dad pulled him back to the car and soon they arrived at

the rehab center. The admitting nurses quickly found all the pills
he'd stashed in his shoes. They checked him in, and Jared spent
about a week detoxing his body before he was able to enter into the
full rehab routine. The detox consisted of buprenorphine to ease him
off the painkillers (so he wouldn't go through an immediate withdrawal), along with some muscle relaxers, Tylenol, and sleeping pills
to gradually ease off all the symptoms he experienced. "It was bad,
but it was better than that week when we'd quit pills without anything," he says.

Jared spent that first week mostly isolated from the other people
in the rehab center. He had a roommate, though.

"This guy had 'wet brain,' which is almost like brain damage. It
comes from really late-stage alcoholism. He had gone totally crazy—
he'd been drinking cologne by the time they brought him in. He
wouldn't talk and he couldn't stay in his bed. As far as I know, he never
left the detox wing."

Once Jared started to come out of his detox, the center sent
people his own age to his room to talk to him about the program
and slowly assimilate him into rehab.

"I did not buy into the whole God shit," he says, echoing Heather's
sentiment. "For the first twenty-eight days I was there, I was, like,
'This is fucking horseshit and all of you people are totally insane.'"

Jared's other main issue with rehab was that he not only had to
stop taking pills, but also stop drinking and doing any other kind of
drug as well.

"I was, like, this is *not* what I signed up for," he says. "Then
someone who worked there, who was an ex–pill head, told me, 'If
I had more fun doing pills than I do now, I would go out and do pills
again.' I was, like, 'You're full of shit.' But then he said, 'Were you
having fun on pills? Because usually people who are having fun on
drugs aren't in here.' And he was right. Being on drugs was horrible,
and I'd already forgotten that."

Jared was initially supposed to stay in rehab for twenty days. He
ended up staying for four months.

"They felt I wasn't ready to leave yet, and deep down I knew they
were right," he says. "The thing was, I had no idea what the fuck I

was going to do with my life. That was the scariest part. Once I got over the physical pain of detox, it actually took about three weeks for me to start feeling somewhat human. You get over the bad hump early, but you're still a long way from right."

After being in the program for twenty days, Jared went on the antidepressant Effexor, which he still takes today. And once he realized he was going to be in rehab longer than he initially thought, he knew he had to come clean with his boss. "She was so cool about it," he says. "She said that as long as I was definitely going to come back, then she'd hold my job for me."

Jared still fought the idea of a "higher power" guiding him through his rehabilitation. "What I realized," he says, "is that my higher power is just a piece of myself, and when I want to get in touch with it for strength, I can."

By the time Jared left rehab four months later, he was hungry to get his life back.

"I was motivated in a way I hadn't felt since before I'd ever done pills," he says. "I started to remember what I wanted to do with my life. It's like my whole pill life was just this crazy sidetrack that I became so obsessive with that everything else just faded away. And then I remembered, 'Oh yeah, I wanted to have a career and become financially independent.'"

There were a couple of other guys in Jared's rehab center around his age who were wrestling with the same problems. So they made a pact, to "try and fuck a lot of people and really kick ass at work."

Jared did just that, but he also hooked up with a sponsor, attended regular AA and NA meetings, and began trying to mend his relationship with his parents.

"They got me out of that life," he admits. "They saved my ass. Now I'm on a payment plan with them to repay all the rehab costs, which is superfortunate for me. A lot of people don't have that option. But my dad still doesn't believe that addiction is a disease. In his mind, he just thinks, 'You fucked up.' And I have to let him believe that. I'm done trying to explain this thing to people who don't get it."

Jared admits he is always tempted to go back on pills. "That shit sticks in your brain like a hook or something," he says. "I still think about pills every day. It's almost like your brain used to be this certain way, and then you do something like what I did to it, and it becomes warped, like a piece of driftwood. It's never going to unwarp."

Joseph Califano from CASA thinks this is an apt analogy. "Whatever the substance, the brains of addicts are 'rewired,' becoming predisposed to cravings," he wrote in *High Society*.

"My view of pills is not normal, and it never will be," Jared agrees. "It just is what it is now. I have dreams about buying pills and snorting them. The way I deal with it is to play the whole scenario out, right to the end where I ended up in rehab. Mentally, you can't just start over with pills. There's no reset to the beginning, where none of this happened."

Jared is proud now to admit that his idea of fun is going shopping for CDs, or staying home and watching a movie, or going out for coffee with friends. He's also learned how to deal with his social anxiety on his own.

"It just takes work," he says. "It was a lot harder at first, and sometimes I'll still get it bad. I'll try to avoid social situations, but if I have to, I know I won't take the shortcut I used to. When I was on pills and felt able to talk freely, I felt like I had all this confidence, but I don't think I was actually saying anything interesting. Now it takes work and practice to go out, but that's the way it's supposed to be. The other thing that helps is that there are always others. You find AA and NA people everywhere. It's like this whole underground network of people that you don't have any idea exists until you become a part of it. And it *doesn't* exist, until you need it to."

CHAPTER **13**

Hunting and Shutting Down

ONCE I RETURNED FROM Tennessee, I slipped fast and easy back into living inside my protective bubble of pills. Like Jared, I'd gone through withdrawal and come back out of it fine. I saw no reason to put myself through that torture again. If I ever had to go through withdrawal again, I knew I could deal with it. But I was also still reeling from my experience in Oak Ridge. I couldn't handle seeing someone so strong become so weak. And to be perfectly honest, I also just really missed being high. But my methods of obtaining the pills I needed were becoming stranger and stranger, and none of them had anything to do with doctors.

My older sister Erica invited me over to her house in Brooklyn for a party. She runs a childbirth education center called RealBirth, where expecting parents can take all sorts of different classes on childbirth preparation. Her business had been growing fast—she had just opened a new location—and she'd just signed a book contract. She dedicates her life to helping women find ways to cope with pain, but I just popped pills for mine.

When I got to her house I found that her kids were with their father at his place, but her friend Lana was there, a woman with long, straight dark hair and sparkling eyes. I'd always liked Lana a lot because of the way she doted on me. She always wanted to know who I was dating and fussed that I was too skinny. She was breaking open a bottle of wine. We toasted Erica's success and assuaged her feelings of nervousness about getting her book done on time.

Lana had recently been in a nasty car accident and messed up her knee pretty badly. Someone had run a stop sign and slammed into the side of her car, twisting her leg around. "They gave me Percocet," she told us, "but I can't stand the way it makes me feel, so hazy and out of it. I'm just taking Tylenol now."

My entire body grew stiff and attentive. This was my game of chess, and I had to make the right move. If she was holding and not using pills, they needed to be mine.

"Ugh, I know," Erica said. "Remember that time I threw my back out and they gave me Vicodin?" she asked me. "It made me so sick, I stopped taking it after the first day."

I remembered it well. I'd spent the night at her house while she was stretched out flat on the floor. We watched old movies, and I was high out of my mind from the pills I'd snuck when I'd given her the first dose upon returning from the hospital. I'd stolen the entire bottle from her the following week. She'd never even noticed, because she had disliked the effect so much that she just switched to over-the-counter pain relievers and acupuncture.

As I racked my brain about how to get my hands on Lana's Percocets, the conversation turned to my recent stay at Bobby's in Tennessee. Lana was shaking her head. "She was very lucky to have survived that. My parents had long, drawn-out illnesses. I never want that to happen to me. I want an exit plan."

Erica nodded. "Me too," she said. "I just want to figure out a way to make it painless and not messy so that it doesn't affect the person who finds me."

"I just got a screener of a documentary about this exact same subject sent to me at work," I said. "I'll bring it over next time so you guys can watch it."

We were on our second bottle of wine by now. "So what don't you like about Percocet?" I asked Lana. "I have to admit, I kind of like them." I kept my voice even, nonchalant. "A friend of mine gives me one every now and then, and it calms me down if I'm having a stressful day."

"You can have them," she said flippantly.

"Really?" I asked. But it was too eager. Wrong move. She looked at me over her glasses. These were educated adult women, not dumb kids from MySpace who I could just give money to for pills. This transaction required more finesse. I filled up everyone's wineglass again.

"I'm kidding," she said. "I wouldn't feel comfortable doing that. It's illegal."

I changed the subject, went back to talking about the idea of exit plans. "I want one too," I said. "I'm just not sure how I'd do it. Maybe the old car-running-parked-in-a-garage thing. I like the idea of just being able to fall asleep."

Lana shook her head. "I just want some sort of pill I could always have on me. No mess, no fuss, just pop it when it's time. I know they must exist out there somewhere."

"I'll make a deal with you," I said. "I'll use all of the research tools available to me at the magazine and our library to find out the easiest, cleanest way to go, in exchange for the rest of your Percocets."

Lana was happily buzzed on wine now. "Deal," she said. "Just remember, I don't want it to be a mess."

I spent every free moment at work that week researching ways to commit suicide. The sooner I could find the right method, the sooner I could get my hands on the Percocets. I knew Lana wasn't looking for any sort of immediate answer, but I was having fun with my research. I cracked up a little too loudly and drew looks from coworkers when I read that one of the entries on how to commit suicide on Wikipedia was beheading yourself. Clearly not right for Lana. It seemed to me that the easiest and most painless way to go was to OD on the very pills she already had mixed with some benzos. But many times these suicide attempts aren't fatal and the person is stuck with severe liver damage. Although it helped if you wrapped a plastic bag over your head right after taking them. Cyanide pills just didn't seem pleasant (convulsions, foaming at the mouth) and impossible to get one's hands on.

After lots of research, it seemed the easiest way to go was a heroin overdose. I knew where to get heroin, but couldn't imagine letting Lana know that: she was far too straight. We were meeting again for a dinner party at Erica's house that weekend, so I brought all my findings along with a copy of the documentary I'd told them about.

I cornered Lana and told her everything I'd found out. She wasn't pleased with any of the options, especially the heroin. "That's just seedy," she said.

"You should become a member of the Hemlock Society," I said. "They have counselors you could talk to."

She waved her hand dismissively. "Already a member," she said. "Not a fan of any of their methods."

I was crushed. No free Percocets for me.

I spent the rest of the night playing board games with my niece and nephew. Eventually I saw Lana getting ready to leave and I got up to say good-bye. As we were hugging, she slipped a plastic sandwich baggie full of pills into my hand.

"Just be careful with them," she whispered. "I'd never forgive myself if something happened to you."

"Please," I scoffed, "These will last me about a year. Thank you so much!" I gave her a big kiss on the lips.

The pills were gone in five days.

The next large haul that came in was from Emily's new boyfriend, yet another mop-haired boy. Only this time he was an artist instead of a musician. I guess that was a step up. He always wore short ties and suits, with no underwear, leading me to quickly discover why she liked him. He worked at a gallery owned by a man who was dying of some hideous form of cancer.

Emily called me up one night. "Johnny's boss is really sick," she said. "The cancer is just getting worse."

"I'm sorry," I said. I didn't know the guy; it just seemed the polite thing to say.

"Yeah, it's horrible," she said hurriedly, "but the point is, the pain has gotten so bad that they've moved him off OxyContin and onto

Dilaudid. The gallery can't make its rent this month, and he wants to sell off all of his Oxy to pay for it."

I ran to my computer to check my bank balance. I'd been storing money from my *Jane* paycheck in a savings account in an attempt to get myself out of debt once and for all, but, well, fuck that.

"How much does he have?" I asked. "And for how much?"

"Tons. Sixty milligrams each. And he doesn't even know how much they are worth, he's selling them for $10 apiece."

I almost dropped the phone. On the street they were worth $60 a pill.

"Send Johnny over with everything he has left," I said. "I want the entire lot."

I felt good about this deal. Not only was I getting what I wanted for a ridiculously good rate, I could fool myself into thinking that I was also helping to support the arts. I bought everything he had left, around seventy pills in all.

By this time my subletters had moved out and I had my old apartment back on the Lower East Side. It was a two-bedroom and I needed to find a roommate fast, so I'd found one on Craigslist, a Goth girl from southern California who immediately painted her bedroom red with alternating black vertical stripes. I kept mostly to myself, hiding out in my bedroom, high, watching movies. Since she was essentially a stranger I was paranoid that she was looking through my room whenever I was at work. I was now keeping my pill stash in a fireproof safety lockbox under my bed. I'd open it every other day and refill Clover. The problem was, I didn't know what to do with the key. I needed an excellent hiding place for it. I didn't want to keep it with my house keys, because what if I lost them one night when I was out drunk? I'd have been fucked, since this lockbox was the real deal: it weighed a ton. For a while I was moving the key to different hiding places in my room every day. First it was inside the medicine cabinet (we each had our own bathroom), but then I got scared she would borrow contact lens solution or something. For a while it stayed tucked between two books on my bookshelf, but then I became convinced she'd want to read one of my books. I finally found the perfect hiding spot. I had a Donnie Darko toy, a fourteen-inch model of Frank the Bunny that had a button on the back you could press and it would repeat quotes from the movie. It came with an interchangeable head of James Duvall with his eye gouged out and a platform stand that had a model of the mailbox where Donnie leaves his letter to Roberta Sparrow. The mailbox even opened up, and there was a tiny letter addressed to Roberta inside. My lockbox key fit perfectly inside the mailbox, and when the door was closed you'd never even think that it would open. The toy and its stand sat on my windowsill with the two Gelflings from *The Dark Crystal* and a poseable model of Cutter from the *ElfQuest* comic series. It was the perfect hiding place.

My father was planning on coming to stay with Erica for Memorial Day weekend, and he was bringing his other children, my twin half-sisters and half-brother, so they could see New York City. They were the same age as my niece and nephew, so the kids usually all played together the one or two times a year we saw them.

When they arrived, we spent the day at the American Museum of Natural History and wandering through Central Park. I took them to the ferris wheel in Toys R Us in Times Square and bought them loads of candy. One of the editors at the magazine had let me fill up a shopping bag of products they no longer needed from the beauty closet. When we got back to Erica's house I dumped the bag out on the living room floor. The twins and my niece dove in, dividing everything up, but I think maybe I was a bit more excited about the loot than they were. Afterward I felt guilty for assuming that just because they were all little girls, they would be excited by free shampoo and lipstick. One of the twins was a chess champion in her state, and she barely took anything from the pile. I wanted so badly to make a good impression on these girls, since I saw them so rarely. I barely knew them, but felt so much love for them anyway. They were both rail-thin, with long dark hair and enormous doe eyes, and I couldn't help but feel protective of them.

Throughout the day I had watched my father interact with them, saw the way he doted on them. It was uncanny how he had created a new family that was almost an exact replica of the one he had originally left behind. My half-brother was five years older than his twin sisters, the same age difference between Erica and my younger sister and me, Nyssa. Nyssa and I were a year apart, and had always pretended to be twins when we were little. She still has friends who believe we're twins—we look exactly alike, which helped keep the lie alive. When we were in third and fourth grades, she had really short hair and I had really long hair. When we met strangers we would tell them that I was the girl and she was the boy, and our neighbors would constantly get us mixed up.

It was hard not to be jealous of my half-siblings for having my father when we hadn't. But it wasn't a malicious jealousy at all, just a sad one. I made a point that first day of keeping my distance from my father. He was working as a truck driver now, and I knew he could barely support his new family. It was only a matter of time before his second wife would divorce him.

I knew he could tell I was avoiding him, and he let me. I'd been popping pills all day and my vision was starting to blur as I watched my sister and him cook dinner in the kitchen. I tried to play a game of chess with the champion twin, but she checkmated me after something like six moves. I knew I was rusty from not playing for a while, but damn, she was good. And I knew it wasn't just because I was high.

I went into the kitchen and saw that a bottle of wine had been opened. My sister's new boyfriend was there too, which helped take the pressure off me having to speak to my dad. The three of them were laughing and chopping vegetables for a salad. My sister opened a window because the kitchen was getting hot from all the pots bubbling on the stove and whatever was baking in the oven. The sun was starting to set over Carroll Gardens. I took a seat at the kitchen table and stared out the open window at the row of brownstones. I poured myself a glass of wine.

"How's work?" my father asked me.

"Fun," I answered. "I just went to LA to interview Hilary Duff for the cover."

"Who's that?" he asked.

"Never mind," I said.

"It's your granddaughter's current favorite pop star," my sister told him. "Which goes against everything I've tried to teach her."

It was strange to think of my dad as a grandfather when he was raising children of his own. I watched him add a large amount of pasta to boiling water as he and Erica talked about kids and parenting. Their voices faded away into the steam rolling off the top of the oven. The scene was intimately familiar; when I was younger there were always huge dinner parties at my grandparents' house. My sisters and I would play in the basement or the living room while the adults and their friends drank and cooked in the kitchen. I looked out at the kids all playing together in the living room and shivered. History had repeated itself.

My wineglass was empty, but it was being refilled by someone. I tried to remember more about the dinner parties from when I was young. I must have been five or six. The kids would eat in the living room, while loud bursts of laughter would come from the dining room. There was a large open passthrough separating the dining room from the living room. The adults could easily check in on us but it was usually us spying on the adults. We could see them reflected in the glass picture window that stretched along the back of Bobby's house. We almost always stayed overnight after these parties, but it would take a while to fall asleep because of the swearing and roaring coming from downstairs. My younger sister and I would share the sinister room with the slanted ceiling.

Erica called her kids in to set the dinner table, and my father quickly told his kids to help out. I stood up and took my glass of wine with me to make room for them. The children swarmed around the table, dropping plates and napkins haphazardly, eager to get back to their game. I stumbled a little while leaning against the wall. I knew I needed to eat something soon.

We finally all sat down. Plates were heaped and wine was poured. The kids were done almost as soon as they started and rushed off again, this time to play on the patio on my sister's roof. Politics were being discussed at the table, so I got up with my wine and went into the living room to check my messages. I don't discuss politics at the table. I think it's gauche.

"Come on, we're going to the roof," my sister called out, so I followed them upstairs. The view from her roof is stunning; you can see the whole downtown Manhattan skyline. The night was clear, so we could see every window in every building. They'd brought more wine upstairs and we all sat around the patio table while the kids played tag on the roof.

"We're going to take the kids to Coney Island tomorrow," Dad told me. "Want to come?"

"Sure," I said. There was a light from the stairs shining directly behind him so all I could see was an outline of his head. I squinted my eyes, trying to take in more of his features. Everyone said I looked like him. I didn't think so, but I tried to view him impartially to see what I might look like when I got older. All I could make out was his soft, quiet voice, talking about the plans for tomorrow.

I was drunk. The roof swirled for a minute, and I clutched the table to steady myself. Erica and her boyfriend went downstairs, dragging the kids kicking and yelling behind them to put them to bed. They said they were going to clean the kitchen and retire too, and my dad told him he would be down in a few minutes to help.

We sat there quietly for a minute or two, neither of us saying anything.

"I think," I said, "that there is something wrong with me."

"Well, yes," he said.

I looked at the city and it looked back at me. "There are a lot of things I don't remember," I said. "About Oak Ridge."

"You've always had that ability, ever since you were a little kid, to just block out whatever you didn't want to know," he said.

I could feel a weird feeling coming on, naked and ashamed, even through my drunken pill fog. "Like with what?" I asked.

"Oh, I don't know, anything," he said, shrugging. "It's just something I've noticed about you through the years."

"Sometimes I think something might have happened at Playland, that old day-care center," I said. I paused, debating whether or not to say what I had to say next. "Or at Bobby's house," I finally said. "I feel strange there, especially in the old room I always stay in."

He shook his head vigorously. "Playland was a foul place, but no one at our house *ever* would have done anything inappropriate," he said.

He was quiet for a minute, but I could see his eyes concentrating hard on the table in front of him as he struggled with what to say next.

"There was always so much drinking going on," he finally said. "So many different people around. It's possible someone came up to your room while they were drunk, since the bathroom is right next to that room. Maybe someone sat on the bed with you. Maybe even tried to hug you because everyone loved you guys so much. Maybe their hands accidentally went somewhere they weren't supposed to, by mistake, and you misinterpreted it."

That's the last thing I remember him saying. I blacked out.

I opened my eyes and I was on my bed at home, on top of the covers, naked except for my underwear. There was spare change covering my body—nickels, dimes, and quarters stuck on my skin.

I looked around me, panicked. I had no idea how I'd gotten there. The last thing I remembered was being on the roof with my father, and then it was one thirty in the afternoon the next day.

I searched around the room for my phone, finally finding it underneath a pile of clothes wadded up in front of my bathroom door. There were seven missed calls, all from my father's and sister's cell phones, and a few texts from Emily and Stephanie. I could see that there were voice mail messages, but I couldn't bring myself to listen to them. I turned on my air conditioner because the room was swelteringly hot. I stood in front of it for a minute, cool air blowing over me, and tried to massage the red coin tattoos out of my skin. When the room cooled down I crawled under the covers and played back everything I could remember about the night before. No matter what, I still stopped blank after the last thing my father had said to me.

It had sounded rehearsed, like an excuse he had been telling himself for years in order to forgive someone else.

I fell back asleep, clutching Ollie close to me, feeling him purr against my chest.

I woke up later to my phone vibrating on my nightstand. It was my sister.

"Where have you been?" she asked. "We've been trying to reach you all day. We're getting ready to leave Coney Island."

"Sorry, I'm hungover," I mumbled. "I must have drank too much last night."

"Aww," she said. "Do you feel okay enough to meet us for dinner? We're going to Noodle Pudding," she said, naming an Italian place in Brooklyn Heights.

Noodle Pudding, I repeated in my head. That's what I felt like.

"Yeah, sure," I said. It was the last thing in the world I wanted to do. I had the shakes. But I would go because of the children. I had to put on some sort of front for them, especially after ditching out on going to Coney Island with them. "What time?"

"We have a six o'clock reservation," she said. "I know it's early but, you know, the kids."

I rolled out of bed, fished Clover out of my jeans pocket, swallowed two Oxys, and got in the shower.

I arrived at the restaurant before any of them. I thought about smoking a cigarette, but I didn't want the kids to suddenly turn a corner and bust me. I refuse to smoke in front of children, and I'd told my niece the year before that I'd already quit after Erica had told her that "Uncle Josh smokes sometimes." I had been mortified. I think it had been a ploy on my sister's part to guilt-trip me into quitting, since she knew my niece would bring it up in front of me. She's outspoken that way. It's one of the things I love about her.

I could see them coming from a few blocks away, a mob of children swarming around three adults. My niece was riding on my sister's boyfriend's shoulders. They looked like such a family. My heart ached.

I tried to maneuver it so I would sit far away from my father, but the kids had specific people they wanted to sit next to so after four different rounds of chair switching I found him next to me. He put his hand on my shoulder.

"You feeling okay?" he asked. "We missed you today."

"I'm sorry," I said. "I drank too much."

"Me too," he said.

"Do you know what time I left?" I asked him. "I don't remember getting home."

He looked surprised. "You don't? You left around 1:00 A.M. Remember? I tried to get you to take a cab, but you refused."

"I took the train?" I asked. I was mortified. I must have looked like a nut job to other passengers. I hoped I hadn't puked. "I don't really remember anything from shortly after Erica took the kids down," I said.

He looked really disturbed. "You don't remember anything I told you?" he asked.

"Some stuff," I mumbled.

"You don't remember us hugging and lying down on the roof bank?" he asked.

Erica and her boyfriend were giving us a funny look and laughing.

"Jesus, no!" I said. "What are you talking about?"

"I thought it was weird at the time, but you were really drunk," he said. "You wanted a hug. It was really nice, you've never been that affectionate."

Closing my eyes does not make me invisible.

"You really don't remember anything I told you?" he asked, quietly, just to me, after everyone's attention turned to something else.

"Just the stuff about how I might have misinterpreted some stuff," I said.

He nodded. "Well, that was mainly the gist of it," he said.

I hadn't touched any of the wine that had been ordered for the table because of my hangover. The pills were doing nothing to stop it, so I filled up my glass.

I avoided them the rest of the holiday weekend as much as possible. I could feel myself going dark, shutting down. I knew I wasn't running on logic anymore. Something had snapped inside my head, and whatever good feelings I had for the world had been replaced by a simple engine that ran on one thought only—to get through the day until tomorrow. It was as if my brain had blinders on and I was living in tunnel vision.

Since there was no work that Monday I went swimming. I zoned out, meditating with the rhythm of lap after lap after lap. When I got to the locker room I showered quickly and changed. As I was zipping up my fly, a large, broad-shouldered man walked past me. There was no one else around. He maneuvered between my locker and me, suddenly grabbed my face with one hand, and pushed me up against the other wall of lockers.

"I want to pull those pants off you," he whispered.

He let go of my face, caressed my cheek, winked, and walked off.

I stood there, stunned. I was used to guys watching in the locker room, sometimes even pulling out their dick and waving it around. It goes with the territory in most male locker rooms in New York. But no one had ever grabbed me before. There was something so off about what he had said. It wasn't like any other sort of come-on I'd heard. It was foul and it sounded *young*, like what a pedophilic teacher would say to a first-grader.

I could feel tears welling up in my eyes as I finished getting dressed but I sucked them in and created a white wall in my head. I walked out fast, briefly considering reporting him to the staff but not willing to go back even ten minutes into my past to relive that moment. I went down into the subway, blinders on again, full force.

The platform was empty except for a young woman in a skirt standing about ten feet away from me. I glanced at her as I leaned against a column.

Out of the corner of my eye I saw a flash of movement and I turned. The same woman was now lying on the cement floor, twitching violently, her skirt riding up around her thighs. I rushed over and knelt next to her, and she was suddenly still, her eyes focusing on me. She sat up.

"Are you all right?" I asked. "Should I call someone?"

She stood up and I handed her bag to her. "I'm fine," she said brusquely.

"Should I call an ambulance? Or one of your friends?" I asked.

"I'm fine," she snapped.

"Okay," I said, backing away. "But I'm going to just stand over here. I'll be on the same subway car. If you need anything let me know."

She nodded but wouldn't make eye contact with me. The train came and I kept my eye on her the whole time. She looked at the floor.

My stop came before hers. I briefly considered staying on the train and following her home, but figured that would just creep her out. There were other people around now to help her if she needed.

When I got home I sat on the edge of my bed. Ollie climbed into my lap and I stroked him absentmindedly. I stared at the wall for a while, and every time I could feel the shakes coming on I forced them back. I needed to get out of there. I called Joey. I knew he was always up for a drink. Or a vial of coke. He had always been a master of escapism, and I needed to crawl down in there with him. He was at dinner but told me to meet him at his house later.

I took three pills out of Clover and swallowed them with a glass of water that had been on my nightstand for at least a week. It had been almost a year since I'd moved back to New York City, so psyched to start my life over and get my career back on track. I'd taken care of the career, but I'd already given up on the life part. The only life that felt real or safe was the one on pills, the one where everywhere I moved, a warm bubble surrounded and followed me, protecting me. Outside of that bubble the world was cold and harsh, like a February wind whipping over my face. After about twenty minutes I felt the invisible force field start to rise up again around me. I sank into it and let its soothing heat thaw out my skin.

I ordered my own coke that night so I wouldn't have to rely on Joey's. I asked the delivery guy for the twentieth time if he had any good pills to sell, but as usual he only had Xanax. I didn't care about benzos, I had buckets of them left over from online deals. I rarely took them anymore. I found that it was always good to carry some around with me in Clover, though. I could use them as currency at parties or bars and trade for favors, drinks, or, if I got lucky, opiates. Plus I liked the way it made me feel to be able to flash Clover anytime someone I had just met complained about being stressed. I doled them out like Tic Tacs, and it made me feel needed.

As I got ready to meet Joey I did a few lines while listening to Glass Candy. *Fantastic Planet* played on my TV with the sound off.

I met Joey at a bar around 11:00 P.M. He was with a group of friends and the night was on, immediately. The entire group rotated from the bar to the wall to the bathroom. It was like a ballroom dance where we all switched partners. Everyone had their own blow, and we'd rotate who we brought to the bathroom with us. Stall door shut, keys out if someone had a bag, or thumb and forefinger curled together facing up to create a flat surface if someone had a vial (like me). I'd picked up Joey's lingo, "Give me your paw," when I needed to pour a pile of coke onto someone's hand. I refused to pour lines on the backs of toilet tanks, like some people. There was something so disgusting about it. Forget the fact that there would be four of us crammed in a stall with piss covering the floor and scads of toilet paper stuck to the walls. I had my limits.

We bar-hopped the entire night, whole conversations disappearing into the holes in my brain as soon as they were finished. The pills kept me steady. I could drink and do as much blow as I wanted, but I could always feel the protective bubble around me, keeping me on my feet, keeping my words from slurring. I'd see Joey pointing and laughing at me, and when I asked him what he was laughing at he would imitate my face, a dopey smile with my eyes always looking up somewhere toward the ceiling. He kept his arm propped up on my shoulder whenever he stood next to me.

We ended up back at his house around four thirty and fell into bed. We fought—he kept trying to pin my arms down and I'd kick upward and slam him into his window, the bookshelf.

When I woke the next day my body hurt worse than my head. I stumbled out of his room and into the bathroom, trying to stretch my arms. My legs were covered in bruises, and there was a huge bloody scrape on my right knee.

When I got back to his room his eyes were open.

"What the fuck did we do last night?" he asked. "I'm covered in bruises."

"Me too," I said, sliding in next to him.

He propped himself up on one elbow. "Joshua," he said. "This isn't cool. I don't want to hurt you."

"So don't," I said.

We dozed off for a while, and I woke back up around five. He was still sleeping. I slipped into my clothes and left.

I was done with processing events and information that weren't work-related. I was ready to go on autopilot as far as real life was concerned. Books written by Dennis Cooper and Bret Easton Ellis had informed my entire adolescence, and I learned from them at an early age that when things got to be too much, the best way to deal was to simply not care.

I checked out. I floated through work, starting my pills earlier each day, always still surprised at how much I was able to accomplish on them. Part of my job was to top-edit the display copy, meaning I was in charge of all the headlines, dek intros, and photo captions for the entire book. I liked this part of my job because it meant I got to work with every single editor on staff. I was also now top-editing all of the front-of-the-book fashion coverage, in addition to writing and editing features and cover stories. I was busy, and it was a good distraction, but at least once or twice every week I would show up to work still drunk, and every single weekend I would binge myself to the point of becoming nonverbal. Pills were always my base high, and coke was a steady constant, but suddenly I found myself doing Ecstasy and K as well. I was disgusted with myself—I wasn't some fifteen-year-old kid. I'd find myself in giant lofts in Brooklyn, wandering around parties in nothing but my underwear. Or suddenly it would be 10:00 A.M. and I'd be lying in the sand on Long Beach, with no idea how I'd gotten there, head to head with three other people, all of us still snorting coke under our beach towels while families plopped down with coolers and lawn chairs around us.

But the most significant part of that summer was an accidental introduction to someone with access to Candyman.

I'd always thought Candyman was a rumor, a myth. Supposedly, if you had an in, there was a man who would show up at your apartment with a briefcase full of every kind of pill you could imagine for sale. I'd begged strangers who mentioned him for his number, but I was always told he wasn't taking on new clients. I needed to befriend a current client if I had any hope of becoming a customer.

It finally happened one night when I was out at a club with Joey. I ended up sitting next to a girl named Kelly on a banquette. She had short blond hair and was wearing high-waisted jeans, boots, and a tank top with no bra and one strap that kept sliding off of her left shoulder. We started talking about pills and before I knew it I was trading four of my Valium for two generic hydrocodones that she pulled out of a small Comme des Garçons pouch. I swallowed them immediately with vodka from the giant bottle sitting in front of us. This was the other great thing about hanging out with Joey and his friends: I never ever had to pay for a drink. Somehow they could just show up at pretty much any bar or club and get free bottle service and drink tickets

"What's your source?" I asked.

"Candyman," she said.

"Really?" I yelled. "You have to give me his number!"

"He's not taking on new clients," she said shaking her head. "He does fine with the ones he's got."

"Please," I begged. "You've got to let me order with you next time you call him. I'll pay you a service fee."

She laughed. "You don't have to do that. Let's trade numbers."

I got hers and then called her phone so she'd have mine, just as Joey came and flopped down next to me.

"Make me a drink!" he demanded. "Who's that?" he asked, pointing at Kelly.

"This is our bottle, but you can have some." He was wasted.

"It's cool, she's with me," I said, and poured him a drink.

I texted Kelly the next day, determined not to let this opportunity go by. I was sick of always having to scramble for my next source. Even though MySpace and just asking around had given me a relatively steady supply, I was desperate for a regular, solid source so I'd never have to worry again.

She texted back around 7:00 P.M.: "Going to call tomorrow at 8. Meet me at my place. $100 minimum." She gave me her address, about ten blocks away from me.

The next night I left work early. Before stopping at her house I went to the bank and took out $600, and then picked up a few beers to bring with me, just to be polite.

It was a little awkward at first since she was pretty much a total stranger and we were both still hungover from two nights before. But we watched episodes of *The Simpsons* while waiting for the delivery guy to show up. I pictured Christian Bale from *American Psycho*, impeccably dressed in a suit with a luxurious briefcase.

But it wasn't the actual Candyman who came, just one of his runners. He looked like any other dreadlocked drug delivery kid.

The runner pulled off his backpack, pulled out a metal briefcase, and opened it up to reveal hundreds of tiny plastic baggies in neat rows. He handed us a menu, with a complete list of everything he had that day. There was no Vicodin, but plenty of Dilaudid, Oxy, and morphine. He also sold weed, mushrooms, Ecstasy, MDMA, Adderall, Valium, and Xanax. I was in heaven.

I thought I was some sort of big shot, whipping out my $600, but the runner just shrugged. "I've got dudes in the West Village who drop several thousand at a time," he told me.

Clearly I'd been hanging out with the wrong people.

I settled on thirteen 4-milligram Dilaudids, two 80-milligram morphine pills, one 100-milligram morphine pill, and one 80-milligram Oxy. I'd spent enough money to qualify for their special, which meant I got to roll a ten-sided Dungeons and Dragons die and call two numbers. If I got one of them right, I got my pick of anything I wanted out of the box. I called 7 and 9, and 7 came up. I cheered, maybe a little too loudly, and asked for an extra Oxy. After Kelly made her deal and the runner left, I sat and drank a beer with her.

"Um, don't tell any of my friends I did this," I told her.

"Don't worry about it," she said. "I don't even know those guys that well."

"So you don't mind if we do this again?" I asked.

"Anytime," she said, swallowing a Dilaudid and washing it down with one of the Coronas I'd brought.

Access to Candyman changed everything. I never had to worry about where my next haul was coming from. I kept it a secret from Joey. I had barely spoken to Emily that summer. I'd been too busy with Joey, and she was dating some semifamous artist from the Midwest and was always traveling out there to see him. I knew he kept her in pills, so I didn't feel like I needed to tell her about my new connection.

As fall started, I could no longer deny the effects the drugs were having on me, no matter how hard I tried. I was growing increasingly paranoid, and became convinced I was having signs and visions. Joey is an avid collector of taxidermy specimens. One night, after we had gone back to his house almost blackout wasted, I felt something fall off the wall and hit me on the head while we were having sex. I just shoved it to the side and kept going until Joey suddenly stopped, a look of horror crossing his face. He jumped out of the bed. "Don't look at your face," he demanded.

It felt wet suddenly, and I reached up to feel it. I pulled my hand back and it was covered with blood. I leapt up and looked in the mirror. My face was soaked red.

"What's happening?" I asked, terrified.

Joey didn't answer. He had picked up his camera and was eagerly taking pictures of the scene.

"What the fuck?" I screamed, scared out of my mind. I couldn't tell where the blood was coming from. I looked down at the side of the bed to see what had hit me. It was a cloven hoof from a deer or an antelope or some other animal.

I ran into the bathroom and Joey followed me with the camera. I splashed water on my face, but it just made the blood run more, creating a bigger mess. Joey finally put the camera down and and started wiping my face and head clean with a washcloth. We discovered the source, a nasty split directly between my eyes. Half an inch in either direction and I'd have been blind in one eye, the cut was that deep.

I sat there shivering on the toilet in just a towel while Joey kept cleaning me up. All of a sudden his roommate and some guy she had brought home were standing in the doorway.

"Holy shit," she said. She was topless and leaned in to get a closer look. "That looks mean."

The guy who was with her moved her away and leaned in. "I used to be an EMT," he said. "You're going to need stitches."

"I'm not going to the hospital," I said, trying to angle the towel so nothing was hanging out.

"Do you have any medical tape?" he asked Joey, who nodded and got some out of the medicine cabinet.

"We can try to just pull the skin together with the medical tape," the stranger said. Joey pinched my wound shut while the guy made an X with the medical tape over it. It stung, badly, and I could feel my skin tighten in the center of my face as the glue from the tape affixed itself to the inside of my wound. I stood up and looked in the mirror. I looked gaunt, haunted.

"Thanks," I said and shuffled off to Joey's bedroom. A massive bloodstain was smeared into the wall above his bed. I pulled a sheet partially over me, lay down on the bloodstained pillow, and passed out to the sounds of Joey's camera clicking away.

Since it was a legitimate, painful head wound I felt justified taking extra pills over the next few days. But I was disturbed—not so much by Joey's glee with the incident, because, to be perfectly honest, I'm glad now that there's photographic evidence out there of what happened, but, come on, how much more of a clue from the universe did I need? I'd been sleeping with someone I shouldn't, high on drugs, and a fucking *cloven hoof* falls from the sky and clocks me between the eyes! I'm not religious in any way, but I like to pay attention to signs and patterns, provided I'm sober enough to recognize them for what they are.

But in the end, it wasn't anything so dramatic that made me end things with Joey. It was old-fashioned jealousy. I didn't trust him at all. And while a lot of that was most likely a side effect from the pills, there was still the fact that for every night I spent out with him, there were four or five others during the week where I had to work and he was out partying with his crew without me at bar after bar. He could never tell me what he'd been up to the night before; he always, always blacked out. Anytime he wanted to show me a photograph on his camera, he would quickly scroll through the ones that showed a crew of young guys in his living room, partying shirtless after the bars got out. Sometimes I'd freak out, scream at him, or cry, demanding to know what had happened, and he'd never give me a straight answer. I hated what I'd become—a shrill, rage-driven addict consumed with fear that he was cheating on me. But I couldn't stop.

Everything came to a head after we took a trip to his grandmother's house in Massachusetts. She was in the hospital for some sort of surgery. We brought Ecstasy.

The inside of the woman's house looked exactly like Laura Palmer's home from *Twin Peaks*. Everything had been frozen in time. Outside, it was cold, gray, and rainy. As it got darker we sat down at the kitchen table and Joey handed me my tablet. I'd found an old puzzle of tropical birds in his basement and started working on it while I waited for the Ecstasy to kick in. He helped with the puzzle, but after about twenty minutes we both got up from the table and silently wandered off to different parts of the house. He headed to the parlor; I headed to the TV room with all the old photographs of his family.

There was only one of him, one I'd seen before. He was around five, dressed in a sailor outfit, a devilish but innocent grin on his face. My heart ached. I knew the reason I was really so drawn to Joey. His past was eerily similar to mine. He too had a father who'd left when he was really young, and he'd also been mostly raised by an older sibling who had left at the first opportunity. He'd once told me that he had shut down so completely that he hadn't even known how to have an emotion until he was nineteen. He'd been overweight in high school and hadn't had any friends, but once he graduated he starved himself, eating only one meal every other day, and suddenly he became skinny. With that, came friends.

"Josh?" I heard him call from somewhere in the house. I went through the kitchen, which was impossibly yellow. Everything was yellow. The toaster, the refrigerator, the plates, the calendar. I got out of that room quickly.

In the dining room, everything was blue, even the chandelier and placemats. I whimpered a little under my breath.

"Josh?" Joey's voice was closer now. I found him sitting in the front parlor, standing over a massive old-timey radio housed inside a wooden box the size of my dresser.

"Help me figure this out," he said, fiddling with the knobs. I knelt down beside him and flicked the On switch. The room was flooded with the sound of Lawrence Welk. Joey made a face and went to change it, but I grabbed his hand.

"I kind of like this," I said.

He indulged me for about thirty seconds before rolling the dial. The bursts of static were horrific. I was rolling on the sofa, turning onto my stomach, and smashing my face in the fabric until he passed a 1970s station that was playing "Amie" by Pure Prairie League.

"Stop!" I yelled. I jumped up and started spinning wildly around the living room. Joey stood in one place and did his shuffling little jig while the song played on. I felt myself topple near a table full of framed photos and empty candy dishes but caught myself against the wall. Joey grabbed me and we fell into the shag carpeting, rolling around hugging and shivering. The Ecstasy was really dopey, not speedy at all. *Melting, melting, melting* I kept thinking, but then I realized I was saying it out loud.

I wriggled out of my clothes until I was only in my underwear and jumped up and headed out the front door toward the lawn.

"Wait," Joey called. "Someone's gonna call the cops!"

I jumped back inside and turned the front porch light off so the neighbors couldn't see me. There was a soft drizzle of rain coming down, but the cool air caressed my skin. Joey came up behind me, and we stood there on the front porch for a long time, staring out at suburbia, not talking. All of the houses around us were dark. I thought I saw a slug moving toward my foot, but when I bent down it was just a curled-up wet leaf. I'd been hoping it really was a slug. I used to keep them as pets when I was a kid, in empty Miracle Whip bottles with air holes punched through the top lid with an ice pick.

"Let's go inside," Joey said, "I don't like it out here."

We went back in, up the stairs, into the guest bedroom. As in most suburban homes, it was being used as a giant storage closet. Boxes of old clothes waiting to be donated to the Salvation Army were scattered across the floor like boulders. A large basket of dusty yarn sat on top of one of the two dressers cluttered with porcelain animals, stacks of old lace, and frameless prints of ships and plants. It had a canopy bed. Do they even make canopy beds anymore? They were everywhere when I was a kid—my own mother had even slept in one. Infantilism personified.

We had sex for hours. I was so blitzed that half the time I didn't even know what I was doing. At one point there was a body part in front of my face I was pretty sure I had never seen before on anyone.

We got up strangely early the next day. Joey packed us into the car. It was still wet and miserable and foggy outside, and depression took hold of me like a body bag. I took two Dilaudid, and that seemed to help a little. We drove two hours to the Edward Gorey museum, located inside the actual home of my childhood idol. My grandmother Bobby had introduced me to Gorey, inscribing my first copy of *Amphigorey* with the words, "To Joshua, who has a keen sense of worth." No one had ever used that sort of language with me before, and I'd always equated my love of Gorey's drawings and words with that first feeling of recognition from someone.

After the tour, and after spending way too much money at the gift shop, we drove around Massachusetts aimlessly in the rain, trying to find a decent place to eat. Joey wanted Olive Garden; I was resisting.

His digital camera was sitting between us, and I picked it up and scrolled through photos from the night before. The scene quickly changed to pictures of strangers from different bars Joey would go to late at night without me. Hot guy after hot guy, shirtless, arms around each other. I could feel my jealousy rising but kept it in check until I came across one of Joey with his arms draped all over a ridiculously good-looking guy (by my standards at least—long dirty hair, facial scruff, a T-shirt with holes in it).

I put the camera down and stared out the window. I knew what I had been getting myself into with Joey. He was a charmer. Even when I was out with him and it was obvious we were together, he'd never think twice about taking some cute young boy into the bathroom to give him drugs. And the problem with cute, young guys is that there is a never-ending supply of them. I suddenly felt impossibly old. I was wasting my life pretending I could still party like a twenty-two-year-old and, worse, reacting to insecurities so deep they'd grown roots into every organ in my body. I pressed my cheek against the window, tried to get the coolness to reach my brain, tried to stop the jealousy spiral I could feel coming on and keep it contained inside my opiate bubble so that I would never let it out.

I wanted to believe I would never be able to live the life Joey lived. I loved my drugs, but I'd rather have done them on the sofa, watching a movie and cuddling with someone, than out at some gay bar with the constant threat of someone stealing what was mine. I didn't have Joey's heart, I just felt like one of a long string of guys he used to make himself feel better about his world. His own cocaine use had slowed down substantially lately, but he constantly had one or more full vials on him to give out bumps to boys, to get himself inside that locked bathroom stall with them. And I suddenly realized that what had started out as pure escapism for me had turned into something much more confusing and clichéd. I didn't know whether I was in love with Joey or just addicted to him.

•   •   •

As weeks went by I got progressively crazier and crazier. I started staying in alone most nights while Joey was out partying. I would eat myself up inside, imagining him stumbling home with a different stranger each time. I was obsessed with two things—my painkillers and my fear of Joey cheating. Every time I started to emerge from the warm bubble, the pain of not being able to trust anyone in this world swept over me, so I'd swallow more and escape back into the mist.

I begged Joey to concentrate on his photography. He'd gone to school at Rhode Island School of Design, and I thought that if I could get him excited about work again he'd stop partying so much. But I knew my efforts were half-assed. I wanted him to stop partying during the week, when I had to be at work, but on the weekends I fully expected him to be his normal party self, to keep me supplied with drugs and drinks, and we'd recover together the next day under the blankets, holding onto each other for life while the pain of the night before rippled through our bodies. Drug love is so powerful: it's the one time you know exactly what the other person in your life is feeling physically, and it unites you.

The end came abruptly. After a week or two of his promising to show up at my house "after just one more drink" and then never showing, I gave up. I was getting more and more responsibility at work, and it empowered me. I took a bunch of Dilaudid, went to his house, and told him I couldn't do this anymore.

He just nodded. "I'm not ready to change yet," he said. "I don't want to."

And that was that. I stopped doing coke and stopped drinking to excess—but I kept my pills. They got me through the day, through the subway ride home, through the loneliness of eating a frozen pizza for dinner every night. They were as natural a part of my routine as showering or feeding the cat. I wasn't interested in dating. Kelly kept me fully stocked, making sure to call me whenever she placed an order with Candyman. I'd also made friends with an editor named Maria at another magazine in the building who shared my love for pills. We'd recognized each other one night at a bar when I was still with Joey, and I had traded her some Valium for her hydrocodone. We each preferred the other.

One day at work I realized Clover was empty, and I started to feel nervous and sweaty. I knew I had more pills at home, but I wasn't sure I could wait that long. I texted Maria to see what she was holding. She wrote back that she had already left for the day, but she had a few Percocets in a baggie in her bottom desk drawer that I could help myself to.

I went to her floor and, ignoring the glances from her coworkers, went straight to her desk and began rummaging around. I couldn't find the pills. I checked every drawer, but there was nothing. I even started going through her files, wondering if she had accidentally slipped them inside one of folders. Nothing.

I called her from the elevator bank. "There's nothing in there," I said.

I could hear a lot of loud voices behind her.

"Fuck, maybe I grabbed them and put them in my purse," she said. "Hang on."

I listened to her fumbling around. I was getting more and more anxious. I didn't even really like Percocet that much compared to other opiates, but now that I thought it was near and within my grasp, I wasn't going to give up. "Oh, shit, here they are," she said, getting back on the phone. "I took them after all. Sorry. You can come get them if you want."

"Where are you?" I asked. I still had some work left to do, but it could wait until tomorrow morning. I was out of there.

"I'm one of the guest speakers at an ed2010.com meeting," she said, referring to a social network website for junior-level editors. "It's kind of informal, like a speed dating thing. Just come down." She named a bar just above 14th Street on the East Side.

When I arrived, I was led to a back room in the bar filled with hungry young journalism school graduates and editorial assistants, desperate to get ahead in the field. I stood in the doorway and surveyed the crowd. They were mostly women, dressed in fashion business casual, resumés in hand and rotating from table to table. There were about ten senior-level editors from different magazines sitting at the head of each table, doling out advice and listening to story pitch ideas. I recognized maybe half of the senior editors, waved to the ones I was friendlier with, and wondered why the hell no one had ever asked me to sit in and speak at one of these.

I finally made out Maria sitting to one side, talking animatedly to two girls who were hanging on her every word. I considered waiting for the break when everyone would switch tables, but all those eager young faces were making me uncomfortable. I marched over to Maria's table.

She looked up at me, surprised. "That was fast," she said. And ever so smoothly she reached into her purse and pulled out an envelope. "Everyone, this is Joshua Lyon. He's a senior editor at *Jane* magazine."

I felt myself blush and mumbled a "Hi, everyone."

"Josh left his ID card on my desk by mistake," she said, handing me the envelope.

"Thanks," I said. "I owe you one. Good luck, everyone." I turned and got the hell out of there as fast as I could, having to walk down the entire aisle with tons of eyes on me. I got outside, hailed a cab, tore open the envelope, and swallowed the pills.

CHAPTER 14

Horror Hospital

I WAS CURLED UP in the corner of my bed, trying to concentrate on an episode of *Heroes* and failing, when the pain started. It was sharp, insistent, and constant, located in a three-inch line just beneath my belly button. I was confused. I thought by this point I wasn't supposed to ever feel any pain. I ate a frozen pizza, thinking I was just hungry, but it didn't go away.

I had a date that night, my first since I had ended things with Joey. I had been really excited about getting back out there, because I knew my isolation was starting to become a real problem. I had little patience for anyone outside the office or for anything that didn't have to do with the magazine. I felt totally isolated, even in rooms full of people.

The pain was getting so bad that I texted my date and canceled. I crawled under the covers and fell asleep with my knees hugging my chest.

I woke up two hours later, shaking, covered in a cold sweat. *Something's wrong,* I thought to myself, then said it out loud, to Ollie, who was on the pillow next to my head. I sat up and turned on the bedside light, and the room swirled. The sharp pain in my belly made me double over, and I gasped. I knew I had to get to a hospital.

I put on jeans, a T-shirt, and a hoodie, bent over the entire time. It was around 1:00 A.M., and I clung to the banister all the way downstairs and out into the street, where people were still spilling out of bars, screaming and laughing and stumbling. *This is what it is like to be truly alone*, I thought. I was invisible, in excruciating pain, in a crowd full of blind eyes.

I hugged the sides of buildings and made it to the corner, and got a cab almost immediately.

"Beth Israel, Emergency Room," I said.

The city was alive as we drove up First Avenue, huge groups of drunk people, screaming, wandering into the street against the light so that my driver kept having to slam on the brakes, tossing me forward. I groaned and clung to the door handle.

We were there in under ten minutes. I limped into the ER, sitting down in the first chair I could find. I explained my symptoms to the admitting nurse, showed them my insurance card, and was told to wait, but was called in almost immediately.

I was taken to a small plastic chair near the main nurse station inside the ER. A woman who looked absurdly like a weathered version of Daisy Duke but in a blue smock took my temperature and I explained how I was feeling. She pushed against the painful area under my belly button and I winced backward. Then she stuck her fingers lower down and to the right, and pain exploded throughout my entire body.

"*FUUUUUUUUUCKKKKKK!!!!!*" I screamed. "Oh, god, sorry," I said quickly.

"Hon, it looks like you've got appendicitis," she said, kneeling in front of me. "We've got to do some blood tests, but I'm betting that's what it is. And we've got to get that thing out of you."

I hated myself for it, but I started to cry. Appendicitis is so lame—it's about the most common ailment imaginable. But still, there was no one there to hold my hand.

"Don't worry about a thing," she said. "We're going to get you hooked up to some morphine so you won't be in pain."

I stopped crying immediately. *Sweet.*

The nurse took blood and another nurse wheeled over an IV drip and plugged it into my arm. She attached a bag of morphine. "You ready?" she asked. "You're going to feel fine in a second."

I nodded and she released the valve that shot the morphine directly into my bloodstream.

Nothing.

I waited. After a minute or two the nurse came back and gave me a knowing smile. "You feeling better?" she asked.

"Um, I don't feel a thing," I said. "My stomach is killing me."

"That's weird," she said, and fiddled with the tube. "It's definitely in there."

"I, um, might have a kind of high tolerance for medication," I said.

"Well, we'll give you another dose then," she said. She attached a new bag to my IV and let it rip. This time I felt the morphine rush into my body. But it went straight into my head, causing everything to go white and hazy for a minute. I was instantly high. But the pain in my belly stabbed right through the morphine, and the feeling didn't abate an ounce.

I wasn't an idiot. I knew what was going on. My tolerance for opiates was through the roof, and no amount of morphine was going to help.

The nurse helped me up and led me down a hallway. I passed a bed with an old woman lying on it who looked like she had a fist bulging out of the inside of her neck, as if there was a person inside her trying to rip through her skin. She was alone, her head pushed back, eyes closed, mouth open. Tiny stick legs poked out from under her dressing gown.

The nurse brought me to a bed near hers. There was no private room, just an open area with curtains you could pull around yourself. She tossed me a hospital gown and told me to put it on. I waved my arm catheter at her. "You're gonna have to take this out first," I slurred.

She unhooked it and stood behind the curtain while I pulled my clothes off. I wasn't sure if I was supposed to leave my underwear on but it felt too tight against my skin, so I pulled it off and slipped into the robe, my bare ass hanging out behind. I sat on the bed and told the nurse I was done.

She pulled the curtain and hooked my arm back up to the tube. I was doubled over in pain. "I'm gonna need more of that," I said, pointing up toward the bag of morphine.

"Wait until that bag is empty and we'll give you a new one with a higher dosage," she said. She frowned. "It should be working though."

"It's not," I said. She left and I pulled my cell phone out of the plastic bag they had given me to keep my clothes in. I curled up and stared at it. I had no idea who to call; no one was going to be awake. I tried calling Emily, Stephanie, even Joey. Nothing. I knew I couldn't call my sister. Her boyfriend was out of town and there would be no one to watch the kids.

Another stab of pain shot through my belly as a doctor told me I had to get x-rayed. I got out of bed, leaning on my IV pole for support. It had wheels, so I let it pull me forward as I followed the doctor down the hall, my ass still bare. A nurse rushed over to tie my robe for me. As I waited outside a door for the x-ray technician to finish up with another patient I saw someone being admitted, a guy my age covered with tattoos, unconscious on a stretcher. A girl dressed in a hoodie covering most of her face stood by him, holding his hand, talking urgently with a doctor. An overdose.

Amateur, I thought.

It took two separate x-rays to get my entire torso. Apparently I have abnormally long lungs. I found this new fact comforting. Since so many opiate overdoses are caused by respiratory failure I figured the extra room in there couldn't hurt.

By the time I got back to my bed my morphine bag was empty, so I buzzed the nurse and asked for more. I got a new bag and felt the delicious warmth surge through my veins, hitting every spot except the one it was supposed to hit inside my belly.

My head was swimming as the overdose kid got rolled into the room across from me. I watched a nurse pull his clothes off and put a robe on him. They kept his underwear on. As I was watching them,

I suddenly noticed a large, grinning clown sitting on a shelf above him, hiding in the middle of all the medical equipment.

I made some sort of gagging noise and tried to sit up, terrified. The clown dissolved back into a mess of heart monitors and wires. I kept my eye on it, and every so often the equipment would shimmer and the clown would appear again. It looked just like the one from *Poltergeist* that hid under the kid's bed. I knew he wasn't real, but the hallucination was so vivid, so clear, that I felt like I had to keep an eye on him anyway, just in case he tried to climb down from the shelf and slither across the floor toward me.

A doctor finally came and confirmed that it was definitely appendicitis, but I'd have to wait a few more hours for an operating room to free up.

"Don't worry," he said. "We'll make sure you're comfortable." He patted the morphine bag and saw it was almost empty. "We'll get that filled back up," he promised.

I couldn't sleep, so I sat on the bed for hours, eating the pain while my head swam in frothy white waves. I'd curl up, move my head to the foot of the bed, try to half sit up with my head between my knees— anything to stop the stabbing pain. Nothing worked.

At 7:00 A.M. I called Erica, knowing she would be up and getting the kids ready for school. I explained what was going on, and she got a little hysterical and promised she would be there by the time I woke up from surgery. I felt a little better after that. Emily also called around 8:00 A.M. and promised she would be there as soon as possible.

I was wheeled up to surgery around 11:00 A.M. A nurse shaved my pubic hair, since they were going to do a laparoscopic procedure. A doctor stood over her while she shaved me and explained that they would only make three small holes—one on my left side, one where my pubes used to be, and then they'd go in through my belly button to pull my poisoned appendix out.

"Can I keep it?" I asked.

"It's considered hazardous material," the doctor said.

"When you seal up my belly button after, can you make it look a little nicer than it does now?" I asked. "There's this weird bump in there."

I was babbling. "We'll see what we can do," the doctor said. I was wheeled through corridor after corridor, and I watched the ceiling glide by, thinking *This is what dying people see.* And then I wondered how many other people had thought the exact same thing.

Suddenly we were in the operating room. I was lifted onto a table. A new tube was put inside my arm catheter and I blacked out, just like Joey on a coke bender.

Erica was standing beside me when I woke up.

"They went like this!" I said, waving my arms around in the air in front of me, trying to show her how they had performed the surgery, and passed back out.

When I opened my eyes again a fat nurse was standing at the foot of my bed. "Keep your eyes open!" she barked, but I passed back out again.

The third time I came to, I tried to force my eyelids to stay open, but they were made of stone. Erica was wringing her hands. "I have to go, the kids are home alone," she said.

"S'fine," I slurred. I looked around and saw I was in a recovery room, with about fifteen other people who were coming out of surgery too.

"You have some friends waiting for you outside. I'll send them in."

She left and was replaced by Emily and Stephanie, who stood on either side of me, fussing with the sheets and pillows. The fat nurse returned.

"We need your bed, we're moving you to a chair," she said. Stephanie lifted me with one arm and Emily grabbed the other, and they slowly walked me over to a reclining armchair and eased me down. Every step was a knife wound in my torso.

"I want to go home," I said, but suddenly Joey was striding across the floor of the room, with a huge bouquet of flowers and a giant shopping bag.

"Hey, Tiger," he said softly and rubbed my head. "Here," and he pulled out a new pair of pale blue American Apparel underwear and some knee socks. "I thought you might need some fresh underthings," he said.

The nurse came over and told me I just had to wait for a doctor to come check on me, and that I could go home after. I just had to pee for her first, because they'd put a tube up inside my penis while I was out and needed to make sure everything was working right again. That explained the stinging pain.

"Want to try and go?" Joey asked. I nodded, and he half carried me over to the bathroom. I brought my IV stand in with me and leaned on it while I tried to pee. I felt like I had to, but nothing happened.

I came back out and Joey walked me back to my chair.

"I have to go, I'm deejaying tonight," he said, "but call me if you need anything."

I watched him walk away, wishing he would stay, wishing that he would carry me home, put me to bed, stay with me all night.

Emily nudged me. "Dude, you're gonna get Vicodin!" she said.

For some reason Erica had taken my cell phone home with her. She explained later that it made sense at the time because she thought that this way she could keep in touch with my friends if they called for me. I called her from Stephanie's phone and asked her if she could bring it back to the city. I didn't have a land line at home, and the thought of being alone post-surgery with no way to contact anyone just seemed like a bad idea. But I could hear in her voice that it was late and she didn't want to leave the kids alone in the house. If they woke up and found her gone they would have freaked. So I told her just to bring it to me the next day.

I was finally discharged around midnight, with my first-ever legal prescription for Vicodin. Stephanie filled the prescription for me at a CVS next to the hospital while I waited, doubled over on a chair inside a Chinese takeout joint. I'd tried to make it the one extra block to the drugstore but whatever heavy-duty pain drugs they had me on were wearing off and I could barely move. I watched people rush by the window. The smell of greasy noodles and duck sauce made me want to vomit.

Stephanie finally came back. "I'm so sorry that took so long, there was a huge line. At midnight! So weird." She handed me the bottle, and I asked her to get me some water so I could take them right then.

She helped me into a cab, rode with me, brought me upstairs to my apartment. The Goth roommate wasn't home and Steph was worried. "Do you want me to stay with you tonight?" she asked.

I told her no, that I was fine. I just wanted to sleep. She tucked me in and I promised to call her in the morning as soon as I got my phone back from Erica.

I passed out quickly, the anesthesia still working its way out of my system. I woke back up a few hours later though, and couldn't move. My entire body was on fire with pain and if I tried to move even an inch, every single nerve ending in my body would explode. I tried to reach for the bottle of Vicodin on the nightstand but couldn't grasp it. I called out for my roommate a few times, but there was no answer. As I lay there, unable to move and alone in my bed, I finally felt the full weight of my mistakes and my addiction. I'd fucked everything up and I was alone because of it. I deserved to be lying there in the dark in agony. I'd abused the safety bubble and it was nowhere to be found now. I'd never experienced loneliness that deep before, in the dark, unable to move, no one to hear me or help me. There was no sleep anymore. So I focused on the pain. I experienced it, embracing it for what it was for the first time ever in my life, as a warning system that my own body was using to tell me that something was very, very wrong.

And suddenly it felt good. It made me feel alive. Maybe my emotional pain that the pills erased was no different from this reaction to surgery; it was just my brain telling me that everything was wrong. And I needed to listen to it, to fix it, instead of hiding from it. If my body was capable of producing those nociceptors in my fingertips that told me when I was touching something hot, then why wouldn't my depression, my anxiety, my fear of the world be just another symptom that my brain was touching its own hot stove somewhere up in there? I now knew I needed to get my fingers off the burner.

After an hour or two I was finally able to shift myself closer to the nightstand and turn on the light. I tried to sit up a little, but that was too much. I reached for the Vicodon bottle and the glass of water I'd heard Ollie lapping from a little earlier. I studied it, looked at my name spelled out near the name of the substance I'd spent countless hours chasing. *After this bottle*, I thought, *no more*.

CHAPTER 15

"All of This Foam Came Out of My Son's Mouth"

JARED, CALEB, HEATHER, ME—All of our collective experiences had hit us physically, spiritually, economically, and emotionally. But so far we had all been lucky—none of us had overdosed and not come back. According the Drug Abuse Warning Network, which collects emergency room visit data for SAMHSA, the number of opiate-related visits leapt 24 percent in just one year, from 2004 to 2005. And according to the DEA, opioid painkillers are now a factor in more drug overdose deaths than cocaine and heroin combined.

One of those deaths took on almost Shakespearean qualities. The case involved a handsome forty-nine-year-old man named James Dean, and his son, James Dean Jr. Yes, those are their real names.

I first met James Dean face-to-face in a cinder-block room at the Warren Correctional Institution in Lebanon, Ohio. We'd been exchanging letters back and forth for several months about his case. Of course I had a very particular image in my mind about what he would look like, but nothing prepared me for either his height or his row of razor sharp teeth. They're so pronounced that I had to ask him if he'd had them filed.

"Nope, they're all mine," he said, but he wasn't smiling.

James grew up with two brothers in a white, middle-class family.

From the get-go his life was pretty tragic. His father was shot and killed when James was five. James is unsure of the exact details, but he was always told that his father was the innocent victim of a stray bullet during a shoot-out.

He smoked pot with his cousin for the first time when he was thirteen. "I was, like, 'Sure, I'll try it,'" he says. "I guess that was pretty much my attitude toward life, even when I was young. It might have something to do with my name, I don't know."

He graduated high school with a certificate in electronics and joined the navy immediately after, along with his brother. Right after boot camp, his brother got leukemia; he died eighteen months later. James himself was honorably discharged in 1981, and went to college at the University of Cincinnati for electrical engineering. But he started using cocaine and drinking heavily, and eventually dropped out of college. He had a series of rocky relationships, one of which produced a son, James Dean Jr., with a woman named Laurie Bender. They called James Jr. Jimmy. A few years later he had another son, Jason Dean, with another woman. His continued partying destroyed his relationships with both of the kids' mothers.

By 1992, James was sick of the misery his drug and alcohol addiction had caused him. He wanted to get clean. He decided that the best way to do that was to go to prison to detox, so he walked into a gas station in broad daylight, punched the clerk in the face, and stole all the money out of the cash register.

I have only his word on this story as far as it goes; it seems a flawed sort of logic, to say the least. He testified that he had actually robbed the clerk to get more money for cocaine, but whatever the reason, his plan worked. He was sentenced to six to fifteen years for robbery, got off cocaine, found God, and earned an associate's and a bachelor's degree from Ohio University. Four years and eight months later, he was released and paroled to his mother's house.

He tried to rebuild relationships with Jimmy and Jason, with little success. He initially stayed clean and sober and became actively involved in the local church, but after failing to create a relationship with his sons, he fell back into drugs and alcohol.

James started his own flooring subcontracting business with a friend and worked his ass off for the next year. In 1997 he fell in love with his mother's best friend's daughter, a woman named Lynda, and they were married. It was another messy relationship, and they divorced in 1999 because James had returned to his old partying ways. But they got back together again in 2000 and moved down to Fort Myers, Florida. Right before this, James hurt his back badly on a job and had to take six months off. He was diagnosed with degenerative disc disease, with bulging discs. He started physical therapy, chiropractic therapy, and massage, then got workman's compensation. And he got his first prescription for oxycodone.

"At first I didn't like them; I'd just give them to friends," he says. But after moving to Florida, Lynda got pregnant, and they were having a hard time paying the bills, and James quickly realized he could sell his prescriptions to make money.

James eventually found a doctor who prescribed him one hundred and twenty 80-milligram OxyContins, one hundred and twenty 10-milligram Lorcet, ninety 4-milligram Dilaudids, and one hundred 2-milligram Xanaxes—every month.

"Then I started liking the pills," he says. "They were drugs I didn't go out of control on. I wasn't staying up for days wired, like I would be on cocaine, and I could work like a beast on them because they took the pain away."

He was eating his pills morning, noon, and night, and when the doctor's prescriptions ran out, he found another doctor who would give him what he wanted.

"When I first started going to him, he had an office," James remembers. "A few months later I was meeting him in a Denny's parking lot, where he'd sell me prescriptions of whatever I wanted for $100 each."

When their baby, Jacob, was born, they discovered he had CHARGE syndrome, a genetic condition that comes with a litany of life-threatening problems, like heart defects and breathing problems. Even though James was at this point a serious pill addict, he knew he had to make money and get insurance to help with the surgeries Jacob required to live. He got a job at Lowe's, and because of his newfound, pill-induced work strength, he became a department manager within six months. But lifting all day aggravated his back, and he was legally prescribed oxycodone again, along with Percocet and Demerol. He'd take what he needed for his pain and sell the rest to help pay for his baby's mounting medical bills.

Prior to and during this entire time, James's relationship with his two other sons, Jimmy and Jason, was strained. Neither of the children's mothers wanted them hanging out with their father because of his past. But James claims that he kept continuing to reach out to both of them.

After fifteen months at Lowe's, James went through upper-management training and was promoted to a different store location, in Highland Heights, Kentucky, in 2003. Highland Heights is right on the border of Cincinnati, so James moved back up north, along with all his prescriptions, to start work. He was staying temporarily at a condo owned by his mother while searching for a new home for his family. Lynda and Jacob had remained behind in Florida until James could get everything settled.

Here's where things went to hell, and fast. According to James, a few months before he moved back to Ohio, Jimmy had come to visit him at a relative's house in Tennessee. Jimmy saw James slipping some pills to the relative. According to James, Jimmy said, "I could sell those things in Cincinnati for fifty dollars apiece."

James had been selling his pills for significantly less, not quite realizing how huge the market really was.

James claims that once he moved back up to Ohio, Jimmy, now nineteen years old, came to him and asked to borrow $1,000 for a paternity test on his newborn son, because he was having doubts that he was the actual father. James told him that he wouldn't have that kind of cash until he sold his house in Florida, so Jimmy asked if he could sell some of his father's pills to make the money. James agreed and gave him enough Xanax and OxyContin to make $1,000 on the street. But he swears that he made his son promise he wouldn't take any pills himself.

"I wasn't even thinking," he says, and starts to cry. "I guess I thought it was something we could do together. When you sell drugs with someone, there's a bond. It's sick, but it's real."

It's sick, but I get it.

A few nights later, after Jimmy had been selling his dad's wares, he and his friend Steven showed up at the condo with some beer. They seemed slightly buzzed. James made them something to eat and then fell asleep in a recliner in front of the television.

"I woke up early in the morning," James remembers. "I found them both on the bedroom floor. Steven was snoring, loudly. Jimmy was in a praying position, on his knees, as if he was bowing down. I said, 'What are you doing?' I got no response. I walked over and shook him, and he just kind of rolled over."

Instead of calling 911 immediately, he called Lynda in Florida to talk him through CPR. Then he called 911 and continued trying to resuscitate Jimmy.

"Suddenly, all of this foam came out of my son's mouth, and blood started pouring out of his nose," James said quietly.

When the EMTs and the police arrived, James made no effort to hide the OxyContin. He gave them his prescription bottle and told them that he thought the two boys had overdosed on them. "But I told the police that Jimmy had stolen them," he admits. "I lied about it. I was in a state of shock. I question myself about it to this day."

Jimmy was pronounced dead on arrival at the hospital. Steven spent several days in the intensive care unit on a ventilator system before being released.

James was initially indicted on several counts: for involuntary manslaughter, aggravated trafficking in drugs, corrupting another with drugs, and drug possession—all felony charges.

James's lawyer, Kenneth Zuk, was able to work out a deal with the state of Ohio in which all other charges would be dismissed if James pleaded guilty to two counts of corrupting another with drugs. These are second-degree felonies, with fines and mandatory prison terms of two to eight years. He would not be eligible for judicial release or community control. James knew that by entering this plea he might have to serve both sentences consecutively instead of concurrently. His sentencing hearing was set for April 7, 2004, at the Claremont County courthouse, by the Honorable William Walker.

Emotions were running extremely high, so much so that Judge

Walker had to begin the proceedings with a warning. "We have a lot of folks here today who have an interest in this case," he told the courtroom. "I caution you because if there is a problem in the hallway or in the courtroom, the deputies in the building here have strict instructions to take those matters seriously and get them under control immediately. Which may mean someone might get taken into custody, and we don't want that to happen here today."

The state brought in several individuals to testify against James. The last two were Jimmy's mother, Laurie Bender, and his stepfather, Will Bender.

Will Bender's testimony was interesting. While all the previous witnesses put the blame directly on James, Bender admitted that "Jimmy wasn't the perfect kid."

Of course not, that's because there's no such thing as a perfect kid. James told me that Will Bender had once called him in the middle of the night, demanding that James find some sort of protection for Jimmy because he had robbed someone of a kilo of meth that was now sitting in their home. James claims he stayed out of it, but that Jimmy ended up selling the meth out of Laurie and Will's home.

When Laurie Bender, Jimmy's mother, took the stand, all she said was, "I don't really have a whole bunch to say today. A mother shouldn't really have to take this position. It's a shame that so many lives have been deeply affected. It's a good thing to have drug dealers out of society and incarcerated. Eighteen years is definitely not enough in exchange for one life, but I know that James is convicted of guilt. I know that James Dean will have guilt in his heart for the rest of his life."

Laurie Bender tracked me down when she found out I had been speaking with James Dean. We spoke and emailed at length about many things, including James's accusation that they had allowed meth in the house while Jimmy was alive, but usually we just talked about Jimmy's life. Most of our conversations were off the record, though, and I won't violate that trust. But she did insist that she never allowed drugs in the house, and that Jimmy was a depressed kid. "He always tried to please everyone," she told me, "but he also seemed to know that something bad was going to happen to him."

I was also able to track down Steven, the boy Jimmy was with when he overdosed. But despite my credentials, Steven was afraid that I was personally affiliated with James and that James was trying to track him down. Steven refused to grant an interview.

James Dean's sole defense came down to his lawyer, Kenneth Zuk:

> First of all on behalf of Mr. Dean and myself, I want to state that we recognize that there is nothing that we are going to say or do that's going to take the hurt away from anybody in this situation. A lot of people have a lot of bad things to say about my client, but he is capable of doing extremely well when he's not under the influence of drugs, when he's not dealing with an addiction, and when he's not taking substances that are controlling his life. The prosecution has his records from his employment. When Jim is not dealing with an addiction, he has a personnel file full of commendations. There are some circumstances that took place here that no one ever could have imagined. When he got hurt on the job somebody gave him pain medication. It took the progression that it does with an addict. And so he started seeking them illegally, and as he has freely admitted in his pre-sentence investigation, he went beyond what was prescribed for him. He crushed them and snorted them. By the time he moved to Cincinnati, his mind and his body were out of control. He admits that he was involved in illegally trafficking in this with his son. His son was involved as well, and that's one of the things that I don't think people really understand. The State's own evidence has in [Jimmy's] handwriting his ledgers of who he was selling to, how much he was selling. I know people don't want to hear this. The victims in this case were involved in the drug scene just as much as the Defendant. That doesn't excuse what James did. He gave the drugs to his son for the purpose of his son selling them. He's going to have to live with it for the rest

of his life that he helped put into motion what resulted in his son's death. He doesn't express himself well, but I've sat in a room with him repeatedly. I've seen the genuine and deep remorse that this man has over what happened. He knows that you're not going to give him the minimum sentence. What we are asking the Court to do is to take into consideration what this man is capable of accomplishing when he is not under the influence of these substances.

The sins of the father.

It's clear that Jimmy was just as involved as James in the small-time Oxy ring they had going on. I should be more shocked about this case. I know I should feel that what James did was despicable. Intellectually, I know that to be true. But I also know what it's like inside that bubble. You really do feel like nothing can ever go wrong when you're on pills. I've given away so many benzos to friends and strangers in my past, someone could have just as easily taken one of my Valiums, continued to binge-drink and do blow, and then never woken up.

James knew what he was doing was wrong, and written testimonies from witnesses refute his claim that he only gave the drugs away for the paternity test, that there was actually a much larger drug ring going on between father and son. But both testimonies incriminate Jimmy as being just as much a part of the problem. A woman named Bridget Cassidy wrote she had been with James and Jimmy shortly before Jimmy's death. She witnessed them discussing how much money Jimmy would owe James. They argued, and eventually agreed on $8,500. Bridget warned Jimmy that he was going to kill himself, presumably by taking any of the pills, and James agreed, saying, "You can't be doing shit like that, boy."

Jimmy allegedly replied, "Shut up, I know what I'm doing."

Another woman, Suzanne Wolfinbarger, reported overhearing a conversation Jimmy had with his father about how many Oxys they had left. Jimmy was trying to get his father to sell him Oxys for $30 a pill, but James said no, they were worth $40 or $50 each. "Haven't I made you enough money already, son?" James asked.

Jimmy supposedly replied, "Yeah, but I want more."

Despite how tragic this case is, James was right in asserting that the dealing connected them together in a way they'd never been able to before. Which, if you take the drug selling out of the equation and try to see it as a family issue, you can look at in two ways: James was trying to do whatever he could to help out the son he abandoned, no matter how morally wrong. Or, Jimmy was trying to impress the father he had never known by going into business with him. The sad fact is, no one will ever really know what happened. There are too many people contradicting each other and no concrete proof that Jimmy was already a wild child or that James was the original corruptor. Of course James never should have given Jimmy any pills.

The judge's decision was based on James's own written statement—the fact that he had tried to use his own dead son as an excuse, putting the blame on Jimmy for asking him for money for a paternity test, and maintaining that Jimmy was the drug dealer, not him. James was initially sentenced to serve twelve years and pay $20,020, but his sentence was later reduced to eight years, with no appeal.

When last James heard, his other son, Jason, had been arrested twelve times for selling drugs and sent to jail. There he met an inmate who knew James. Through this connection Jason sent word through the jail system to James that he still loved him.

"That's the last I've heard from him," says James. His release date is set for April 18, 2012.

Rather than just being tossed into a cell and left to rot, it's too bad that James can't be transferred out of state, to the Sheridan Correctional Center, seventy miles outside of Chicago. Sheridan is one of the first large prisons that focuses on drug and alcohol rehabilitation. It provides treatment and job training to repeat offenders. Early data suggests that prisoners who complete the program and do aftercare once they are released are about half as likely to be rearrested.

The prison itself first opened in the 1940s as a juvenile facility, but it was closed during George Ryan's administration. (Ryan is the ex-governor of Illinois who was sentenced in 2006 to six and a half years in prison for racketeering and fraud.) While the now notorious ex-Governor Blagojevich was campaigning for election the first time, he promised to reopen the Sheridan Correctional Center, dedicate it to substance abuse treatment, and make it a national model.

The 1,300-bed facility started training staff in November 2003 and admitting inmates in January 2004. In order for an inmate to be eligible for the facility, he or she has to pass a screening test developed by Texas Christian University. It's a series of questions designed to provide a snapshot of an inmate's drug and alcohol abuse history. If the inmate is considered eligible after the test, the screeners next take a look at the inmate's crimes. Sheridan doesn't accept inmates who have been convicted of murder or sex offenses. The third criterion is how much time the inmate has to serve. Eligible candidates must have a minimum of nine months and a maximum of twenty-four months left on their sentence; this means that prisoners from other in-state facilities can also transfer in.

According to Sheridan's warden, Michael Rothwell, the facility is run as a holistic program—one that looks not only at addiction and chemical-dependency issues, but also at academic, vocational, and cognitive behavioral issues as well.

"It's like a three-legged stool," he explains. "If you pull any one of the legs, the stool falls over. Our inmates are constructively engaged seven hours a day."

Inmates participate in one-on-one and group therapy sessions that focus on different needs for different inmates, such as grief or anger.

The vocational and educational activities aren't designed to just pass the time. They are specifically set up to meet demand occupations in the state of Illinois—everything from welding to culinary arts. Sheridan works with several organizations, like the Safer Foundation, which helps with job placement in different communities. Anyone who leaves Sheridan has at least a ninety-day aftercare community-based transitional plan. There are also community advisory councils, which are citizen groups that help integrate inmates back into the general population.

"There are thousands and thousands of inmates that come back to Chicago," Rothwell says. "It's foolish for the communities not to say, 'Hey, we need to take some ownership in helping them transition into coming back.'"

There are other prisons that have small-scale versions of the Sheridan program, but Sheridan is unique in its size and community involvement. "It's a much more comprehensive effort to integrate services inside the prison and outside, based on this behavioral continuum," Rothwell says.

So why aren't all drug offenders sent to prisons like this one? Why are we wasting millions and millions of tax dollars every year to let prisoners sit in a cell, only to come right back for a repeat offense because they have learned absolutely nothing except how to avoid being raped and how to score cigarettes?

Money, of course. Initially, these facilities are obviously more expensive to set up. But in the long run they save untold amounts of money. "Legislators are always juggling the resources that are getting scarcer and scarcer," Rothwell says. "It all comes down to this— do you fix your potholes, put money into education, or pay for treating inmates?"

Joseph Califano Jr. agrees with Rothwell. He told me that Governor Schwarzenegger had been proposing similar programs in California but couldn't get them through the legislature. "The politics of it are very difficult," he explained. "But if we treated everyone in prison who needs it, and we only succeed with 10 percent of them, in one year the treatment pays for itself. The problem is, when I talk to state legislators, what they say is that their constituents want computers in the classrooms, they want more mass transit, and they can't justify providing treatment to criminals. It's just a tough political call for them."

The inmates are going to lose every time, and it's shortsighted thinking like this that keeps our country wasting money by pouring funds into programs like DARE that do nothing, instead of into ones that will not only help people with their addiction issues but also benefit society in the long run and save tax dollars now used to fill our prisons with returning addicts.

CHAPTER 16

Escape to (and in) the Midwest

I MANAGED TO STAY clean for about four months after my appendectomy. It wasn't hard. I asked for and received a refill on my bottle of Vicodin and weaned myself off slowly to ease the withdrawal. Work kept me distracted, and I started swimming every single day after leaving the office late. By the time I got home, I would pass right out.

Then, out of nowhere, *Jane* folded and I was out of a job. I had devoted a total of six years of my life to the magazine and my identity was wrapped up in it. I spent anywhere from nine to fourteen hours a day with my coworkers; they were family. I had started my career out in magazine promotions—basically, throwing parties. But I wanted to write, so when I heard that a photo assistant job was open at *Jane*, I fought hard to get it, even though I knew nothing about photography. I knew most of the articles at *Jane* were written in-house, not freelanced, so I thought that if I could just get my foot in the door, I could start pitching story ideas and work my way up. That's exactly what happened. I was so proud of the magazine we put out. It was fun, funny, and controversial, and I'm pretty sure that no magazine like it will ever exist again, at least on a large scale. Especially one targeted to women. We had forty-eight hours to clean out our desks.

I think all of the staff, particularly the editorial department, went into a state of of shock that lasted months. The few friends from the magazine who knew about my pill problem came to me for benzos. I pretended I didn't have any, but by the time we all met up at Lakeside Lounge for our big farewell party I was already high on Candyman's morphine. I'd been keeping some in my safety box under my bed because even though I'd been sober, it was easier to be sober knowing there was something within reach if I ever really needed it. And I needed it. I couldn't deal with people I loved trying their hardest to remain upbeat. My morphine bubble numbed me—I couldn't face the magazine's death sober. According to Joseph Califano, this is typical of substance abusers and addicts, who experience repeated cycles of abuse and addiction followed by periods of relative abstinence and effective functioning. Addiction is a chronic, relapsing disease, not an acute one.

I hate it when I fit the pattern.

Late in the summer, Emily and I decided we needed to get out of town. She wanted to visit the artist guy she'd been dating long distance. His mother lived near her hometown in western Pennsylvania, near the Ohio and Kentucky borders, and we could meet him there. She had friends we could stay with, ones she swore we could score pills from.

When we arrived I rented a car at the airport, a huge black SUV with zero visibility from either side and behind. The only direction I could see was forward—a problem because the vehicle had a tendency to pull to the left. At first I thought it was the effects of the Dilaudid I'd taken to get me through the flight, so I was relieved to discover that my weaving all over the road was a result of mechanical failure, not my own reflexes. We drove into the pitch-black countryside, long stretches of winding road with multiple slams on the brakes to avoid the cats, raccoons, and skunks that kept darting in front of the car.

"Just hit it," Emily sighed after some brown, shapeless creature waddled out in front of us. I couldn't bring myself to do it and swerved headlong into the oncoming lane instead.

Forty-five minutes into the trip I discovered the high beams, which made the drive much less terrifying. Every half mile or so we'd pass a dilapidated house with a sagging roof and a rusted car parked out front. Scarecrows were everywhere, hung on crosses in front lawns in honor of the season. I wondered if the residents just put a bag of stuffed straw over the heads of their front-lawn Jesus, to save money.

Emily's boyfriend was named Jess, and his mother lived in one of these same houses off the highway that you barely ever get more than a glimpse of as you drive by. We pulled into a gravel parking lot. A massive barn loomed before us. Moonlight streaked through the slats in the wood from the other side of the structure, making it appear lit from within.

We got out of the car and headed toward the side porch, which was covered in vines and flowers and a small stone with the words "Go Away" carved into it. A picnic table off to the left of the porch was covered with more pots and flowers. Half-eaten tins of cat food were scattered along the border of one railing. The yard and porch felt neglected yet cared for at the same time—there was an odd sort of order to the chaos.

As we walked up the front steps, a piercing, drawn-out scream came from inside the house. Emily and I grabbed each other. Jess appeared at the front screen door, totally unfazed by the sound as he welcomed us inside.

"What was that?" I asked as we shook hands, and a woman appeared behind him, arms open wide.

"I'm Julia!" she exclaimed as she hugged Emily, then me. I liked her immediately. She had long hair that was just beginning to gray. She wore baggy sweatpants and a sweatshirt with deep armpit stains, but her eyes were bright, her smile broad. A black cat ran circles around her feet, and I noticed saltwater aquariums everywhere, with neon anemones swaying in the bubbles of the air filters. A tiger fish glared out at me from one, and countless striped orange *Finding Nemo* fishes darted around.

The same piercing scream came again from another section of the house, and I jumped. Julia threw her head back and laughed a witchy cackle, beckoning me to follow her into another room. Along the walls were six enormous, ornate birdcages, large enough for me to climb into, and massive colorful birds clung to the outside bars. I looked down, expecting to see the carpet covered in bird shit, but it was mostly contained inside the cages and a footwide layer of surrounding newspaper.

"I rescue them," Julia explained as a macaw flew from its cage and landed on her shoulder. I ducked down instinctively, but as soon as I saw how docile it was, I reached an arm out toward the nearest bird and it climbed up onto my shoulder. It was all green, with bright yellow eyes that met mine with an even gaze.

"Hi," I said.

"Hi," it muttered back.

Emily and Jess were having a lovefest reunion in the other room, leaving me alone with Julia.

"I hear you're working on a book about pills," she said.

"Trying to," I answered.

"Well, are you going to interview me?" she asked.

"You like pills?" I asked. The green bird on my shoulder fluttered its wings, knocking them into my ear. I eased it back down onto its cage.

"Love 'em," she said and threw her head back and cackled again.

"Well, then, let's talk," I said.

She led me into the living room, where three more elaborate saltwater aquariums bubbled away. The television was set to a football game, which she muted. Emily and Jess disappeared up the dark staircase. Julia picked up a book called *Magic and Medicine of Plants* and handed it to me.

"You ever heard of bindweed before?" she asked. "It's supposed to have hallucinogenic properties. I had it growing all over my backyard. The flowers look like white trumpets."

"Never heard of it," I answered. "Ever try it out?"

"No, no, you have to know how to do it just right, and I don't," she said.

"Back in high school, I heard you could trip if you ate a whole package of poppy seeds, so I did," I said. "I just puked for hours."

Julia nodded wisely. "Bad idea. Now, what we had when *I* was in high school were Quaaludes. The Rorer 714s."

Her eyes got all wide and that huge smile spread over her face. "You had to be near a chair or a bed when you took one of those. It was the ultimate down. Drugs were plentiful when I was growing up. Jess was born in 1973, and back in 1965, 1966, I had a bunch of older sisters. Everybody would just go down to the park every day and get stoned, and there were massive amounts of pills. I remember my mom coming into my bedroom one time, and I had, like, two thousand pills on my bed."

"Jesus, what kind?" I asked.

"I had Black Beauties, I had reds . . . reds were the best. I think reds were better than 714s. I remember this girl falling forward in a plate of spaghetti taking reds. I was over at her house for dinner, and she just fell forward right into her food. To me, they're a great escape. Now that I'm older and my body's creakier, I use them a lot for pain relievers, too."

"What about opiates?" I asked.

"Oh yeah, I'm definitely into opiates. A lot of women my age like them. I'm fifty-three now."

"Do you get them from legitimate doctors here?" I asked.

"No," she said, as a bird shrieked in the other room. "My doctor recently gave me a three-month supply of Ambien, but I have a girlfriend that gets me sixty Vicodins a month."

"But where is she getting them?" I asked. "Is she overprescribed for something?"

"No, she gets them from somebody else who has fibromyalgia. That's a nerve disease, and all the nerve endings in your skin hurt. It hurts so bad you can't even wear clothes. Very, very painful, but this way she can make a little extra money. I usually give a bunch of them to Jess. I'll call him and say, 'I have fifty,' but he usually takes so long to get down and see me that I'll have, like, fifteen left by the time he gets here."

I wanted her to adopt me.

"I've always been a big pothead," she continued. "I've been smoking pot since I was fourteen, and if I could only have one drug the rest of my life, it would be pot, hands down. But pills make everything go a little easier. When I take a pill at work, I get three times as much work done."

"Do you ever just try to get some from your own doctor?" I asked.

She got up and drummed her fingers gently along the wall of one of the aquariums. "I'm not that bad that I'm going to fake injuries to go to the doctors," she said. "I know people who do that. It's their career. That, and doctor shopping. There will always be somebody trying to make money off their pills. That girl who sells those Vicodins to me, she makes a good buck off of them."

"Are you ever worried that your connection is going to dry up?" I asked.

"No, because you can always find them on the street."

"What about OxyContin?" I asked.

"Actually, I don't like Oxys, because they keep me up," she said. "I like to go to sleep. With the Vicodin I have to time the pills, so I'll take my last one at two or three in the afternoon. I have a lot to do when I get home from work, as far as feeding the fish . . ." She trails off, staring deep into the bubbling coral of the aquarium nearest the couch we're on. "I love my fish tanks."

"Okay," I said, trying to get back on track. "So you give away a lot of pills to Jess. Do other people ever come to you, knowing you have this connection?"

"Oh yeah. I sell pills, too. Usually I just give them away, because I'm overly generous. I sell weed to my friend who works at the pet store, and I give him some pills, too. And he had a problem for a while, because he lost the top half of his finger in an accident. I don't know what kind of accident he had, but he lost half of his finger, and he got addicted to painkillers from that."

I narrowed my eyes and looked at the tiger fish. It was staring at me. It wanted my finger.

"Someone told me a story recently about a guy who broke his own leg to get painkillers," I told her.

"I'm not that bad," she said. "I'm just a child of the 1960s and '70s. I mean, I've shot heroin at a Black Sabbath concert."

I was radically, pointlessly, jealous.

"The person that shot me up messed my arm up, and I got a big abscess. It was real bad, I could feel it going right through my arm. It was very intense. You just . . . when you feel it, you know there's a couple of minutes before you do the nod. I don't really like getting to that point. I like somewhere in between that point. I like to be able to function."

"Which is why pills work for you," I said.

"Exactly. People will always say there's an epidemic of drugs, and there *is* an epidemic of drugs in this country. You don't have to be a genius to figure that out. They prey on the weak and I have an addictive personality. And not just with drugs. With food, animals . . . I just like how they make me feel. It's a great escape. I live pretty much like a hermit. I really like my solitude, and I like being alone with my animals. Of course, I get preached at by my son."

"About what?" I asked.

"I'll make jokes with him about taking twelve Vicodins a day and he'll gasp. I'm just kidding with him. I only take a couple a day."

"But isn't it kind of weird for him to be preaching to you, when you're his supplier?" I asked.

"Jess's father left when he was three weeks old, so I raised him all by myself," she said. "Jess is like *my* father—he watches over me. It's not a normal mother-son relationship. There was a point when Jess was vacuuming and doing my laundry and all kinds of stuff, and he was telling people his mom was a drug addict and he had to do all this stuff, but that's just hype. Because the whole time I was raising Jess, there was never a time that I was not able to take care of him."

Her body language wasn't exactly defensive, but there was a sad edge creeping into her voice.

"Do you consider yourself a drug addict?" I asked.

"Yes," she said, with no hesitation. "But I can quit whenever I want." And she threw back her head and cackled her wild laugh while the birds screeched in unison in the other room.

Before we left that night, Julia pulled out a coffee mug with a

Native American woman painted on one side of it. Inside was an orange prescription bottle. She opened it up and dropped several hydrocodone pills into our waiting hands, like a housewife on Halloween doling out candy to the eager and overfed brats that we were.

We drove to a bar about forty minutes away to meet a friend of Jess's named Elliott. Both Jess and Emily had promised me that this guy had good pill stories for me. I'd spoken to him over the phone a few times over the summer, and from what I'd gathered so far, he'd grown up pretty normal, in a middle-class family. He'd been prescribed Ritalin in the second grade for ADD.

"I don't even remember how I felt before Ritalin," he told me. "After, I remember my life as a continuous series of being really psyched about things, then hating the world. I didn't understand it."

He eventually got Adderall added to his ADD cocktail. "It just got automatically prescribed to me," he said. "I didn't think anything of it at first, until a friend of mine who knew I had a prescription started asking me for them. I didn't really know why, but then I looked closer at the bottle and it said 'mixed amphetamines,' and I said to myself, 'Hmmm, amphetamines, huh?' So I did some research on the drug scheduling system and found that Adderall was a Schedule II substance. I realized I had an endless party for free. And it was fun."

Years later, around 2005, he was working at the local recycling center. On the job, he met a guy named Gary, who had been in a nasty car wreck years before: he'd fallen asleep at the wheel and driven into a ravine. He'd messed up his chest really badly, his clavicle was now positioned way too far over, under his chin. Gary had prescriptions for both Vicodin and OxyContin to deal with the pain. He'd take what he needed but had leftovers, so he asked Elliott if he knew anyone who wanted to buy some.

The Oxys were 40 milligrams and Gary was willing to sell them for $17 each, which was less than half the street value. Elliot's friend Sam had always talked about how much he loved painkillers but could never get any, so Elliot told Gary he could easily get $17 from Sam.

"When I told Sam about the opportunity, he gave me $170 for ten," Elliott said. "I wasn't really interested myself—I guess I just had this idea that OxyContin was too intense. But soon after I sold Sam his first bunch, we skipped class and both took one. We ended up lying on the floor and watching old Genesis videos, almost crying because it sounded so beautiful. It was weird. I never even knew I liked Genesis. At least it was the Peter Gabriel era. Anyway, after that, I started buying my own pills."

After Elliott's night of old-school Genesis worship on OxyContin, he started taking pills about once a week, recreationally, with his friend Sam. Sam would give Elliott money to give to Gary.

Elliott would deliver the pills to Sam and then Sam would give him just one. "Every time I did it, I'd think, 'Oh, I don't need to do that again,'" says Elliott. "But as months went on, Gary started giving me Vicodin for free at work every now and then, just for fun. But then I started wanting them outside of work, so I'd meet him at these weird, sordid places like gas stations or car garages."

Gary was being prescribed ninety OxyContins a month, but once Sam started buying regularly from him, he always ended up selling out within a week or two. "I had to start waiting a few weeks in between my pills, and it drove me crazy," Elliott told me. "Gary was keeping only a few OxyContin for himself, because he had to submit to regular drug tests so his doctor knew he was actually taking them, and that there were no other drugs in his system that would interfere with the prescribed narcotics. He would save a couple of Oxys for himself and take them a few days before each test."

We've already heard of some doctors doing this, and the DEA believes this sort of drug testing is a good idea from a commonsense standpoint. But they can't officially recommend or enforce it because it strays into the practice of medicine as opposed to the legal application of the Controlled Substances Act. As a federal agency, they leave it up to the discretion of medical boards.

Gary thought OxyContin made him too slow, which is why he preferred to sell it and keep only what he needed for his tests. He much preferred his Vicodin, and as time went on, he became more and more hesitant about selling or giving any away to Elliott.

"I'm pretty open about my drug use," Elliott said. "And it got to the point that if I couldn't find any pills, I'd just ask people. If someone was talking about pot, I'd just say, 'Hey, dude, know where I can get painkillers?'"

Elliott doesn't believe that he was physically dependent on anything at the time. "It was more of a behavioral thing," he explains. "It's a problem I have with impulsivity." For a while, he even slowed his drug use down after one particularly nasty incident involving a Fentanyl patch and a bunch of Gary Numan songs.

"Sam was taking the pills I was getting him from Gary at the recycling center, and taking them up to Cleveland to trade with other junkies. He got really into Fentanyl patches; he'd bring them back, bite them open, and suck the fluid out of them."

Fentanyl patches, such as Duragesic, are applied to the skin and deliver an extremely strong opioid analgesic: a single patch can control pain for up to three days. They are mostly used to treat people with intractable cancer pain. They are also usually only provided to patients who have developed a tolerance to other pain medications. It's recommended that patients have a tolerance equivalent to 60 milligrams of morphine a day for at least a week before going on the patch.

Sam gave Elliott a couple of patches, and one night Elliott sucked the liquid out of both of them.

"I was at my mom's house," Elliott remembers. "No one was home—she was out of town. I remember getting really excited about downloading a bunch of Gary Numan songs, or something weird that I normally don't like. That *always* happens to me when I'm high. The next thing I know, it's morning and I'm lying on my mom's bedroom floor covered in puke. I totally cut my drug use in half after that scare."

I can guarantee you that there are millions and millions of teenagers and adults who have had similar experiences with alcohol. You drink too much, you pass out, you wake up covered in puke and think to yourself, "Whoa, never again," or "Shit, I'd better take it easy for a while." It happened to me countless of times as a teenager—the "normal" time period when, if you're a budding drinker, you test your limits and discover what works for you and what doesn't. It's messed up, but those kinds of stories don't faze me in the slightest. I'm used to them, I've seen them, I've been there.

There are two main dangers in passing out while drunk: you may aspirate your own vomit into your lungs or you may stop breathing—too much alcohol depresses the respiratory center in the brain. The same dangers exist with Fentanyl, only more so. Just one Fentanyl patch contains enough analgesic to relieve pain for up to *three days*.

Think of it this way: when you're out at a party you can usually tell when your friend has had too much to drink. You see him stumbling around with a bottle and waving someone's underwear, or babbling incoherently about some old episode of *The Facts of Life*, or falling down a flight of stairs. (Guilty on all counts.) In this circumstance you may try to help by putting your friend in bed and checking on him periodically to make sure he's still alive. In extreme cases, you may take your friend to the hospital.

But Elliott was alone when he took a massive dose of a powerful substance contained in what seemed like a very small amount. No one thinks he's going to die from one Jell-O shot. And being alone is standard practice for a pill user: pills (and patches) aren't social drugs, even though the media loves to portray the dangers of "pharming parties." Sure, they exist, but usually in a much more casual way. When a bunch of the guests trade some pills at a cocktail party it doesn't become a pharming party. It's still just a cocktail party where some pills happened to be traded.

Elliott was lucky he didn't die that night. But it still wasn't enough for him to realize he should quit opiates. He did what any normal college kid would do after waking up covered in puke. He just decided to slow down for a little while.

When Emily, Jess, and I arrive at the bar Elliott is easy to spot—the one lone twenty-five-year-old emo-looking kid, sitting in a small-town college bar. Jess and Em left me alone to talk with him. We slid into an outdoor booth, ordering beers.

"How's school going?" I asked him.

"It could be going better," he answered, tossing his bangs out of his eyes and taking a sip of beer. "I asked my doctor for more Adderall to help me out."

"And?" I asked.

"He said no. I think I'm pretty much flagged in this town as a big-time drug user. But he's understanding about it; he tells me he wants to help me but doesn't think Adderall is the right way to go. So he put me on another drug, called Strattera. I started four days ago, but it hasn't begun to work yet."

Strattera is a relatively new drug for treating ADD. It's supposed to help people focus, but in a nonstimulating way.

"I can already feel the side effects, though," he said. "I'm impotent, for one thing. And I have dyspepsia. I'm always thirsty."

With that he flags down our waitress and orders another beer. I order one too. The beer is intensifying the effects of Julia's hydrocodone and I feel a rush of guilt. I'm acutely aware of the hypocrisy of interviewing someone for a book about drug abuse while I'm on drugs.

Elliott pointed to a set of railroad tracks across the street from the bar. "I know someone who died on those tracks," he said. "This kid who also used to do a lot of pills. We started a band together, made a few demos, but it never went anywhere. One night we were hanging out here at the bar. Two hours later, he was dead. We got hold of the police report, and all signs point to suicide, but it was officially ruled an accident. He was legally drunk, but the report said that after he lay down on the train tracks, as soon as the train started coming, he pulled his hoodie over his head and curled up into a ball."

I could see the tracks over Elliott's shoulder, empty now, no trains in sight.

"After he died, I just didn't have the energy to keep up with my drug habit for the first few days, which is pretty strange considering I was addicted. But I didn't react immediately. I was in shock. It took me a few days before I could even cry, and even then it wasn't until I finally took some pills."

I could relate. As much as pills are an escape from your emotions, after a certain point, they become the *only* emotion, the only one you know how to function with, a surrogate inner life.

"When I'm not on opiates, I feel like a robot," he said. "They get me out of the robotic mode. And sometimes I get sadder when I'm on them, but it's a sadness that feels more human to me."

He tells me that he is back to doing Oxy mainly, but that his friend Sam has cut down a lot because of a new girlfriend.

"It's mostly an alone thing now," he said. "I don't really have many more friends besides Sam. There's been an awful lot of unreturned phone calls. People realized I was doing a lot of pills. The annoying thing is that any lectures I've gotten on my drug use have taken place here," he said, waving his arm, gesturing to the bar around us.

"It'll be from some drunk guy who has heard through the grapevine that I do a lot of pills. They'll say things like, 'Man, you've got to stop doing those drugs. *I* don't do them.' And meanwhile he's puking on himself."

"Do you want to quit?" I ask him.

"The last time I stopped cold it was really bad," he said. "I mean, it wasn't like *Trainspotting*, where you see dead babies crawling on the ceiling and stuff, but I had diarrhea and the shakes and serious depression, and I couldn't sleep."

"What do you think it would take to make you stop for good?" I asked, as a pill wave rolled through me.

"You don't do pills to intentionally fill a void," he tells me. "It just happens unintentionally, and you stick with it. Maybe schools should teach social skills classes instead of drug-warning classes so you can learn how to meet the right person. Because what I've felt when I'm in love is far more potent than any drug. That's how I know that I'm not a junkie. When I look back at the times when I've had love, I want that so much more than the drugs. It was the only time I wasn't abusing pills so much."

He finishes his beer, gestures for another. "But then again," he continues, "too much self-reflection will just make you neurotic. I don't know who I am whatsoever."

CHAPTER 17

Harm Reduction and the Future of Painkiller Abuse

LOVE MAY BE MORE potent than any drug for Elliott, but these days the preferred method used to ease addicts off painkillers is buprenorphine with naloxone, usually prescribed as Suboxone. Buprenorphine is the opioid that Dr. Bodkin had been testing for use with depression in the 1990s and the drug Jared was given in detox. Naloxone (or Narcan) in its pure form can temporarily reverse an opiate overdose and restore breathing; it is usually injected to quickly kick opiates off the brain's receptors. The combination of the two drugs helps addicts because the opioid staves off the cravings, while the naloxone prevents abuse if you try to snort or inject it.

In 2000, Congress passed the Drug Abuse Treatment Act, a measure allowing physicians who meet certain guidelines to use approved opioid drugs to treat opiate addiction on an outpatient basis. Buprenorphine was approved by the FDA for this purpose in 2002. Doctors have to apply for a waiver and prove that they meet the guidelines. During the first year they may treat up to thirty patients. After one year, they may treat up to one hundred patients. The reason for this cap is to make sure that doctors are able to provide adequate referrals and other forms of addiction treatment for their patients.

But the sad fact is that many addicts aren't going to seek out treatment for themselves. That is why I favor harm reduction outreach programs having access to naloxone. If our real goal with the war on drugs is to save lives, then why not put the one drug that can save a life directly into users' hands?

Many people would argue that this would give users a free pass to take whatever they want. If they OD they can just come right back and go on using the next day. This may be true initially, but in at least some cases the trauma of overdosing and nearly dying might be enough to give users pause and seek out more aggressive treatments for their problem.

The Chicago Recovery Alliance (CRA) has been particularly vocal in its campaign to get naloxone into the hands of heroin and other opiate users. (For the record, they claim that the whole Adrenalin-shot-in-the-heart scene from *Pulp Fiction* is total bullshit—it needs to be administered intravenously.)

CRA's most important rule is never use alone; this might be problematic for pill abusers since they often lead such solitary drug-use existences. CRA's website, www.anypositivechange.org, has all sorts of opiate-use safety information and can tell you how to get access to naloxone and the proper way to administer it.

"The Chicago Recovery Alliance started its naloxone program in early 1997," says Dan Bigg, the director. "I've had many people overdose in my life; it's a very painful experience to have a friend die. Naloxone is the perfect antagonist to any and all opiates. It was determined by the DEA to have no potential for abuse. It's been out there used in the medical setting since 1971. It's really looked at as a pure antidote."

Naloxone training and distribution has become a well-known practice within most harm reduction centers. "I'd say at our center, 99 percent of the requests for naloxone are coming from opiate users themselves," says Dan. "But sometimes someone will bring in his mother, and the mom will say, 'Can I have my own in case my son loses his? Because I've encountered him overdosing and it would be nice to have something to actually do instead of watching my child die in front of me.' In Cook County, overdoses kill somewhere between eight hundred to one thousand people a year; it's a bigger killer than HIV and hepatitis and infectious diseases combined. We've received seven hundred and fifty-one reports of pure reversal with naloxone to date."

Dan is hoping that someday naloxone will be available as an over-the-counter drug.

Just as parents who know their child has a peanut allergy keep a prescribed epinephrine auto-injector on hand, people who suspect their kid, friend, or loved one is abusing opiates should be trained in the use of naloxone and have an injector kit in their house.

But there are two main problems with this. Few parents like to admit to themselves that their kid has a drug problem, and even fewer are going to take the time to go to a harm reduction center to get the training they need. Most people think of harm reduction centers primarily as needle exchange programs for heroin addicts. But they provide all sorts of counseling, HIV education and testing, access to buprenorphine treatment for opiate addiction, and naloxone training. I won't lie to you—these centers (many of which are located in inner city areas) can seem pretty scary to a white, suburban parent. The only thing I have to say to that is, parents, get over your illusions. If your kid has a bottle of Oxy hidden in his backpack, he is in no better situation than anyone else you might see milling about outside an HRC. And the people you will come in contact with *there* are at least taking responsible steps toward treatment and the spread of HIV.

"I heard from a guy from Rochester, New York, who was trying to keep his brother, who was using opiates, safer," says Dan. "He was willing to do whatever it took to get his hands on naloxone, even fly to Chicago. Luckily he was able to find it in one of the New York programs. Once you realize naloxone is out there and what it has the potential to do, it's hard *not* to have it as part of your life."

I agree with this with all my heart. So much so, that right after I got off the phone with Dan, I walked five blocks down from my apartment to visit the Lower East Side Harm Reduction Center to get properly trained and have my own naloxone kit. I've slipped up enough times in my life with pills, and still spend my fair share of time around other users, that it just seemed morally irresponsible not to know how to bring someone back from an overdose.

The Lower East Side naloxone program started later than CRA's, in 2004. They were working with the New York Academy of Medicine on a study of its effectiveness, and it proved to be a success. Most of the current funding for the program comes through the city. The center also gets a lot of businesspeople in suits who show up after work at night.

"These people are really responsive to the naloxone program," one of the counselors tells me. "They're chipping [slang for occasional use], they're not really fully in the lifestyle. Since they aren't using as much, they have a lower tolerance and are in more danger of overdosing. They know that and really want access to naloxone just in case."

I told the counselor about the book I was working on. I admitted that I had slipped up after getting clean the first time and wanted to have naloxone on hand, just in case. My training was done by a charming, fast-talking, slightly frazzled woman named Yolanda, a recovering addict herself. She was utterly thorough in teaching me how, when, and where to inject naloxone. Having already talked to Dan, I felt ahead of the game, but she gave me a ton of take-home literature and some sound advice.

"When you call the ambulance," she said, "don't tell them that it's an overdose. Tell them your friend has stopped breathing. They'll come faster that way."

I don't know why this surprises me. It shouldn't, but it also depresses the hell out of me.

I signed a form stating that I had gone through training, and then she took me to meet with the prescribing psychiatrist who works on the premises. We talked about my reasons for wanting naloxone: that I didn't feel I was in any immediate danger but that I liked the idea of being prepared, and my desire to help anyone I might happen to be around who was overdosing.

When it was over, Yolanda brought me a small blue pouch containing my naloxone and all the materials that come with it. Yolanda and I had already gone over everything that came in the pouch during my training, but when I got home I took everything out and lined them up on my coffee table.

There was a bottle of 0.4 milligrams of naloxone, a sterile 3-milliliter needle, alcohol prep pads, rubber gloves, a copy of my naloxone prescription ("In case the cops bug you," Yolanda had told me), my certificate of completion for opioid overdose prevention signed by a member of the NYS Approved Opioid Overdose Prevention Program, a pamphlet in Spanish and English on how to use all the materials, and my favorite thing of all, a single-use Bio-Barrier Face-shield for administering the "kiss of life" to someone who is overdosing. I love the idea of being a hero, but I'm deathly afraid of cold sores.

To this day, I carry the pouch around with me everywhere I go. Luckily I've never had occasion to use it, or have someone use it on me.

I was disappointed that harm reduction wasn't mentioned even once at the DEA's first ever National Symposium on Pharmaceutical Diversion, which took place on November 2, 2007. The symposium brought together a panel of experts in law enforcement, industry, public policy, science, health care, and medicine "for a public discussion on the complex issues surrounding the diversion of pharmaceutical drugs and efforts to combat this growing problem in America today." It was also a chance to tell the world about the new anti–prescription drug ad campaign the DEA was launching. I sat in the auditorium for three hours. Here's what the conference boiled down to. John Walters, the director of the Office of National Drug Policy Control, read off a bunch of stats; he then talked about how the DEA is targeting rogue Internet pharmacies. The ONDPC announced that it has partnered with the National Association of Chain Drug Stores to provide open letters to parents to teach them to control substances in the home and dispose of pharmaceuticals properly. Stephen Pasierb, the president and CEO of the Partnership for a Drug Free America, talked about how kids believe prescription drugs are safe to use because they came from a doctor; he also pointed out that these drugs are important and vital to the medical community and we need to educate America about this.

Next up was Joseph Rannazzisi, the deputy assistant administrator of the DEA Office for Diversion Control. He talked about the evils of Internet pharmacies. Then we heard from Sharon Brigner, the deputy vice president for the Pharmaceutical Research and Manufacturers of America. She talked about how PhRMA had partnered with DARE (ahem, *useless*) to create a curriculum for fifth, seventh, ninth, and twelfth graders about abusing prescription products. PhRMA also joined up with Partnership for a Drug-Free America to talk with health-care providers who encounter prescription drug abuse to find out what kinds of resources they need. A good step, I think. Dr. William Jacobs Jr., the president of Nexstep Integrated Pain Care, Inc. (a chronic-pain facility in Florida) emphasized the importance of getting opioids to those who need them and called for mandatory training in medical school curriculums on how to better assess the risk of substance abuse in patients. According to him, this doesn't currently exist. He also talked about NASPER, the National All Schedules Prescription Electronic Reporting Act. This is a nationwide prescription-monitoring program that would replace the current patchwork of individual state programs. NASPER was passed unanimously by Congress and was signed into law by George Bush, but so far remains unfunded.

The American Pharmacists Association sent Michael Moné to advocate on behalf of giving pharmacists access to patients' universal electronic medical records. No! This idea flies in the face of all privacy and ethical issues in the book. The only people who should have access to your medical records are your doctors, and in certain specific situations, members of your family.

Francine Haight is a nurse and mother who lost her son Ryan to a prescription drug overdose from pills he bought online. She formed a nonprofit organization called Ryan's Cause that focuses on education for families and communities about online pharmacies. Which is great, except that when Francine spoke about her son's overdose, she said he overdosed on Vicodin. This simply isn't true. Ryan Haight died from a combination of generic hydrocodone (Vicodin), morphine, Valium, and oxazepam. Francine's vilification of Vicodin alone at this national symposium, which was being broadcast live on television and picked up by media outlets everywhere, is, frankly, irresponsible. Misconceptions like this only contribute to the world's fear of using opioids for chronic pain relief. I feel terrible about Francine's loss, but she should have been clearer, especially in this massive forum, that the biggest danger comes not just from buying drugs online, but mixing the illegally bought prescription drugs together and with other substances.

Lastly came Lieutenant John Barnes from the Prince William/ Manassas Narcotics Task Force. Barnes spoke about trying to quell the sale of prescription drugs by the people who were legally prescribed them.

There was a Q & A session afterward. Unfortunately, since the symposium was open to the public, it attracted a bunch of student activists who used this opportunity to get close to DEA officials in order to bitch about why medicinal marijuana hadn't been legalized everywhere yet. I had my hand raised constantly, but was never called on.

The main point that I wanted to raise was why isn't anyone focusing on the actual nature and study of addiction itself? Isn't that where the heart of all this is?

A few months later, during the Super Bowl, I saw one of the new educational diversion control commercials that the symposium had promised would be coming out. In it, a drug dealer was complaining that business was down because his customers were now dipping into their parents' medicine cabinets.

They still weren't getting it. This was just one small fraction of diversion. Any drug dealer worth his salt carries at *least* benzos on him these days. It was "Just Say No" all over again.

It turns out that what may actually be the future cure of addiction is a vaccine. In the March 3, 2008, issue of *Newsweek*, the cover story's author, Jeneen Interlandi, wrote, "In the current jargon of the recovery movement, addiction to alcohol, drugs or nicotine is a 'bio-psycho-social-spiritual disorder.'" Sounds about right to me. She continued, "The emerging paradigm views addiction as a chronic relapsing brain disorder to be managed with all the tools at medicine's disposal. The addict's brain is malfunctioning, as surely as the pancreas in someone with diabetes."

It's too bad that paradigm didn't exist back in 2000. Dr. Alexander DeLuca might still have his job at Smithers.

The National Institute on Drug Abuse's director, Nora Volkow, is quoted as saying, "The future is clear. In 10 years we will be treating addiction as a disease, and that means with medicine."

An addiction vaccine would work the same way as a normal vaccine, but instead of targeting bacteria and viruses, the new vaccines would go after addictive chemicals. The proposed vaccines have drug molecules that have been attached to proteins from bacteria, and it's that bacterial protein that sets off an immune reaction. A cocaine vaccine has already entered its first big human trial, and vaccines against nicotine, heroin, and meth are also in the works.

Forget for a moment that this development raises all kinds of serious ethical questions. I know that if my mother had come to me at age nine to be vaccinated against future drug use instead of just having me sign that lame Nancy Reagan card, I would have run away. I'd probably have ended up somewhere a lot worse off than I am today. The real issue is that, no matter what, we are a supply-and-demand economy, whether it's for something legal or not.

No vaccine is going to change that.

CHAPTER 18

"Boredom Is God"

IT'S BEEN THREE YEARS since Heather left rehab, and her relationship with Derek couldn't be stronger—they're expecting their first baby. "I have to say," she tells me, "that being pregnant is better than any narcotic. I have no cravings for pills at all, and I feel relaxed and calm all the time. Which is weird for me, because I've always had so many panic issues my whole life. There's a part of my brain that's, like, 'When is the other shoe going to drop?'" She laughs.

Her pregnancy has healed her relationship with her mother too. "We talk every day now, it's been a total 180 degrees."

The big concern for both Derek and her has been whether to have an epidural, because of her past experiences with narcotics. There is a nonnarcotic version of an epidural, so I put Heather in contact with my childbirth-expert sister Erica to help explain all the different options that are available to her.

"My mom tells me, 'You can't say now if you're going to take the pain medication or not, and it's not like you're taking it to get high,'" Heather says. "I'm just not making any promises right now. I'm open to all options. I mean, I was never one of those girls who sat around and was, like, 'Oh, one day I'm going to have a baby.' But obviously, I am super, super excited."

• • •

Caleb is still living in the one-bedroom apartment located inside his parents' garage, but now his girlfriend has moved in too. "We don't have to pay rent, and I have a measure of independence," he says.

He's still getting his methadone and Oxy from the Christian with a love for booming sermons, only now Caleb has graduated to selling pills himself. The man sells Caleb 80-milligram Oxys for $25 apiece, way below their street value. Caleb, in turn sells them to other people at a markup, to make extra cash.

"I have one customer who is in the military, and somehow he gets around their drug testing. He's sort of a hokey guy, so I mark the pills up for him. But then I have another guy who is really sharp who buys them off me for $30, but he'll buy in bulk so I walk away with a lot more cash. He in turn drives out to the suburbs, marks them way up, and sells them to kids out there."

I ask Caleb if he gives any sort of kickback to his original source, since he's making so much money off him.

"No, but I probably should. We've developed such a good friendly business. I'm the only one of his customers that he still only charges $25 a pill."

Caleb originally planned that half of the profits he made from his drug deals would go into the bank and the other half would go to his own recreational use. But it's been more like an twenty-eighty split. He still does methadone when he's between Oxys to stave off withdrawal.

"The idea is for me and my girlfriend to eventually save up enough money to buy a house, instead of living in apartments and having all our money flow out into rent and bill expenses."

But with his drug money basically being pissed away, his main source of income is music, creating sample beats that get bought up by large television corporations for use as background music on programs.

"With the music publishing checks, I put about 90 percent of that into the bank and spend the 10 percent on Oxys," he says.

I ask him if he wants to quit.

"I totally want to stop," he says. "But for me, it's not because I've fucked up anything major, it's exclusively about my pocketbook. I feel like I function really well, and I love being on it. But I hate not being able to save money the way I want to. I want to have kids someday, have the home and everything. I have about $40,000 saved up already, but I shudder to think how much more I'd have if I didn't do pills. I don't even want to think about it."

The trouble is, Caleb and his girlfriend are utterly codependent. He'll argue that they've already spent too much money one week on pills; she'll pressure him and his resolve will weaken. And vice versa.

"Neither of us have the option of doing any kind of treatment," he says. "Our families know nothing about this lifestyle. If we want to stop, it will have to come from total willpower."

This sounds like bullshit to me. "What about going on Suboxone?" I ask. "It's easier to get off than methadone."

"I have a bottle of it in my drawer," he tells me.

"So why aren't you taking it?"

"I guess," he says, "because deep down, I don't really want to stop."

Jared has been completely sober for four years now. He's been promoted to a full editor within his Boston publishing company and his specialty is acquiring comedy books. He's been in a steady relationship for two years, remains on the antidepressant Effexor, and attends AA or NA meetings once a week.

He worries sometimes about what would happen if he ever had a medical condition that required him to take painkillers. "If it was absolutely necessary and impossible to get by without them," he says, "I would make sure I had someone else who knows about my history administering them to me and hiding them."

"There were times where I didn't go to an AA or NA meeting for months," he says. "But now I'm strictly once a week, including additional therapy."

Like Heather, Jared is still bothered by all the higher power talk that goes along with AA and NA, but he has stuck with it anyway.

"The thing that got me was that you don't have to do anything you don't want to. You can go and sit and still be using. Just because someone tells you to do something, it doesn't mean you have to do it. It's just good to go and listen. For me, I know that these people know something about the subject, and it's worth listening to what they have to say."

This surprises me, because I'd always been under the impression that if you are on something, you should *not* show up at a meeting.

"The rule is that you're not supposed to speak if you are on something," Jared explains. "You're supposed to listen. But the rules are also pretty meeting-specific. If it's an established meeting that has been around for a while, it usually develops its own culture. There's one group I go to where you can't even mention drugs, and another where it gets down and dirty and people say anything they want. It's a matter of finding the right one where you feel comfortable with the level of disclosure."

Jared still doesn't believe in God, but that certainly doesn't stop him from attending meetings. "God is defined as your understanding," he says. "The whole idea is putting your trust into something that isn't your own brain, because your own brain is all messed up. The language of the meetings says 'God' a lot, and I think that drives people away. It certainly drove me away in the beginning. But now I look at the higher power stuff as simply a tool for living after you've stopped doing drugs. The primary goal of these groups is to stop using, so even if you can just take away a sense of belonging and an understanding that these people have experienced things similar to you, well, I think that's worth something."

Out of everyone I interviewed for this book, I worry about Elliott the most. He has dropped out of the psychology department at Kent State University and signed up for an associate's degree at a branch school for graphic design. "I can't draw, so I can't get into the bachelor's program at Kent," he says. "The branch school is almost like a community college for people who just want regular local jobs, so I'll probably just find me a little job around here or something."

Instead of doing opiates, Elliott has switched back to Adderall, in addition to Celexa, his antidepressant. He now has a legitimate prescription for both, but is taking double the prescribed dose of Adderall. Whenever he goes out, he also caps it off with Soma, which he gets from his friend Sam for $2 a pill. "It just sharpens my senses somehow," he says. "It makes me able to talk to people and then not take rejection too hard."

I ask him if he really feels like he's getting constantly rejected when he doesn't take pills.

"I don't try without them, that's the thing. If you don't try, then you can't fail, right?"

The night after our last phone interview, I got a series of texts from Elliott. I knew he had been speeding hard on several Adderalls when we'd spoken earlier that day, and on top of that, he texted me that he had just drunk an entire bottle of Robitussin and taken a Tylenol 3 (the kind that contains codeine). *I'm rubbing God's belly*, he wrote.

I tried to convince him to stay with his friends and not go off by himself, but he was insistent on going home to listen to Velvet Underground alone. We texted throughout the night; I was terrified he was going to overdose. But by the next day he was fine. It had felt like he had been reaching out to me, and I remembered something he had told me the day before.

"I think I have the emotional response of a serial killer," he'd said. "You know how they say they kill so they can feel something? It's like that with human relationships for me."

Elliott wants desperately to connect with someone so he can feel. He can't connect with someone unless he's on pills, but when he's on pills, he doesn't care about anything. It's a vicious circle, and in his case, one that is still in continuous motion. The last I'd heard he had taken to snorting Imodium to get high. Apparently he read somewhere online that it was possible.

• • •

A few months after Emily and I returned from Ohio, Jess left her for another woman. She was totally blindsided. Even though it had been a long-distance relationship, it had felt solid to her. She'd known him since college, and during our trip they'd started talking marriage. But almost as soon as it was on, it was off. He ended it over the phone.

I went to her apartment the day it happened. A few of her other friends were there consoling her too, so I palmed her a Dilaudid and she smiled gratefully and disappeared into the bathroom for a moment.

Pills, in a way I hadn't even realized, had primarily defined her relationship with Jess. Emily and I had both retreated so deeply into our own heads that there wasn't much communication going on between us anymore. She was the female me. She was high every time she had been with Jess, on hydrocodone provided to the two of them by Julia and morphine provided by me via Candyman (morphine had become my latest favorite, and I'd wanted to make it hers, too). Whenever Jess had come to New York to visit her, they'd take pills straight away, splitting an 80-milligram morphine, the effects of which would last about two full days. They would stay in bed the entire time, their pupils too pinpointed to face the outside world. Appetites nonexistent and muscles limp.

"Believe me when I tell you that at the time, it felt like we were the only two people on Earth," she tells me now. "We were on the edge of something—maybe it was death—but it felt bigger than us and we were humbled by it. When we took away reality, essentially, that's when he could love me. Or that's what it feels like now."

I can still taste the reckless jealousy at this thought. At no point in my life, besides the occasional nights with Everett, had I had a partner who did pills as much as me and would want to disappear into the fog together.

Before meeting Jess, Emily used to tell her shrink that if she could just fall in love, she wouldn't need the pills. Of course that was a lie. Our need for pills made us immune to anything resembling real love. All it did was temporarily fill the void, and when the high wore off, we were the same depressed, pathetic people. She would pick endlessly at her spilt ends, and I would stare endlessly at any blank surface I could find.

"My shrink likes to say that people who take drugs are hypercreative and hyperaware—they have no patience for the slow grinding work of joy," Emily says. "But they're searching for something that they have intuited must exist. Like how people are always saying that true love takes time and work and it's not always fireworks and unicorns. For me it has to be everything at once. I want to get there yesterday. I want to jump in with everything and worry about the consequences later. With Jess, it was a rush and now it's over and done and he doesn't love me and I'm out of pills."

Emily and I went to our first NA meeting together, in a mammoth community center located off of Houston Street. She got more out of it than I did. I was restless and couldn't concentrate, but she interpreted the experience in a way that worked for her. "The twelve steps are supposed to be about helping an addict slow the fuck down," she explained to me after that first meeting. "To feel what we're supposed to feel and experience it all, even if it's painful, or worse, boring. We're supposed to get to joy. But to get to it authentically, the way you're meant to over the course of a life. And for me, that experience is the 'higher power' of the program. Boredom is God. And if I can get through that, I can turn that god into love."

The problem for me with this theory is that when I was a child, I made a promise to myself. I was ten, a year after I'd signed Nancy Reagan's card. I was already supposed to be in bed, my lights were out, but I was crouched by my front window, which faced the street. I could see Erica, who was sixteen, sitting on the steps below me. Soon a white van with no windows screeched to a halt in front of our house and the side door of the vehicle slid open. I could see it was packed with other teenagers, and a Duran Duran song poured out into the street. Erica ran down the front steps and leapt inside. The door slammed shut and the van sped off until the street was silent once more. I wanted to be in that van, sitting in the back, surrounded by friends, doing God knows what and driving to nowhere. All I had was the dark bedroom behind me, a silent house, and a gaping and waiting bed that I didn't want to go anywhere near. I wanted an escape and I swore an oath to myself with such conviction that it has been forever burned into my brain: *I will never lead a boring life.*

Emily has managed to stay off pills, but she is now a regular pot smoker. She refuses to give that one last drug up. "I'm too conscious now," she says. "I'm too hungry. Pot takes off the edge, but not with the same sense of isolation that pills gave me. I really do want to be happy, and I really do want to feel loved. If I'm absolutely honest with myself, I spend as much time thinking about pills as I do romanticizing my time with Jess. That's just what life is. I miss them. I miss them. I miss them."

It was a new psychiatrist who started to get me back on my feet. Ever since my last psychiatrist had moved to San Francisco, I'd avoided therapy. But after staying in bed for three straight days, curled up in the fetal position, unable to move, eat, or shower, I finally went to my general practitioner and asked for help. I told him that I thought I was suffering from severe depression but I left out the pill-popping part. I had lost seven pounds, and he was concerned enough about the way I looked to get me an immediate appointment with the psychiatrist who worked down the hall. I came clean to the shrink about the pills.

"Opiate addicts tend to be suffering from the most severe forms of depression—they feel totally empty inside," he told me. "The pills act as a security blanket, a protective bubble from all that hurts."

He'd nailed me in two sentences, even using my mental language about the bubble. We started out on antidepressants—Wellbutrin and Lexapro, and a prescription for Klonopin for when my anxiety got particularly bad. We had a long discussion about the Klonopin and whether I could be trusted with it, given my history. The antidepressants changed everything, though. I no longer wanted to hide in my room, watching movies alone. I wanted to go out again, be social and rediscover my friends. But most important of all, this new doctor challenged me. He didn't let me sit and babble away like my last one, he forced me to examine the words that came out of my mouth, to uncover the reasons why I say and do the things I do. He didn't tell me anything; he made *me* discover what's going on inside my head. It's an ongoing process, and one that has nowhere near run its course.

I still don't go to NA meetings for support. I appreciate their existence but I think that more than my discomfort with the higher power stuff, my resistance comes from an unwillingness to tell a room full of strangers what's really going on inside my head. Which is ironic, since here I am writing a book about exactly that. But I don't have to look at you, or have you slap me on the shoulder and say, "Good work, man," while stacking up a pile of metal folding chairs in some church basement after I've given a qualification. That would make me feel ten times more vulnerable. I'm still slowly climbing out of the bubble.

And Clover is still never far away.

CHAPTER 19

One Year Later

AN OLD FRIEND, Kate, had a new, younger girlfriend whose father is a politician. The girlfriend decided she wanted a massive blowout for her twenty-fifth birthday. Her parents rented her a farmhouse compound upstate with ten bedrooms, a barn that contained a pool table, darts, Ping-Pong, a full basketball court, and a massive field with a fire pit on top of a hill that overlooked rolling green hills. A bluegrass band from Bard College (excuse me, an "old-timey music" band—they insisted on being referred to as this) was hired to play. They also rented a giant Moon Bounce.

I discreetly popped the hydrocodone I'd bought from a friend on a whim the week before. The pills had become like Advil to me. I had to take five before I even felt the slightest wave of relief, but I figured that even with my continued access to Candyman, I should always buy pills whenever they were offered, just in case anything ever happened to him. By the time we arrived at the farmhouse, I was ten pills deep and felt only vaguely nauseated. They must have been pretty old. But I still had six Dilaudids inside Clover.

It was dark when we pulled into the driveway, but the house and nearby barn were flooded with light, and people poured out the front door to see who the new arrivals were. I was immediately accosted by two blonde acquaintances who rushed me upstairs, showed me my bedroom, and popped chocolate hearts stuffed with 'shrooms into my mouth. From that point on the weekend dissolved into forty-eight hours of continuous ingestion. The mushrooms never ran out. There was a never-ending supply of keg beer and tequila. I snorted coke, Dilaudid, Adderall, and Xanax. I smoked pot and kept eating my supply of shitty hydrocodone pills. I hurled myself around inside the Moon Bounce, daring the mesh sides to give way and send me flying out into the field, but they held strong. During the old-timey music band's set, the guitar player somehow lost all of his clothes except his baseball hat. His penis was shriveled tight up to his body against the chill night air. I was surrounded by kids ten years younger than me and I consumed ten times as many chemicals as any of them. I avoided my face anytime I passed a mirror inside the house because my eyes seemed to have retracted a good inch deeper inside my skull. I kept a hood draped over my face as much as possible. I was sharing a bedroom with slanted ceilings and two twin beds in the back of the house. My roommate was a girl with a mess of long wavy brown hair and a never-ending supply of cocaine. We'd usually try to go to sleep at the same time, staring up at the sharp angles above us and pretending that we were living in an episode of *Little House on the Prairie*.

I spent the weekend avoiding my hosts, Kate and her girlfriend. I knew they could tell I had been separating myself with the kids who held the hard drugs, and I felt their disapproval. They had wanted this to be a chill, relaxed weekend of friends. I wanted to obliterate my mind, because a twenty-three-year-old painter had just dumped me after I'd asked him to get an HIV test with me. We'd gotten messed up on blow and had unprotected sex a few times, but he couldn't handle the thought of getting tested and told me he didn't want to see me anymore. I knew this meant I had to get tested again, and was furious with myself for ending up back in the same place I was after Everett.

The truth was I'd been using again in secret for almost two months. There had been no major catalyst—I'd just floated right back into the bubble one day.

By Sunday, as everyone was packing up to leave, my body was

shaking uncontrollably. I only had two of my hydrocodones left. I'd left the rest of my Dilaudid at home, figuring they'd be wasted up here since I knew there would be so many other drugs available. Now I was panicking. I was terrified I wouldn't be able to make the trip home with just these two lame pills, and I barely did. I shook the entire time and kept up a steady stream of nervous babble to keep my mind off my body.

We made it home and I hit the lockbox immediately. My back was killing me—I'd had a small cyst removed from it right before I'd left for the party. It had been located right in that center spot on your back that's impossible to see from any angle in a mirror. I could feel the area with my hands, but it felt weird, just a small mass of stitches that stung when I touched them. I ate Dilaudid. The pain left. I forgot.

It took me three days to recover from the weekend. I stayed on the couch eating pills, still shaking, under blankets. I watched television until it just became nonsensical light and sound before my eyes. I drifted in and out of sleep, my dreams influenced by whatever was on, to the point where I had no idea if I'd actually watched a program or made it up entirely in my sleep.

I had an appointment to get my stitches removed on the following Wednesday, so I forced myself into the shower, into some clothes, into a cab. When I got to the dermatologist's office she told me to remove my shirt.

She was silent for a second.

"You ripped all your stitches out," she finally said. "I told you not to do any heavy lifting or exercise!"

"I didn't!" I said. I thought for a moment, rolling time backward in my mind.

"Oh wait," I said. "I jumped around a lot in a Moon Bounce."

She sighed. "I guess I never told you not to do *that*. I'll have to add that to my list of things I tell my patients not to do." I felt her run a gloved finger gently across the spot where the cyst had been.

"Well, it's a wet, red and white mess now. It'll definitely scar. I'll take out the stitches, but you need to make sure you keep it clean and bandaged and put this ointment on it twice a day," she said,

handful of hospital-style antibacterial packs. I felt the
out of my back, pulling on scabbed-over skin. It was a
it I could feel my skin resisting, trying to hold on to the
threads it had grown around.

I promised to call if anything weird happened to it and left,
climbing into a cab, careful to lean forward so my back wouldn't hit
the seat on the bumpy ride home.

That night I managed to pull the bandage off by myself, but I
couldn't reach the spot to apply the antibacterial gel and reapply a
bandage. Frustrated, I called the painter I'd just broken up with. Despite his weirdness about getting an HIV test I'd stayed friendly with
him, and we'd met for coffee a few times since he only lived three
blocks away from me.

"I can't deal with open wounds," he said. "They just really gross
me out. Sorry."

The only other person I could think of was Joey. He had started
dating someone new, and I almost preferred the idea of having an
infected abscess on my back than asking him for help. But he came
right over to clean my wound and dress the small gash.

"Why did we break up again?" he asked.

"Drugs," I sighed.

He kissed me before he left, careful to avoid the center of my
back when he hugged me good-bye.

The next day I got an email from Kate. She called me out for
keeping to myself during the party and doing too many drugs. I was
pissed. My immediate response was, *Fuck you, it was a party, we were
all there to have fun.* But one phrase in her email stuck out.

"More than anything in the world," she wrote, "I wish that you
would finally just say good-bye to pills. You are such an amazing,
beautiful person with a uniquely tender soul, and you have so much
awesome shit going on in your head and in your heart. It's utterly
heartbreaking to see all that beauty and life get smothered and
squashed by drugs. But that's exactly what happens. They take the
light out of your eyes, Joshua, and that is the biggest tragedy."

I knew she was right.

The light *was* going out of my eyes. For some time now, every time I'd looked in the mirror, I'd seen a dead person staring back at me. There was nothing behind the glassy, viscous surface of my eyes. They were strictly a functional body part now, incapable of conveying an ounce of feeling except maybe during a hysterical, manic laughing bout whenever something struck me as funny while I was fucked up.

I was high again on Dilaudid, but because of Kate's letter I had an overwhelming urge to go to a meeting. I'd been to a few more after my first one with Emily, as support for friends or research for this book, but never as someone willing to take any of it seriously. I looked online, found one in the West Village that started in the next fifteen minutes, walked out the door, and grabbed a cab. Every ounce of my body was fighting this decision, but as the cab made a sharp turn onto Houston, my body whipped a little to the left and I noticed a printed card stuck in the door handle on the opposite side of the backseat. It was a cream-colored card with brown lettering on it and it read: "If I can do what I ought to do, why don't I?" There was one week of a calendar year printed at the top—October 17 through October 23, no year. That was it.

I picked the card up and turned it over. There was nothing on the back. The message spooked me. It was as if the city gods had left this specific card here for me in this exact cab, knowing I'd find it.

The meeting itself was uneventful. It was packed, so I was shoved way in the back and could barely hear the speaker talk about his homelessness before finding sobriety. I was more interested in looking around me, surveying the crowd, seeing what sort of people actually came to these things. I felt a warm, loving feeling coming from everyone, but I wasn't sure if it was just the drugs I was on.

As soon as the meeting was over I saw people start making a beeline toward me, noticing that I was a newcomer, so I ran. People dole out their phone numbers as freely as coffee at these things, and I wanted none of that. If I was going to do this, it would be on my terms.

I went cold turkey the next day. I was residually high until the early afternoon, when I started to feel a nervousness creep around my skin and the inside of my brain. By late afternoon the nervousness was gearing up to a full-blown panic attack, so I took a Klonopin, which knocked me out for a little while. When I woke up I felt like I was coming down with the flu, so I took some NyQuil and slept in a fever state for the rest of the night. By the next morning I was full-on sick. I called Emily and told her I was going off pills, and she came over with juice and saltines. I writhed around on the couch across from her while she looked on with pity and I think not a small amount of fascination, or maybe just digust. My legs were kicking out uncontrollably from the sweat-soaked blanket on top of me. I tried to play it off like I was fine, just a little sick.

"You look like shit," she said. "And it kind of smells in here. Can I open a window?"

I pointed toward the one near the radiator that stayed open without having to prop anything up underneath it.

"How long is this going to last?" she asked.

"How long did it last for you?" I asked.

"I never got this bad," she said. There was no judgment in her voice, but I chose to find it there anyway.

"The last few times it was less than a week," I said as I felt my insides start to roll over. "I think I need to go to sleep now," I hinted and she left, telling me to call her if I needed anything at all. I barely made it to the bathroom in time after she left.

Kate came over next. She brought bananas, more juice, and Epsom salts.

"What am I supposed to do with these?" I asked, shaking the milk carton–shaped container they came in. "Aren't these for old people?"

"Soak in them," she told me. "It'll help with the muscle and bone pain."

After she left, I did. A few undissolved salt granules scratched against my back and feet as I writhed against the porcelain, my muscles still twitching.

This was hell, of my own making.

I could no longer pretend that I could do it on my own.

• • •

My sister Erica drove me to the airport. She was silent as we headed toward the Holland Tunnel. I'm pretty sure she could tell I was high. My head was slumped against the window. I couldn't tell if her silence was disappointment at my state or a struggle to find some sort of comforting words. She was always so in control, always knew what to say, and the quiet was freaking me out. I should have had Emily drive me or just taken a cab so I could just finish up my last bag of Dilaudid in peace.

Once we turned onto Varick Street and got stuck in tunnel traffic it became unbearable. I figured since I was going into rehab I'd better get used to just saying what was on my mind, so I turned to her and said, "I'm scared."

"Oh babe, I know," she said, and I could tell she'd prepared a speech and had just been waiting for the right moment.

"They're going to fill you up with a lot of higher power and God stuff," she said. "*Don't* let it scare you off. That higher power can be anything you want it to be. It can be Ollie, it can be your family . . . well, maybe not all of us, but it can be a fucking stuffed animal or the sky or a plant. Just substitute whatever it is you come up with for God whenever they bring up the word. I'd hate for you to get scared off over a matter of semantics."

"But it isn't just semantics," I slurred. "They want you to actually believe something."

"And you don't?" she asked.

"I have my own thing," I mumbled. "It's private. I don't like talking about it. That stuff is personal."

"Then you don't have to. When they make you say the serenity prayer, just silently say whatever you want in place of God. It can even be something as simple as love."

I couldn't have this conversation—it was too naked. We were in the tunnel now and the traffic was creeping. Exhaust fumes were pouring through the air vents in the cheap rental car she'd picked up. We both laughed nervously about how much we hated being in the tunnel and traded our imagined worst-case scenarios about the river above suddenly caving in on top of us, or having traffic come to a sudden standstill and being slowly driven mad over the course of several days. She told me a story about our stepfather, about how his car had once broken down in the middle of the tunnel and a police car had to nudge him all the way out from behind. I couldn't think of anything more mortifying, except maybe choking during dinner at a fancy restaurant.

When we reached the end of the tunnel I rolled the window down, stuck my head out, and breathed in huge gulps of what I quickly realized was New Jersey highway air. I rolled the window back up fast and tried to concentrate on even breaths. I needed another pill. I had my last four in a small plastic baggie in my right-hand pocket. I propped my left leg up on the seat to block the view of my right hand digging around in my pocket, unfastening the tiny zip lock on the bag, and fished out a pill. I hadn't brought Clover with me for fear of permanent confiscation. I pretended to be intensely interested in something outside the window as I slipped the pill into my mouth, faced forward, casually took a sip of the ginger ale I'd brought along for the ride, and swallowed.

By the time we made it to the airport I was about to pee myself, so Erica pretended to slowly unload all my bags while I ran inside to find a bathroom. But because of the pills it took me forever to start peeing, and by the time I got out all my bags were lined up on the sidewalk, with Erica nervously eyeing a long line of impatient cars behind her.

"All right, this is it," I said. I was too doped up to actually cry, but the weight of self-disgust pulled my shoulders so far forward and down that I looked like an old man, hobbling onward to my last ever evening walk before toppling over in a death roll.

Erica, who usually cries during parades, was oddly stoic as she hugged me good-bye. I read it as disappointment in me, but by that point I knew I was just having a big old pity party for myself. At the rate I was going I would have taken anything slightly bitchy said to me by an exhausted and bored airport security guard as a personal attack on my numerous failed attempts at getting off pills for good.

Few trips are as lonely, depressing, and loaded with finality as a solo trip to rehab. I'd watched my share of the television show *Intervention*, and had always thought how weird it would be to have a stranger accompany you on that journey. But now I wished I had someone with me who knew what was up.

Since I was going alone I was making sure to stay as high as I possibly could until the last possible moment. I think this is typical. I thought of Jared and Heather, high on their final trips too. I can't imagine an addict having it any other way. The flight was boarding by the time I arrived at the gate. I had none of my usual flying fears as we took off—my body was soaring at the same rate as the plane.

I cleaned the grease off the airplane window with my complimentary water and napkin, so I could lean my face against it and stare at the ground below us. Tiny lights, square after square of perfectly angled, plotted-out land. I had to transfer in Atlanta, the exact opposite direction of my final destination in Minnesota. I like the rocking chairs in the Atlanta airport, but I had to walk fast to catch my connection. The flight to Minneapolis was half empty so I got to stretch out my legs on the seats next to me. As we took off I swallowed my last three pills and stuck the small, empty zip-lock drug baggie inside a copy of the *SkyMall* catalog. The finality of this act made me panic. I still had a one last high left on its way, but I knew it was going to be a long slide downhill.

20

Onward

THE ADMISSION PROCESS WAS tedious. A tie-dyed-shirt–wearing technician went through page after page of paperwork, asking all the same questions I'd been asked when I had first called. The nurse brought me a cafeteria tray of crackers, three bananas, and some Kool-Aid, then sat down and asked me all the same questions again while taking my vital signs and weighing me. She asked me when the last time I'd used was and I told her about two hours ago. She made me hold my arms out in front of me, and I was shocked at just how badly my hands and arms were shaking. She had me stick out my tongue, which flopped up and down involuntarily. I knew I'd developed a slight tremor, but I hadn't realized it was inside my mouth as well.

I zoned out. She asked me if I felt like harming or killing anyone, and I started laughing.

"Oh good," she said. "I've yet to have anyone say yes to that, but I'm always a little nervous when I get to that part."

When we were finally done she showed me to a room next to the nurse's station with three empty beds.

"This is the detox room. We'll keep you in here for the first seventy-two hours," the tech told me. He searched my suitcase and made me turn my pockets inside out, confiscating my cell phone, all of my prescriptions, and a bottle of witch hazel because it contained alcohol. He then handed me a pair of flip-flops in a plastic bag. "For the shower," he explained.

I made my way to the bathroom and discovered three showers located around a corner from the stalls, and I stripped down and stepped inside one, pulling the curtain shut. I showered quickly, nervous that I was going to pass out and crack my head open. After I dried off, I put on a pair of pajama bottoms and a T-shirt and drifted back down the hallway full of closed doors with patients' names on them. Some were decorated with photos from magazines or flowers made of pipe cleaners.

As I passed the nurse's station the tech called out that he would be checking on me periodically through the night. "Just raise your hand if you are still awake when I come in with the flashlight," he said. "And I don't knock," he added rather ominously. I took this to mean no sleeping naked or masturbating. He had nothing to worry about on either account. Whatever libido I had left had long been killed, and my body was a scrawny, acne-ridden mess—I had no interest in being naked. I crawled into bed and didn't wake up for nineteen hours, except for a few periodic moments when a nurse would sit gently on the side of my bed and take my blood pressure and temperature.

When I finally opened my eyes for good I could hear people milling about outside my door in the main room. I sat up and my muscles screamed. I couldn't straighten my shoulders and I shuffled, stooped over, to my suitcase to pull out jeans, a T-shirt, and a hoodie. I slid the shower flip-flops on and headed toward the door. I couldn't remember the last time I'd taken any of my antidepressants. I paused before opening the door, steeling myself, then swung it open.

There were maybe twenty people in the main lobby room. All the phones were being used, and some people were sitting at the main table reading or talking. I shuffled over to the nurse's station, avoiding eye contact, but immediately people started coming up and introducing themselves to me. I mumbled hello, avoided eye contact.

"You're up!" the nurse said, waving toward a chair behind the station's partition. "Sit down." She took my vitals again, checked my hands and tongue, which were both still doing the Saint Vitus dance on their own.

"You must feel like shit," she said.

I nodded.

"We're putting you on Suboxone. It will help."

She left and went into a back room to fetch my meds, came back, and handed me a cup filled with water for my antidepressants, which I swallowed in one gulp. I put it down and spilled the orange Suboxone out of the second cup. She handed me the water again.

"Isn't this supposed to just dissolve under your tongue?" I asked, dimly remembering that from my research for this book.

"Really?" she asked. She had no clue.

I slipped the orange pill under my tongue and it slowly melted. It tasted like orange-flavored baby aspirin but much more bitter. I waited for it to disappear completely then drank deep from the cup of water. There was still a sharp metallic taste under my tongue, so I grabbed some candy from the table behind me and sucked on a lollipop. The room had emptied out suddenly.

"Where is everyone?" I asked.

"It's inspirational movie time upstairs in the lounge," she said, pointing to a set of stairs behind me. "You can go watch it or you can go back to bed for a while. It's your choice."

I decided to go check out the movie, so I headed up the stairs, which emptied into a large lounge with windows on all sides. Every sofa and inch of floor space was covered with people. I sat near the top of the stairs, too scared to make my way into the crowd to find a spot closer to the television, but an older guy saw me and moved over, patting the floor next to him. I got up and squeezed in, whispering thanks, and he smiled back.

I got my first good look at the television screen and realized that the "inspirational movie" they were watching was *Priscilla, Queen of the Desert*, which made *no* sense to me because they were at the scene where one of the drag queens was riffling through a giant bowl of pills and plucking out the ones she wanted, chasing them down with a bottle of vodka.

And as my mind went trigger-happy at the sight of the pills, I suddenly realized I was starting to feel amazingly, deliciously, exquisitely high.

I suddenly remembered an interview with one of my doctors for this book, from what seemed like a million years ago. He had told me that if you had been off other opiates for at least twenty-four hours, Suboxone could make you high before it leveled out in your system. I counted back the hours. It had definitely been more than twenty-four hours since my last Dilaudid. I have an incredibly fast metabolism too. I rolled onto my back and looked up at the screen. The movie, which I'd never really liked, suddenly seemed full of lovely colors and gorgeous desert landscapes. I took off my hoodie and stuffed it under my head to make a pillow. I rolled up my sleeves and stretched my arms upward, flexing my fingers. I noticed a large bowl of candy a few people away, so I got up on all fours and crawled over to it, grabbing a bunch of Dum Dums. Another opiate wave hit me as I relaxed back in my spot. I tried to remember what I'd learned about Suboxone. It was buprenorphine, the partial analgesic, but with naloxone added to it. It can get you high at first, but the naloxone keeps you from overdosing or even feeling any effect if you snorted or injected it. Whatever, this was enough opiate for me. I felt incredible.

I was going to love rehab.

Sleep came easily that night, and when I woke up there was a single paper cup by my bedside with my antidepressants and more Suboxone. I still felt a little high from the night before, so I broke the Suboxone in half, took one side and hid the other in my pocket, then took my other pills. I slipped on the same clothes I'd worn before, made my bed, and wandered out into the main room. It was dead silent.

"Where is everyone?" I asked the nurse on duty, a new one I didn't recognize.

"Small group," she said. "Come here. I need to take your vitals."

I sat back down at the patient chair, felt the now familiar pressure on my upper arm as she pumped a small black plastic bulb.

"So, am I going to get to meet with anyone? Like a doctor or a counselor?" I asked. My arms were still shaking pretty badly, but my head felt a little clearer.

"Eventually," she said. "Just rest for now. Go to groups if you want. There's a schedule in your folder. Who is your buddy?"

I remembered something from the night I checked in, I was supposed to be getting a "buddy," another patient who was supposed to show me the ropes.

"It's in my folder," I said. "I'll find out."

"You missed breakfast," she called out after me.

"Not hungry," I said.

I went back into my room and pulled out all the paperwork I'd been given when I'd checked in. My buddy was supposed to be somebody named Chuck.

I fell back asleep until I heard commotion again in the main room. I opened the door and grabbed the first person I could find and asked him if he knew who Chuck was.

"That's me. You Joshua?" he asked. "I'm your buddy. I was just coming to find you."

He had a lazy eye, and I couldn't figure out which one was looking at me. I subtly leaned to the right, then to the left, to see which one followed me the most directly. It was unclear.

"Do you have your paperwork?" he asked. "There's a whole checklist of stuff we're supposed to do together. I've never been a buddy before, so I don't really know how to do this."

I grabbed my folder and found the sheet he was talking about. According to it he was supposed to show me around, sit with me for my first three meals, explain the weeklong schedule, and help me complete something called "20 Questions," a list of pretty generic questions about my substance abuse issues and what I was hoping to get out of recovery. I'd already started working on them. They were basically the same questions I'd been asked when I'd initially called about being admitted and then had to repeat, twice, upon my actual admission. This would mark the fourth time I had to answer questions about what drugs I used and why I thought I used them and how frequently. But one question in particular really bothered me.

It was worded, "Does your use lead you to hang out with low companions?"

Low companions? What kind of classist bullshit was this? I'm sure I was considered a "low companion" to people on many occasions. My answer to this inquiry was, *I find this question incredibly offensive. Every human being has worth, regardless of whether or not they have a drug problem.*

Chuck told me he'd come and grab me for dinner and we'd figure out a time to go over my twenty questions. I went back to the detox room and lay down on my bed. I was feeling violently sick as the Suboxone wore off, and just as I was about to take the half I'd hidden, a nurse walked in with more. I let the full pill dissolve this time under my tongue, not bothering to wash it down with anything, instead seeing if I could get every single tiny, minuscule granule to dissipate. I fell asleep with what felt like sand in my mouth.

I woke up, high. Chuck was yelling at me through my open door. "Let's go, buddy," he roared. I stumbled out of bed and up to the cafeteria for my first official meal. I took one look at the hot-food area and turned green. "There's a salad bar over there for you veggies," Chuck said, noticing my hesitation. For some reason everyone thinks I'm a vegetarian when they first meet me, but in this case I didn't care, salad was all I could handle. I realized it had been two days since I'd eaten anything of substance, but I still had no appetite.

I collected my tray and utensils and followed Chuck's waving hand to the seat he'd saved next to him. As I sat down everyone tried to shake my hand at once, asking a million questions about where I was from and what I was in for. It was too much. I got up to get myself a drink, but all I could find was Kool-Aid. It wasn't the Kool-Aid I remembered getting at friends' houses in my youth; it was some bizarre flavor I couldn't identify. It had an acidic tinge to it, like a liquefied Sour Patch Kid.

I sat back down and picked at my salad, trying to answer as many questions as I could with as few words as possible.

The Suboxone had killed my appetite, so I excused myself early and went back to bed, thankful that the staff was being so lenient with me about participation. It didn't last long though. When I woke up again there was a tech standing in my doorway.

"You should get up and go to a group," he said. "They're starting one upstairs right now."

I stopped by the nurse's station to get more Suboxone, which I split in half and palmed so I'd have more for later, and headed upstairs just in time for the meeting to start. There was a guy I didn't recognize standing at the front of the room. "Welcome to Crystal Meth Anonymous," he began.

I got up and walked back downstairs. The tech gave me a sharp look. "What?" he asked annoyed.

"I don't belong up there," I said. "It's a crystal meth meeting. I don't do that shit."

"Yes, you do belong up there," he sighed. "Everyone is required to attend. We have people come from the outside to lead that group."

"But I hate crystal meth," I said. "I only tried it once, years ago, and it was, like, sick!"

"You can still get something out of the meeting," he said in a tone that signaled the discussion was over. "Go back upstairs."

I went back up, annoyed. The guy at the front of the room was reading a passage from an NA book. I tuned out and surveyed the crowd instead. I recognized almost everyone from the cafeteria earlier, but there was a group of older guys sitting together who I figured must be the meth addicts from the outside. They looked like depressed, middle-aged gay guys. I knew I was supposed to relate to what they were saying in terms of the nature of addiction itself. But once the Big Book reading was over, everyone started telling stories of five-day benders filled with anonymous bare-back sex that ended with them testing positive for HIV and anal warts.

Except for my fuck-ups with Everett and the painter, when I was on pills I'd mostly just watch reality TV on VH1. If I was feeling especially ambitious, I would go get a 7Up from the deli downstairs. Maybe text a few people, just to say hi. This meeting was doing nothing for me, except instilling a guilt-ridden sense of self-congratulation for never becoming a meth head. That said, the stories were fascinating, and the more they poured out, the sadder I became. How had I gotten so lucky? But then I remembered where I was and why I was here.

The routine settled in fast. I was moved from the detox room and placed in a room directly across from the men's showers, with two roommates, both of whom were in for crystal meth and sex addiction. I'd been in rehab for three days and still hadn't met one on one with any sort of counselor. In my small-group therapy sessions I was just told to keep working on the assignments given to me in my welcome notebook. They included what seemed like Sunday school assignments for drug addicts—make a collage poster of my "higher power." Make another collage portraying how being gay has affected my life. Complete a thorough reflection of my chemical-use history and present it in group therapy.

That last one made me nervous. I asked Chuck what it meant exactly.

"You have to make a list, year by year, of every drug or drink you've ever taken, from the time you started using until the present," he told me. "And add up how much it all ended up costing you."

"How the hell am I possibly supposed to remember all that?" I asked. "I got high for the first time when I was thirteen."

He shrugged. "Just estimate as best you can."

I decided to put off that assignment for as long as possible and work on the collages first. During a free period I went into the art room to check out the supplies, which consisted of ripped-up copies of *Maxim, Newsweek,* and *Good Housekeeping,* poster board, glue sticks, and pipe cleaners. A few other collages were spread out to dry. One had a photo of a ripped, shirtless guy from what must have been an Axe Body Spray ad plastered in the center, with the word *Sex* pasted above it. The rest of the poster just had smaller photos of magazine guys or bottles of liquor pasted at random angles with words like *Love, Depressed, Power, Lost,* and *Alive* cut out from headlines and posted above each one. One had the headline, "Taking things for granted" pasted right above a close-up shot of four hot dogs in buns.

I was horrified and cracking up at the same time. I decided to collect as many of these as I possibly could and curate some sort of exhibition on bad rehab art as soon as I got out. I rifled through the stacks of magazines to see if there was anything at all to work with for my own, but the best I could come up with was a three-year-old copy of *National Geographic* that looked like it had been attacked by Freddy Krueger. I made a mental note to ask my friends to send me some decent magazines, and to show the ridiculous collages to my new friend, Richard.

I'd made friends with Richard right after he'd checked in, which was a few days after me. He was a marketing executive from New York, and was inside for cocaine addiction. We became immediate friends, initially because of the other friends we quickly discovered we had in common. But it became more than that. He was wise and funny and bearishly cute. He always had something insightful to say during any of our large-group sessions, and he made me feel guilty for not taking this experience that seriously. Richard really wanted to create a change in his life, whereas I was starting to feel as though my friend Kate had bullied me into this situation. Yes, I knew I had a pill problem. But I'd also had my fair share of late-night coke benders with Kate over the years. There's an unspoken hypocrisy among many drug users—casual ones and addicts alike. People who love pot look down on cokeheads. Cokeheads think heroin users are insane. And heroin users just don't give a shit about any of it.

I was still being given Suboxone, and was still palming halves of it regularly and hiding it inside an envelope in a box of stationery I'd brought with me. After a week I had completely weaned myself off it, but they were still doling it out, and by the time ten days had passed I had a pretty huge stash. I saved it for outings.

Once a week, we'd get to go on some sort of field trip, either to a movie or bowling or some sort of park. It always included a stop at Wal-Mart or Target to pick up essentials. We also had several trips during the week to off-site locations like other NA or AA meetings, or church, but only if you wanted to go. I saved my Suboxone for those trips, so I could enjoy being high in a different atmosphere than the depressing institute I was trapped in. I didn't question my abuse of the system at all. After I had stopped feeling so sick from withdrawal, I was beyond feeling pissed at my friends and was now just flat-out furious that I had agreed to check myself into this place

I didn't need it.

The staff was insane.

My BlackBerry had been confiscated.

None of this was helping my anti-authority complex. I began to look for ways to break the rules, just to satisfy what felt like an incurable itch inside my brain. We weren't supposed to smoke during breaks in small-group sessions, so I always snuck out behind the gym and lit up during our five-minute session release. The dress code said we weren't supposed to wear hats or hoodies—I guess because they hid our faces. I wore both together whenever possible. We weren't allowed to have energy drinks, so I'd buy one whenever we were on an outing and quickly pound it before a tech could see me. My roommates were even more brazen: they would hop out the window and run across the street to the gas station to bring us back cigarettes and Red Bull. (The energy-drink rule especially made no sense, seeing as how the soda machine on the premises was filled with a never-ending supply of Mountain Dew.)

I was constantly stopping by the administrative office to get my BlackBerry out of the safe and check for messages. Richard told me he had done it a few times for work and it was no big deal, so I made friends with the people in the office and they always let me grab my phone after lunch. My BlackBerry was inside a large paper envelope in a locked file cabinet, and after the first few times, they'd just let me open it myself and pull it out, since the key to the file cabinet was always still in the lock. I'd check my messages, reply to the important ones, turn it off, and put it back away.

One day I got an email from the editor in chief of *Spin* magazine, asking me if I'd like to come in and interview for a senior editor position. I was psyched and trying to figure out the best way to reply (definitely interested, on vacation overseas, back in a few weeks?) when the clinical services director, a woman named Susan who had curly gray hair and always wore brightly colored vests with floral, floor-length skirts, walked by. She had a total shit-fit.

"Who gave you permission to use your phone?" she shrieked.

"Ummm . . ." I said, looking helplessly at the staff cowering behind their desks. I didn't want to rat any of them out. "I just thought I was allowed to."

"You're not," she snapped. "You need to get a pass from your adviser."

I was fourteen days into the program at this point and had yet to meet with any sort of adviser one on one. Everyone kept pushing it off, saying, "Keep working on your assignments."

"Sorry." I shrugged, turning the phone off, slipping it back into its envelope, and shutting the file cabinet door.

"And take your hat off," she snapped.

I glared at her, pulled my cap off, and stuck it in my back pocket.

The next morning, after daily affirmations, where we had to go around the room and say three things we liked about ourselves (I usually said, *I have friends who care, I'm a good person,* and *I'm resilient*), Susan, who was wearing another one of her hideous skirt-vest combos, made an announcement. She was carrying a silver stick with a star on the top and metallic blue streamers hanging down from it.

"I think I need to remind you all of a few of our rules," she said sweetly, patting the magic wand in her lap to emphasize each word. "If you have a phone in our safe, you must get a written pass from your adviser in order to check your messages. Also, hats are not allowed. It says this clearly in our rule book."

About half the people in the room were wearing hats. I raised my hand.

"That same rule book says that we are allowed up to fifteen minutes a day on the computer to check our email," I said evenly. "There is no computer here."

"Um, yes, it's broken," she said. "I'll check on the status of that. In the meantime, *no hats.*"

Maybe a third of the people in the room sighed and removed their baseball caps and hoods. I wasn't one of them. Susan and I stared at each other in silence for a few seconds before she said, "Are any more of you going to comply?"

The room was silent. Susan and I kept up our steady gaze.

"All right, then," she said and walked out of the room. Everyone immediately put their caps back on, pulled their hoodies back up, and filed out of the room to go to small group. Susan was seriously starting to piss me off, but she was the least of my problems. I had to figure out a way to reply to *Spin*. I went to my counselor, who I *still* hadn't met with one on one for a session, and explained what happened with my phone.

"Yeah, you're not supposed to do that," she said, tssking a little.

"Well, can I have a pass?" I asked.

"Let's wait a few days until Susan has calmed down," she told me.

I was furious, but I let it slide because that afternoon I had an outing. I celebrated in my usual style by popping a Suboxone right before we left. The outing group I had been assigned to was made up of about ten people, and we had all voted earlier to go to the *Sex and the City* movie. One of the techs, Amy, who was taking us out in the big white rehab van, had to clear any chosen activity with Susan first. Amy came back looking dejected.

"Susan rejected *Sex and the City* as an appropriate activity," she said.

"You're fucking kidding me," I said. "Why?"

"Um, she didn't even know what it was, but she didn't like that it had the word 'sex' in the title. She thought it might be a trigger for some of you."

I looked at the group of people around me—a bunch of older, methed-out gay dudes, one bearded guy who was still trembling so bad from alcohol withdrawal that he looked like he was having a permanent seizure, and my buddy Richard. There was no way any kind of sex portrayed in that film would have been a trigger for any of us. I would have understood if Susan had said something about the fact that there would probably be drinking in the movie, but even that was a lame excuse, since my first night there, Susan had shown us that movie about alcoholic, pill-popping drag queens.

Luckily the Suboxone started to kick in and I relaxed and agreed to go see the new Indiana Jones movie instead. But I was becoming pretty sure that Susan had it in for me.

We drove to the mall where the movie was playing and had about forty minutes to kill before it began, so we went to Barnes & Noble, where I picked up copies of every nature, photography, and art magazine I could find for my collages.

I don't remember much of the movie, I was too busy enjoying my high and thinking how Cate Blanchett looked perfect and how awful it would be to be eaten alive by ants. I remembered poking spiderwebs with my *Star Wars* figures when I was a kid to see if I could get a spider to attack, and then I remembered how obsessed I'd been with my He-Man Evil-lyn toy and how I'd even made her a cloth cape cut from an old blue T-shirt and how her magic crystal ball wand glowed in the dark, and then suddenly the movie was over.

We stopped at Target on the way home. I wandered the store aisles, high, my favorite activity ever since day one on Vicodin, so many years ago. I bought a T-shirt with a lion on it, some linen spray for my sheets to get rid of the hospital smell. I also bought two Red Bulls that I pounded in succession a foot away from the cash register after purchase.

When we got back to the rehab I started leafing through my magazines, cutting out pictures for my posters. It was kind of fun. I felt like a kid working on a junior high art project, and I really wanted to impress the teacher.

I spent all my free periods during the weekend working on my posters, and was embarrassingly proud of the end results. You couldn't see a single white spot of the poster board on either of them. The one that was supposed to be about how I felt about being gay was centered around a blurry photograph of a guy lying shirtless in a pile of leaves next to a tree, surrounded by other images of drawings and photographs of people with animal masks on or bags tied around their heads landscapes by Gustave Courbet, 1970s photos of drunk parents, and a large shot of a car that had crashed into a McDonald's restaurant. The collage was awful and beyond pretentious. I loved it.

The higher power one was harder. I still had no idea what my higher power was. I considered leaving it blank, as an homage to the phrase "God is boredom" that Emily had uttered so long ago, but instead found large photos of a raven and an ancient skull, and stuck them in the center of tons of landscape shots. The earth, animals, and death all seemed like things I could concretely believe in.

I was two assignments down. I raced through my reading homework, wrote journal entries about my responses to them, writing exactly what I knew the therapists wanted to hear. I had pretend "breakthroughs" about discovering my addictive behavior, things I already knew about myself, but faked that they were revelations.

The only thing I wasn't faking at this point were my feelings for my fellow patients. I felt strongly for almost all of them, which I learned is typical for most people entering rehab for the first time. It's much easier to focus on other people's problems than your own. But I think my feelings for them went beyond just that. I'd never been exposed to so much raw pain at once. I wanted to heal everyone. During group sessions, when someone would reveal something particularly horrifying or ask for advice about situations back at home, I would offer up honest suggestions and support. As much as I was resisting the program, I badly wanted it to work for these other people. I just didn't trust that rehab could work for me, because I knew I couldn't trust myself. I was fighting it every step of the way.

I started working on my chemical-use history. I traveled back in time, deciding to break it up into sections: high school, college, and then graduation to the present. I found it was pretty easy to come up with estimations. I remembered when I'd tried different drugs for the first time, my frequency of use. The monetary values were pretty easy to calculate too, although I started growing increasingly uncomfortable as the numbers kept rising and rising, hitting six figures, then, shockingly, seven, since I was told I was supposed to include expense account drinks for work over the years too.

I took another one of my hidden Suboxones that night.

I knew that I needed to get back to the guy from *Spin*, and missed being able to text Emily and Steph whenever I wanted. I hated the idea of having to ask for a pass to use a phone that belonged to me, loathed the authority being lorded over me. So I formulated a plan.

I don't remember how I first learned that I could pick locks—it's just something I discovered how to do at a very early age. And the locks in this particular facility were the easiest kind of all, the ones that only required a driver's license to slip into the slit on the inside of the door, find the curve of the lock, and push it back into the door itself, thus releasing it. I examined all the door handles in the building and they seemed to all operate by this same mechanism. One night during our evening group I slipped out, pretending I needed to use the bathroom, and went downstairs to the art room, which I knew had already been locked for the day. I slid my license in and the door popped open with barely any resistance. I popped the lock on the door handle back in from the inside and gently closed it. The lock stayed firm.

The next day was family visiting hours, and even better, the weather had just turned beautiful, so I knew most people would be outside. Those of us who didn't have visitors were just supposed to use the free time to work on our assignments, but nobody monitored our exact location in the building.

The administrative office was located in a hallway that ended with the cafeteria on one end, and looked directly into the large meeting room on the other. If you turned right at the end that looked into the meeting room, you hit the main entrance and the offices of all the therapists.

My only chance to get in the office was during these visiting hours, when everyone would be outside. Coincidentally, the therapists had scheduled an internal meeting in their main office, directly around the corner from the room I needed to break into.

I knew I needed a lookout, and Richard was game.

"All you have to do is stand at that corner, pretend to be reading, and knock on my side of the hallway if anyone starts coming," I told him. "Make the knocking sound like you're just doing something casual and rhythmic, like you have a song in your head and you're tapping out the notes."

"No problem," he shrugged.

"Do you want me to get yours too?" I offered. But he declined, not wanting to break the rules. *His loss*, I thought, but his will and determination to stick to the program suddenly made me feel uneasy. I buried the thoughts quickly.

The right time finally arrived. I had been pretending to read the bulletin board outside the cafeteria but was secretly waiting for the cook to finish cleaning up and head home. The lights finally went out, and I whistled to Richard, who was sitting in my sightline in the main room. Everyone was outside except for one mother and son who were sitting in the main room, but they were out of sight from the hallway. I could hear the therapists' distant voices coming from around the corner.

Richard took his place at the end of the hallway, leaning casually in a way that he could see if anyone was coming and easily reach around and knock on my side. I pulled out my driver's license and went to work. But nothing happened. I tried three, then four times, but each time I could feel my license bending with resistance. It was starting to tear. I kept digging away at it anyway, until I heard a faint rap to my left. I looked up and saw Richard walking back into the main room. I quickly tried to pull my license out of the door but it was stuck. My body flooded with panic as I kept wiggling it around until it finally slipped out. I followed him in and sat next to him on a couch.

"They must use a stronger lock on the offices," I said under my breath. "I can't get in. Fuck."

"That sucks," he said. "False alarm anyway, she turned the other direction and went into the bathroom."

I felt like I was disappointing him, especially after I'd bragged about being able to get in and playing secret agent by setting him up as my lookout.

I left him in there and went back to my room, stewing inside. I stretched out on my bed and examined my license, which now had a small, crumpled dent in it, just under my photograph. I bent it back and forth. It was too floppy for a firmer office lock. I needed a credit card. But I didn't want to risk mangling mine, since I was essentially trapped in Minnesota. I looked in my wallet, and discovered my old Condé Nast Aetna dental and health insurance cards. I had been paying for Condé Nast's COBRA coverage ever since *Jane* folded. It was the only reason I'd been able to afford rehab, since it was covered under my continued-benefits program.

The cards were white and made out of a thick, firm, yet pliable plastic. Even better than a credit card. I picked up the dental card and headed back upstairs. Richard was still reading and I motioned to him from the doorway.

"Round two," I whispered. "I can't give this up, now that I've started."

He took his position again and I went to work. The door still wouldn't budge. I maneuvered the card in and out, back and forth, trying to get it to slide just enough down the sloping curve of the lock to pop it in, but it wasn't working. I felt the card buckling in resistance, I was mangling it as I shoved harder and harder and just as I was about to give up, the door popped open.

Richard must have heard the sound because I looked up fast at him and his eyes widened. I mouthed *Be right back* and stepped inside the office, shutting the door quietly behind me. I crossed the darkened room, fishing out the two paper clips in my pocket to get at the locked file cabinet, but was relieved to see that the key was still sticking out of it.

I dropped to my knees, opened the bottom file where I'd last placed my envelope, and slipped my BlackBerry and charger inside the sleeve of my hoodie. I could hear the muffled voices of the therapists through one wall of the office. I shut the cabinet door, making sure the key was in the same position as before. I opened the office door an inch, then another, before daring myself to stick my head out and look at Richard. He saw me and motioned me out with a thumbs-up sign. "I can't believe that worked," Richard said, laughing.

"I'm a very determined person," I said.

The following Monday I had to present my chemical-use history to my small group. I thought I'd just be reading my lists out loud, but they sat me down in front of a large easel with a massive drawing pad on it.

"Whatever you do, don't look behind you," one of the patients said.

It was a gorgeous day, so we were having small group outside. I leaned back in my chair, shielded my eyes from the sun, and started reading off my list. I started strong, listing the first time I'd gotten drunk, the first time I'd smoked pot, and then averaging out the frequency with which I'd continued those drugs and others through high school. By the time I'd gotten to my college years I was hunched over in my chair, mumbling out the names of drugs, the cost, the frequency. The list never ended. I kept talking and talking and talking as the sun beat down on me, baking my thighs inside my black jeans, making the crooks of my arms sweat.

My voice was trembling by the time I finished up.

"Are you ready to look behind you?" the therapist asked, when I'd finally wrapped it all up.

"Okay," I said. I couldn't figure out what the big deal was, but felt a sense of dread creeping up on me. I turned slowly in my seat.

The huge piece of paper was almost entirely black with ink. Years and lists of drugs and dollar amounts were crammed together so tightly that barely any white space was left on the paper. *This is what the inside of my brain has become*, I thought to myself. *It used to be a clean slate.*

"Not so confident now, are you?" one of the other patients cackled.

Had I been acting overly confident? I was growing more and more upset. Group was over, and I stood up and walked over to the easel, trying to make out the words listed on it. The writing was so tiny that the words flowed together in one continuous river of ink.

"Can I keep this?" I asked the group leader.

"Sure," she said. "You can burn it at the bonfire tonight if you want. Sometimes that helps people."

So lame, I thought to myself, but suddenly I wanted nothing more than to see this receipt of my past go up in flames. I ripped the giant piece of paper off and rolled it into a poster-sized tube, tucked it under my arm, and headed back into the building.

My roommates weren't in so I pulled my BlackBerry out from its hiding place under the mattress and checked my messages. I hadn't heard back from the *Spin* editor yet, and the messages I'd been getting from Emily and Stephanie were brief and terse. Neither of them were too happy that I'd broken into the office. "Rather counterproductive, wouldn't you say?" read one text. I stuck the phone back under the mattress. I tried to get angry at them, but the anger was being overridden by something more complicated. I couldn't get that black piece of paper out of my head. It sat un-curling on the desk next to my bed and I could see the shadow of darkness inside it. The sum of me: my years of drugs, ripped from my brain and splattered onto a canvas. Everything I'd kept private was now on display in permanent marker. I couldn't wait to see it burn.

My BlackBerry vibrated underneath me, sending a shiver of something that I was beginning to recognize as guilt through my body. I left it under the mattress. Whatever the message was, it wasn't meant for me yet.

The fire grew quickly, its heat and smoke being pushed by the wind directly in my face. My eyes filled with water and ash, but I didn't budge. Everyone was sitting in a circle around the large burning pit, saying their nightly affirmations, which were essentially the same as morning affirmations—encouraging, happy thoughts only, but you could also say things you were grateful for about anything that had happened that day.

The circle started. Someone said, "I love my mom," and the whole group shouted back, "You love your mom!"

I am somebody. YOU ARE SOMEBODY!

I have a family who loves me. YOU HAVE A FAMILY WHO LOVES YOU!

I can work this simple program! YOU CAN WORK THIS SIMPLE PROGRAM!

I'm going to succeed when I get out! YOU'RE GOING TO SUCCEED WHEN YOU GET OUT!

I'm crying, wiping my face with my sleeve. These people want and need help so badly. All of my indiscretions—the rule breaking, laughing at their art projects, the hidden pills, fighting with Susan, breaking and entering and stealing the phone, it flies in the face of everything these people are working so hard for. We are supposed to be a community of people helping each other, and each of my acts so far have been nothing but a slap in the face to their attempted sobriety. And I finally allow myself to accept my own.

It isn't enough that I want to help them. I need to learn how to want to help myself. I can't understand why this is an epiphany, when it now seems like the most obvious thing in the world.

The guilt I feel at not having been taking the program seriously is crushing, but for the first time since I'd gone to take care of Bobby in Tennessee, there's a voice inside me that's clear. Clearer even than my night alone after surgery. My conscience finally and fully emerges from its slumber and takes over. It's my turn to speak in the circle.

"I . . . regret," I say.

"YOU Regrehh . . . wha?"

I sense accusatory eyes facing me. These are supposed to be affirmative remarks only, and patients take this sort of deviance seriously. It messes with their warm feelings of camaraderie. I'm staring into the fire, watching embers glow. When I look up to face everyone, all I see are orange spots before my eyes.

"I'm sorry, but that's all I feel right now," I say.

There's a slight pause and some disapproving murmuring, but the circle of voices move on to the person sitting to my right and the affirmations continue.

I take the rolled-up piece of poster paper that's tucked under my arm and feed it to the fire. I slide it in underneath the logs, into the cave of embers, and watch the ends immediately begin to curl and smoke. It takes longer to ignite than I expect since there are so many layers in the cylinder, but soon, twenty years of drug use begin to disperse into smoke and rise out of the fire and into the sky. I take a stick and prod gently at the poster. There's a flash as the whole thing finally catches fire and then the entire archive burns quickly. Soon there's nothing left but a tube-shaped mound of ash that, using the stick, I blend in with the rest of the kindling, embers, and dirt until nothing of my history remains.

I look back up and the circle of voices has almost made it back to the beginning. The last woman to speak is someone from my small group, an extremely large woman, with sad eyes and stringy hair. She had lost custody of her child right before entering this facility because of her crack habit. She had come into the program straight from a shelter with no clothing except what was on her back. On one of our outings three of us from the small group had pooled our money and bought her some new clothes at Target.

"I am loved," she says, softly and unsure.

"You are loved," I answer back, my voice rising above the others, cautiously hopeful; hungry to believe the words are meant for me as well.

Epilogue

DESPITE MY FLAGRANT ABUSE of Suboxone while I was in rehab, I don't want anyone to be scared of this drug if it's offered up as part of a rehabilitation program. The way Suboxone works is that with steady, continued use, the high quickly dissipates and replaces the craving for opiates. I don't believe it should be a long-term option, though. The quicker you can be weaned off, the better.

When I returned home from rehab after being thrown out early due to insurance complications, I had an immediate, but thankfully brief, relapse. After my head cleared, I sought help from the Lower East Side Harm Reduction Center and went on a normal Suboxone program, one that I didn't abuse. It helped immensely. But during my relapse, I had noticed that single doses of Suboxone were now available on Candyman's menu, which speaks volumes about the drug's potential for abuse. What started out as a hopefully safer alternative to methadone should probably be looked at a bit more closely by those who administer and manufacture it. And I hope by now it goes without saying that if you're a parent or friend who is helping someone go through opiate withdrawal and he has been prescribed Suboxone, you will consider being the one to administer the dose and sit with that person while the entire pill dissolves in his mouth. It's not like the user can hide it under his tongue, since that is exactly where it dissipates.

I have to admit, it's still, even now, difficult for me to write these words about telling people to get help. Because there will always be a massive part of my brain that wants opiates, and feels like I'm betraying users out there by spilling so many secrets about the topic. I dread the idea of becoming some sort of go-to person on how to get clean, of being some sort of "expert" on the topic of addiction. I don't consider myself an expert on anything except my own life. And many times, I doubt even that.

One story in particular keeps me going, though. During my research for this book, one of the experts who has been studying opiate abuse for a long time now told me a story off the record. This particular expert had become so wrapped up in his own research on the topic that he completely failed to notice that his own spouse had become utterly addicted to opiates, after discovering a ring of elderly military vets who were selling their medications to pay for other pressing life necessities. The spouse was able to hide it because *so many* people can easily conceal this type of addiction. It allows you to function normally on so many other levels. The idea that one of the nation's leading experts in the field of opiate abuse had not been able to see that it had infiltrated his own home speaks volumes.

The problem is, we can't treat pill addiction or dependence like any other type of drug addiction. These are medicines that help people and *must* be made available to those in need, so simply going after the drug manufacturers won't work, unless it's to strengthen security measures. I don't have the answers. My only hope is that this book will make the questions clearer and a little louder. As far as the personal details of my life that I've revealed, I could go that whole route that so many memoirists take, and say "I did it just to be able to help that one lonely kid in Iowa who thought he was the only one out there feeling the same way." I've always thought that was kind of a bullshit answer. And frankly, it's culturally irrelevant these days. That "lonely kid" in Iowa doesn't exist anymore. He probably has 678 Facebook friends and a YouTube following that rivals the ratings of most satellite radio shows. I wrote this book to help myself understand what happened to my life.

That said, I *will* be pretty psyched if it helps anyone else along the way.

Joshua Kennedy Lyon
January 29, 2009

Sources

BOOKS

Pain Killer: A "Wonder" Drug's Trail of Addiction and Death, Barry Meier, Rodale, 2003

Drug Abuse Warning Network, 2005: National Estimates of Drug-Related Emergency Department Visits, Substance Abuse and Mental Health Services Administration

Generation RX: How Prescription Drugs Are Altering American Lives, Minds and Bodies, Greg Critser, Houghton Mifflin, 2005

Results From the 2006 National Survey on Drug Use and Health: National Findings, Substance Abuse and Mental Health Services Administration

High Society: How Substance Abuse Ravages America and What to Do About It, Joseph A. Califano, Jr., Public Affairs, 2007

The Science of Addiction, National Institute of Health, 2007

Comfortably Numb: How Psychiatry Is Medicating a Nation, Charles Barber, Pantheon Books, 2008

Sickness and in Power: Illness in Heads of Government During the Last 100 Years, David Owen, Methuen, 2008

NEWSPAPERS & MAGAZINES

Journal of Clinical Psychopharmacology: "Buprenorphine Treatment of Refractory Depression," J. Alexander Bodkin, M.D., Gwen L. Zornberg, M.D., Scott E. Lukas, Ph.D., and Jonathan O. Cole, M.D., Volume 15, No. 1, 1995

Journal of Clinical Psychiatry: "Combining Serotonin Reuptake Inhibitors and Bupronion in Partial Responders to Antidepressant Monotherapy," J. Alexander Bodkin, M.D., Robert A. Lasser, M.D., James D. Wines, Jr., M.D., David M. Gardner, B.Sc. Pharm., and Ross J. Balessarini, M.D., April, 1997

The New York Times: "Sales of Painkiller Grew Rapidly, But Success Brought a High Cost," Barry Meier and Melody Petersen, March 5, 2001

Newsweek: "Playing With Painkillers," Claudia Kalb with Joan Raymond, Ellise Pierce, Sam Smith, Jay P. Wagner, Jeanne Gordon-Thomas, and Alan Wirzbicki, April 9, 2001

Associated Press: "Maker of OxyContin Faces at Least 13 Lawsuits Over Often-Abused Painkiller," July 27, 2001

The New York Times: "The Alchemy of OxyContin," Paul Tough, July 29, 2001

The New York Times: "At Painkiller Trouble Spot, Signs Seen as Alarming Didn't Alarm Drug's Maker," Barry Meier, December 10, 2001

USA Today: "Painkiller Thieves Get More Creative," Donna Leinwand, December 1, 2003

The New York Times: "Drug-Fighters Turn to Rising Tide of Prescription Abuse," Michael Janofsky, March 18, 2004

WCPO News: "Father Gets Jail Time for Son's OxyContin Death," Liz Foreman, April 7, 2004

Time: "Prescription For Crime; Illegal Pills Have Sparked a Wave of Thefts and Criminality that Rural Towns Just Can't Handle," Rex Bowman/Tazewell, March 28, 2005

USA Today: "Ecstasy's Lost 'Its Panache' Among Teens," Donna Leinwand, April 22, 2005

Time: "An Inside Look at a 'Pharming Party,' the Newest Venue for

Teenage Prescription-Drug Abuse," Carolyn Banta, August 1, 2005

The New York Sun: "Dr. Feelgood, Past and Present," September 20, 2005

The New York Times: "Drug Survey of Students Finds Picture Very Mixed," Kate Zernike, December 20, 2005

The New York Times: "When Teenagers Abuse Prescription Drugs, the Fault May Be the Doctor's," Howard Markel, M.D., December 27, 2005

USA Today: "Prescription Drugs Find Place in Teen Culture," Donna Leinwand, June 13, 2006

The New York Times: "Illegal Drug Use by Teenagers Is on Decline, U.S. Study Finds," Micah Cohen, December 22, 2006

USA Today: "Teen Drug Use Drops, with Exceptions; Survey Finds Abuse of Pharmaceuticals Relatively Steady," Donna Leinwand, December 22, 2006

Vogue: "Trouble in Mind," Eva Marar, December 2006

USA Today: "Deadly Abuse of Methadone Tops Other Prescription Drugs; Only Cocaine Kills More by Overdose," Donna Leinwand, February 13, 2007

USA Today: "Painkiller More Available for Abuse," Donna Leinwand, February 13, 2007

Albany Times-Union: "A Disgraced but Popular Doctor," Brendan J. Lyons, February 28, 2007

Associated Press: "Prescription Drug Abuse Soaring," March 1, 2007

Associated Press: "Binge Drinking, Pill Abuse Intensify at Colleges," March 15, 2007

Newsweek: "The Changing Science of Pain," Mary Carmichael, with Samantha Henig, Dan Ephron, and Julie Scelfo, June 4, 2007

New York Post: " 'Oxy' Kids Crisis," Larry Celona and Leonard Greene, June 18, 2007

Elle: "Beyond the Valley of the Dolls," Lauren Slater, July 2007

The New York Times: "Japanese Slowly Shedding Their Misgivings about the Use of Painkilling Drugs," Donald G. McNeil, September 10, 2007

The New York Times: "Drugs Banned, Many of World's Poor Suffer in Pain," Donald G. McNeil Jr., September 10, 2007

The New York Times: "In India, a Quest to Ease the Pain of the Dying," Donald G. McNeil Jr., September 11, 2007

The New York Times: "Experts Debate the Meaning of Addiction," Donald McNeil, September 14, 2007

Los Angeles Times: "Drug Use Down, but Teens Still Abusing Painkillers," Theo Milonopoulos, December 12, 2007

Vogue: "The Quick Fix," Judith Newman, March 2008

Newsweek: "The Hunt for an Addiction Vaccine," Jeneen Interlandi, March 3, 2008

The New York Times: "Methadone Rises as a Painkiller with Big Risks," Erik Eckholm and Olga Pierce, August 17, 2008

US News & World Report: "Teen Brain Might Get Hooked Easier on OxyContin," Amanda Gardner, September 10, 2008

WEBSITES & MISCELLANEOUS

Court of Common Pleas, Clermont County, Ohio—James Dean Hearing Transcripts from March 15th, 2004, March 29th, 2004, April 7th, 2004, and April 15th, 2004

New Jersey State Police News Release: "State Police Division of Criminal Justice Arrest Alleged Members of Multi-Million Dollar Prescription Drug Ring," January 26, 2007

Health on the Net: "Dealers, Family Biggest Sources of Illegal Prescription Painkillers," Alan Mozes, February 9, 2007

CNN.com: "Deadly $2 Heroin Targets Teens," Tracy Sabo, June 12, 2007

The Pennsylvania Health Care Cost Containment Council, www.phc4.org/reports/FYI/fyi26.htm

www.painreliefnetwork.org